T0330358

Elgar Introduction to Organizational Paradox Theory

ELGAR INTRODUCTIONS TO MANAGEMENT AND ORGANIZATION
THEORY

Series Editors: Cary L. Cooper, *Alliance Manchester Business School,
University of Manchester, UK* and Stewart R. Clegg, *School of Management,
University of Technology Sydney, Australia*

Elgar Introductions to Management and Organization Theory are stimulating
and thoughtful introductions to main theories in management, organizational
behaviour and organization studies, expertly written by some of the world's
leading scholars. Designed to be accessible yet rigorous, they offer concise and
lucid surveys of the key theories in the field.

The aims of the series are twofold: to pinpoint essential history, and aspects
of a particular theory or set of theories, and to offer insights that stimulate critical thinking. The volumes serve as accessible introductions for undergraduate
and graduate students coming to the subject for the first time. Importantly,
they also develop well-informed, nuanced critiques of the field that will
challenge and extend the understanding of advanced students, scholars and
policy-makers.

Titles in the series include:

Elgar Introduction to Organizational Discourse Analysis
Marco Berti

Elgar Introduction to Theories of Organizational Resilience
Luca Giustiniano, Stewart R. Clegg, Miguel Pina e Cunha and Arménio Rego

Theories of Social Innovation
Danielle Logue

Elgar Introduction to Theories of Human Resources and Employment Relations
*Edited by Keith Townsend, Kenneth Cafferkey, Aoife M. McDermott and Tony
Dundon*

Organizational Project Management
Theory and Implementation
Ralf Müller, Nathalie Drouin and Shankar Sankaran

Elgar Introduction to Organizational Paradox Theory
Marco Berti, Ace Simpson, Miguel Pina e Cunha and Stewart R. Clegg

Elgar Introduction to Organizational Paradox Theory

Marco Berti

Senior Lecturer in Management, UTS Business, University of Technology Sydney, Australia

Ace Simpson

Reader in Human Resource Management and Organizational Behaviour, Brunel Business School, Brunel University London, UK

Miguel Pina e Cunha

Fundação Amélia de Mello Professor, Nova School of Business and Economics, Universidade Nova de Lisboa, Portugal

Stewart R. Clegg

Professor, University of Stavanger Business School, Norway and Nova School of Business and Economics, Universidade Nova de Lisboa, Portugal

ELGAR INTRODUCTIONS TO MANAGEMENT AND ORGANIZATION THEORY

Cheltenham, UK • Northampton, MA, USA

Published by
Edward Elgar Publishing Limited
The Lypiatts
15 Lansdown Road
Cheltenham
Glos GL50 2JA
UK

Edward Elgar Publishing, Inc.
William Pratt House
9 Dewey Court
Northampton
Massachusetts 01060
USA

A catalogue record for this book
is available from the British Library

Library of Congress Control Number: 2021938695

This book is available electronically in the **Elgar**online
Business subject collection
http://dx.doi.org/10.4337/9781839101144

ISBN 978 1 83910 113 7 (cased)
ISBN 978 1 83910 114 4 (eBook)

Printed and bound by CPI Group (UK) Ltd, Croydon, CR0 4YY

Contents

Figures

Tables

Boxes

About the authors

Marco Berti has always thrived in paradoxical tensions: as a born-and-bred Italian who travelled around the globe to become an Australian; as a management consultant turned academic at a mature age; as a pragmatic businessperson whose sense of social justice drives towards critical management. He has contributed to making paradox theory more sensitive to power, and he has explored the relationship between paradox and logic and the role of paradox in research movements and theorizing. His research interests also include organizational discourse analysis (he wrote an Elgar Introduction to the topic), digital transformation of the workplace, social construction of space, and teaching management ethics in the context of a transforming economy and society. His work has been published in prestigious journals such as *Academy of Management Review*, *Academy of Management Learning & Education*, *Management Learning*, *Organization*, among others. Marco is a senior lecturer at the University of Technology Sydney.

Ace Simpson has a paradox predilection on account of his childhood exposure to eastern philosophy where he learned to perceive the ontology of all things and beings as simultaneously one and different. Through his undergraduate and post-graduate studies in psychology he sought to identify tools to support human well-being, happiness and flourishing – only to discover that psychology at the time was all about mental illness. Disappointment with psychology led Ace to explore human well-being in organizations, considering that people spend more than half of their lives within the workplace. Through research he learned that one of the most powerful happiness and well-being interventions is, paradoxically, to seek the happiness and well-being of others, through acts of compassion. Compassion is laden with other paradoxes including those related to emotion and rationality, altruism and strategy, autonomy and dependence, virtue and vice – topics Ace has explored in numerous research publications with Miguel, Marco and Stewart, the co-authors of this book. Ace is Reader in Human Resource Management and Organizational Behaviour at Brunel Business School, Brunel University London.

Miguel Pina e Cunha first engaged in paradox when, during his PhD at Tilburg University, he realized that there was an enormous gap between the world of theory and that of practice. The linear theoretical model of product innovation didn't match the real practice of organizations. This led him to explore what he saw in practice: improvisation. He explored the paradoxical side of paradox in a paper published in 2002 in *Human Relations* and, since then, has embraced paradox as a lens to explore organizational functioning. He engaged with paradoxical processes such as serendipity (luck and preparedness), positive organizing (positive and negative), genocide (evil in the name of good) and paradox itself (as problem and as solution). He is the Fundação Amélia de Mello Professor at Nova School of Business and Economics, Universidade Nova de Lisboa, where he studies organization as process and paradox, and has recently explored the role of trade-offs, persistence and performativity in paradox theory.

Stewart R. Clegg is no stranger to paradoxes. Educated in a business school as a sociologist he became a Professor of Sociology who forsook the discipline of the Department of Sociology for the discipline of management in the business school. Paradoxically, the discipline of sociology when applied to management is capable of much greater reach than when confined to the substantive specialisms of the parent discipline. In this he has been helped greatly by being deviant: he managed to combine three of the least influential and fashionable perspectives at the time in his PhD (*Power, Rule and Domination*, 1975: Wittgensteinian approaches to language; qualitative research and 'thin' ethnography. Paradoxically, had he been armed with foresight he should have called it 'discourse analysis'). Armed with this basis in deviance he has gone on to enjoy a paradoxically flourishing career across many terrains all powered by power(ful(l) theory applied liberally to accounting, history, project management, evil organizations, positive organizations, professions and much else besides. In an increasingly narrowly specialized, institutionalized and professionalized world he remains, paradoxically, a successful deviant, a deviant professional, a transgressor of orthodoxies in a manner that has become orthodoxy (how para-doxa is that?). Finally, paradoxically, although an Emeritus Professor at the University of Technology Sydney Business School he does not work there and he does not live where his work is acknowledged. Many of his more recent adventures in paradox and other matters have been with the three good friends with whom this book is co-authored.

Acknowledgements

Paraphrasing Gandhi, it takes a community of paradox scholars to write a book about paradox. We therefore gratefully acknowledge the discussions from our colleagues in the EGOS paradox subtheme. More directly we are grateful to colleagues with whom we have written over the years: Arménio Rego, Camille Pradies, Dean Pieridis, Jonathan Schad, Medhanie Gaim, Rebecca Bednarek, Wendy Smith.

Miguel Cunha acknowledges support from the project 'Developing a European Forum on Paradox and Pluralism – EUFORPP', a project funded from the European Union's Horizon 2020 research and innovation programme under grant agreement No 856688. He also acknowledges support from Fundação para a Ciência e a Tecnologia (UID/ECO/00124/2013, UID/ECO/00124/2019 and Social Sciences DataLab, LISBOA-01-0145-FEDER-022209), POR Lisboa (LISBOA-01-0145-FEDER-007722, LISBOA-01-0145-FEDER-022209) and POR Norte (LISBOA-01-0145-FEDER-022209).

Glossary

Term	Definition	Treatment in the literature
Actor	A human undertaking social actions relating to other entities, human or not. Actors are located in networks with other actors, in an ever-changing institutional order, with their consciousness and sense of self being shaped by participation in these networks. Any actor's identity is in a state of becoming, resulting from an ongoing tension between efforts to differentiate self from others (but also from earlier versions of the self) and attempts to achieve a sense of coherence and social identity.	Voronov and Weber (2020)
Circles/Cycles	Enduring patterns resulting from feedback loops that over time reinforce their internal logical, making organizational problems intractable to analyse, manage and change. Circles may be positive (virtuous) or negative (vicious). In any event, they express a dynamic of their own that escapes organizational steering.	Tsoukas and Cunha (2017)
Contradictions	The dynamic tension between opposed, interdependent elements which presuppose each other and form a unity.	Engeström and Sannino (2011)

Dialectic	The continuously unfolding triadic process of change through the transformation of a thesis-antithesis into a synthesis that will compose the thesis for a further tension. The process is historical and conflictual in nature.	Farjoun (2019), Hargrave (2021)
Dilemma	The simultaneous presence of two equally (un)desirable goals/ requirements that cannot be achieved simultaneously.	Putnam et al. (2016: 9)
Dualism	Two attributes are incompatible and mutually exclusive, like oil and water.	Farjoun (2010)
Duality	The 'twofold character of an object of study without separation', like the two sides of the same coin.	Farjoun (2010: 203)
Paradox	'Contradictory yet interrelated elements – elements that seem logical in isolation but absurd and irrational when appearing simultaneously.'	Lewis (2000: 760)
Persons	Human beings endowed with a sense of self and a capacity to conduct self-reflection.	Voronov and Weber (2020)
Plurality	Denotes multiplicity of perspectives in contexts where power is diffuse.	Denis, Langley and Rouleau (2007)
Tension	'An umbrella term (…) to describe the fundamentally tension-ridden character of organizational structures that are constantly merging and becoming.'	Mease (2019: 6)
Trade-off	The simultaneous presence of two forces pushing in different directions.	Byggeth and Hochshorner (2006: 1420)

Introduction

The way of paradoxes is the way of truth.
To test reality we must see it on the tight rope.
When the verities become acrobats, we can judge them.
(Oscar Wilde, *The Portrait of Dorian Gray*)

Normal organizations run on routines. Despite their normalcy to insiders, many organizations appear as a theatre of the absurd to outsiders, a characteristic caricatured with much craft in comedies such as *Yes, Prime Minister* and *The Office*. Other organizations are deliberately ambiguous and opaque, as in the case of clandestine organizations, often making their public projection and private experience starkly dissimilar, due to secrecy, hidden governance and sustained unacknowledgement of their existence on the part of their members (Cappellaro et al., 2021; Stohl & Stohl, 2017). While the routines of the absurd may be hidden from the general public, their oaths, rituals, cyclical events and repetitions are felt even more keenly by their members as they live secret lives. Yet, as the poets know, this is the script for everyday organizational life, not just the absurd and the secretive, as we humans create routines to try and keep absurdity and equivocality at bay. Farson (1996) regards absurdity and contradictions as pervasive, universal phenomena experienced in dealings with organizations and bureaucracies. Along with Nobel laureates Beckett (1958) and Dylan (1966), we would seek to underscore the absurdity of routine and repetition as an endless beckoning (Tsoukas & Cunha, 2017) that paradox disrupts.

Against the shackles of routine we will highlight the delights of disorganization (Cooper, 1986), recursivity (Hernes & Bakken, 2003; Luhmann, 1995a) and wonder (Carlsen & Sandelands, 2015; McCabe, 2016; Sandelands & Carlsen, 2013). Warren Bennis once defended the importance of aiming to create delightful organizations (Bennis, 2000). Since organizational theories have performative effects, in as much as they contribute to forming the objects of which they write (D'Adderio, Glaser, & Pollock, 2019; Garud, Gehman, & Tharchen, 2018; Marti & Gond, 2018), the creation of delightful organizations requires delightful theories (an idea also suggested by Ghoshal, 2005). Delightfulness may be assumed to be a state of great pleasure; hence a delightful theory and practice would be a pleasurable state of affairs. In terms of antinomies, delight is the antithesis of something that is displeasing or disagreeable.

1

Paradox theory is, we believe, a delightful theory of organizations because it challenges the disagreeably taken-for-granted idea that organizations are orderly, logical and predictable entities which, whatever else they produce, create the boredom of routine. Paradox has been an element of so-called new thinking about organizations (Tsoukas et al., 2020). Paradox disrupts the absurdity of repetition. Paradox incorporates the ambiguities of experience, generating dilemmas, tensions and contradictions, the human condition of existential being. Paradox acknowledges that leading and managing occurs in absurd worlds, marked by competing goals, contradictory interpretations and ambiguous causalities. Hence, paradoxical theories resonate with the human experience of organizing in a way that neater and more mechanistic architectonics do not.

This *Introduction to Organizational Paradox Theory* is not intended as a comprehensive compendium of the burgeoning literature on paradox that has emerged, especially in the last two decades (see Putnam, Fairhurst, & Banghart, 2016; Schad et al., 2016 for a review). Rather, it should be approached as a guide to the absurdity of dominant rational architectonics, aimed at readers who intend to venture to an unfamiliar interpretation of those destinations they must traverse each day or who, with Dylan (1966), are simply curious about how to get out of going through all those things twice and more, that they do every day, *ad infinitum*.

Travel guides are inevitably biased: they are addressed to a specific audience (adventure-seeker versus package tour holidaymakers, young tourists on a shoestring versus affluent travellers) and reflect the specific interests and idiosyncrasies of their authors. Coming across a guide to a familiar destination we are sometimes sufficiently intrigued to browse its pages to find out which features and locations have been highlighted and which have been ignored; whether those absurdities in which we rejoice made it to the page or were among the deleted drafts. In doing so we can be irritated by some choices, but also surprised by discovering something new about the place we inhabit. What we take for granted, with which we are ordinarily delighted, may be as absurd as that which we thought disagreeable.

Tour guides, while they may contain maps, are not cartographically representative. A map aims to offer a complete object representation of a specific geographical site, a result achieved (paradoxically) by removing some objects (e.g. trees) and highlighting others (e.g. roads), even by including socially constructed objects (e.g. borders) that are not intrinsic to the territory (Berti, 2017). A travel guide, with all its limitations and idiosyncrasies, stimulates the interest of its readers, even when they are familiar with the place they are being guided to, highlighting aspects that they might find more interesting, offering practical tips and advice on how to navigate the opportunities and threats implicit in the text, providing some illustrations – in the form of images or narrative vignettes – of what can be seen and experienced once they see their destination through the lens of the guide. Our book is more of a guide than a cartographic device. A problem with guides is that they attempt to capture in a static form an everchanging reality: while information about natural features or monuments can remain current for a long time, other aspects risk becoming instantly obsolete (for instance, advice about fashionable hangouts or good restaurants, favoured plays or authors). Guides change as realities alter or are so perceived.

Organization theories are guides to organizing. As such, they are in constant evolution, with new constructs and perspectives continuously added or rejected following theoretical debates and empirical findings (Khorasani & Almasifar, 2017). Of course, guides have their historicity. When social realities change but the guides that inform action do not, increasingly absurd organizational theatrics may be performed. New guides highlight the practices of changing realities while old practices, informed by guides from the past, comfortably correspond to a sense of reality slipping ever further away from contemporary concerns. Paradoxically, the problem of repetition beckons again; the absurdity of the same old things being reimagined with new labels that may delight the younger traveller but is so familiar to those more seasoned. Once the old guides have established practices, cycle, routine and repetition will reproduce them with little variation. Hence, phenomena alerted to by newer guides may be defeated by organizational imprinting (Stinchcombe, 1965). The literature on organizational paradox is very much a contemporary concern, only blossoming emerging in the 1980s (Cameron & Quinn, 1988; Luhmann, 1986; Putnam, 1986; Smith & Berg, 1987). Paradoxes had been observed before in studies of organization, but only as apparent conundrums, to be rationally explained and solved (Blau, 1954; Perrow, 1977); only a few sociologists deeply familiar with Marx engaged with the idea of organizational dialectics and paradoxes (Allen, 1975; Benson, 1977).

Contradictions persist not only because changing realities are refracted through worn-out lenses, but also because they are overlain with many new ones. For those working in the prism of Marx's bequest, one great contradiction trumps all others: the paradox of the great mass of Labour being beheld to the small elites of Capital. The paradox is even more salient since the turn of the century, considering that most democratic countries – after the post-war decades in which the most egregious social and economic inequalities have been redressed – appear to have abandoned redistributive policies and practices (Piketty, 2020).

Even if organization theory, over its illustrious career, has eschewed this fundamental contradiction, it has been alert to more contemporary ones. Where and when contemporary paradoxes arise, they constitute dualisms that demand choice of one or other horns of a dilemma, invoking new routines as resolution of persistent problems. Persistence has its ironies, of course; dilemmas recur – unless organizations *engage* with paradoxes rather than being stuck in routine, repetitions and cycles, they respond in ruts.

In this *Introduction* we meet organizational paradox, a new lens for seeing ruts and rationalities that are increasingly absurd. Organizational paradox is busy being born in a welcoming intellectual community that is not just tolerant of methodological and paradigmatic differences but one celebrating diversity and multiplicity of ideas, building on an inclusive and robust conceptual core (Schad, Lewis, & Smith, 2019). In practice, designs need to be embraced by managers if more delightful organizations are to be its progeny. With this book, we desire to seed that progeny, taking organizational paradoxical approaches out of their intellectual enclave by translating them, as a guide to practice, for managers still captive to disagreeable practices (Ghoshal, 2005).

To account for, as well as take advantage of, the constant transformation and evolution that characterizes organizational paradox theory, we structure each chapter by first providing readers with a succinct description of the 'conceptual core' on which a majority consensus has been – at least momentarily – achieved. Then, since it is important to preserve theory vitality, the boundaries of this conceptual core are tested, by highlighting unresolved issues and remaining gaps, problematizing, revealing and challenging some of the assumptions that bound the paradoxical approach (Alvesson & Sandberg, 2011). Doing this allows us to outline future, still unexplored, possibilities for conceptualization, research and application. Since paradox might seem a very abstract, even obscure, concept, conceptual definitions and theoretical debates are accompanied and enriched by concrete illustrations, vignettes and exemplary cases, demonstrating the pervasiveness of organizational tensions and the relevance of a theoretical framework aimed at understanding and managing them in practice.

Choosing which topics to include in this book was a difficult and intrinsically frustrating exercise, as is the case when compiling lists for any guides. Any inclusion requires exclusion, which is intrinsically controversial and subject to accusations of bias. At the same time, an Introduction is meant to be read as a coherent text (differently from a Handbook, in which chapters can be consulted individually, according to the reader's specific interests). Thus, our choices (summarized in Figure I.1) were motivated by the desire to offer a logical 'itinerary', following a coherent narrative that guides the reader in exploring the paradox literature, which both offers guidance and leaves liberty for wandering, according to individual tastes and interests.

As the caption (which paraphrases the famous Magritte painting, *La Trahison des Images*) states, this map is not really a map, since it describes many possible 'itineraries' that can be traced by following the narrative of this Introduction. In addition to the main storyline, it is possible to retrace one's

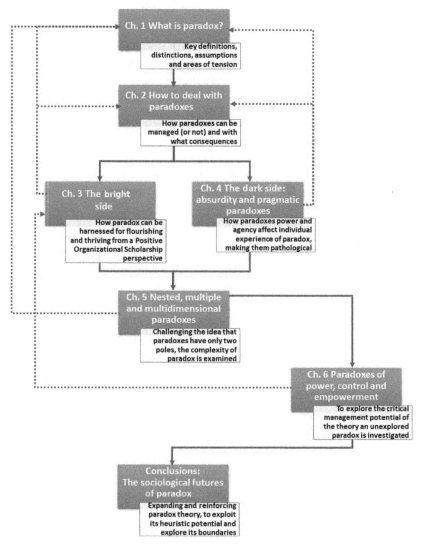

Figure I.1   *'This is not a map'*

steps, for instance to consider the critical management implications (discussed in Chapter 6) of pragmatic paradoxes, or to reflect back on the key definitions of paradox in light of discussion on the nested nature of paradoxes. The dotted line in the picture illustrates some (but not all) of the possible alternative pathways to explore the topic by iterating between chapters. The content of each chapter is outlined more specifically below.

Chapter 1 (What is paradox?) introduces key definitions and ideas developed by organizational paradox scholars, which constitute the currently agreed upon conceptual core of paradox theory. A concise definition of paradox as interdependent and persistent contradictions (Schad et al., 2016) is promoted as a dynamic model of organizing, highlighting the importance of acknowledging paradoxes (Smith & Lewis, 2011), the role of paradoxical mindsets (Miron-Spektor et al., 2018), as well as the latest discussions on the ontology of paradox (Hahn & Knight, 2019). A brief history of the evolution of the concept and of the vital scholarly community that has been studying paradox is provided. The chapter also includes concrete examples of organizational paradoxes and highlights the need to constantly test and expand on this conceptual core, to avoid the reification or taming of paradoxes (Cunha & Putnam, 2019).

Chapter 2 (How to deal with paradoxes) focuses on how paradoxes can be managed, showing the rich repertoire of actions that have been proposed (or empirically observed by researchers) to cope with contradictions. Structural (e.g. separation), intersubjective (e.g. practices) and individual (e.g. oscillation) responses are described, and their performative role in shaping the very tensions they supposedly react to is documented. Moving beyond a binary distinction between constructive responses based on acceptance, which are supposed to harness the potential of paradoxes, and negative ones, characterized by denial, that are thought to lead to vicious circles (Smith & Lewis, 2011), the pros and cons of each response modality are considered, together with the conditions that enable their manifestation.

Chapter 3 (The bright side: paradoxes and positive organizational scholarship) is explicitly meant to act as a precursor to the one that follows, considering the potential of paradox to leverage desirable change. Considering paradox from a Positive Organizational Scholarship perspective, the chapter highlights how paradoxical tensions can be harnessed to manifest virtuous organizational cultures of abundance and generate learning opportunities (Cunha et al., 2020). The chapter further considers the need for navigating contradictions implicit to positive organizational practices.

Chapter 4 (The dark side: absurdity and pragmatic paradoxes) explores the 'dark side' of paradoxes, showing that – under conditions of limited agency and disempowerment – tensions can be experienced by individuals as paralysing, pathological conditions (Berti & Simpson, 2019; Tracy, 2004). By 'zooming in' on individual experiences of paradox, the role of absurdity, power and agency are emphasized, as is the need to create conditions that allow individuals to cope with tensions.

Chapter 5 (Nested, multiple and multidimensional paradoxes) examines the complexity of paradox, going beyond the idea that paradoxes have only two opposite poles. First, we look at how paradoxes can be nested or embedded in each other and then we consider tensions generated by multiple poles, evolving over time, to deepen and make more complex how the phenomenon may be regarded in order to overcome any tendency to 'tame' paradox.

Chapter 6 (Paradoxes of power, control and empowerment) constitutes a purposeful side-trip, to look at a fundamental but underexplored paradox that characterizes all organizations, that between power over (the use of power to control others, which has oppressive consequences) and power to (the capacity to act in concert, producing collective achievement). One implies the other but has opposite and contradictory consequences. We also consider how this paradox can be met through the growing of coactive power, or power with, through processes of collaborative democratic governance. Focusing on this issue helps make paradox theory more 'sensitive to power' and expand its use as a Critical Management perspective.

Conclusions (The sociological futures of paradox: incorporating grand challenges) takes stock of the trajectory of paradox theory and attempts to plot (and direct) its future evolution, highlighting possible ways to expand and reinforce the theory, extending its reach and maintaining its vitality, also in relation to the evolving field of organizational studies and the new challenges of a transforming economy and society.

In concluding, it is important to mention what could appear to be the most important omission in our guide. We have made the choice to focus on the 'material' side of paradoxes, treating them as phenomena that have specific and assessable features and that can be appraised by an independent observer. Yet paradox can also constitute a powerful intellectual prism, a metatheoretical perspective that complements other theories of organization (Cameron & Quinn, 1988; Lewis & Smith, 2014). As a complementary or auxiliary theory, paradox helps to shed light on a variety of organizational theories. By focusing on the contradictions of organizational life, paradox illuminates why things lead to their opposites, how solutions become problems, how success degenerates into failure, and so on. In other words, paradox helps with understanding why organizations are so rich in tension and contradiction, sometimes so absurd, yet with an absurdity that, if interpreted appropriately, can be so full of surprise and creativity. While we do not devote a chapter to the heuristic use of paradox, our treatment of the subject in our guide demonstrates implicitly the potential of a paradox framework to reveal organizational nuance and complexity, debunking the assumption that organizations should be seen as merely predictable mechanisms executing the tasks they were designed to do. Engineering has its place; so too does the theatre of the absurd, and each have their guides. In the one, linear rationality; in the other, paradox. Our aim is to be a guide that uncovers the engineering that scaffolds organizational reality by opening up the theatre of everyday organizational life to more paradoxical accounts. In time, these accounts will lose their sense of playfulness and delight but until then, dear reader, we hope to delight you with the contents of this book so that it is worth the price of at least reading it once … or twice … but no more. Read, begin your enquiry, consider the paradoxes that frame your organizational existence… and cope with them!

1. What is paradox? Tensions, contradictions and oppositions in organization studies

Indeed, even at this stage, I predict a time when there will be mathematical investigations of calculi containing contradictions, and people will actually be proud of having emancipated themselves from consistency.
(Wittgenstein, 1964: 332)

Paradox, once seen by those who write about the organizational machinery as a defect or an extravagant form of inconsistency, is represented in contemporary organizational scholarship as a condition of complex organization. Organization is full of paradox: change vs. stability, planning vs. emergence, exploration vs. exploitation, to name only some of the most frequently discussed. From what is increasingly known as a paradox perspective, organizations are more than the site of occasional and specific paradoxes; they are intrinsically paradoxical. These paradoxes are not just situations of rational choice between alternatives if only because organizing may be a means for emotional and political expression (Petriglieri & Petriglieri, 2020).

Binary oppositions demanding choice are replaced in paradox perspectives by dualities that necessarily coexist. What is a paradox? How can organizations be understood through a paradox lens? To discuss this question, the book can be read as a contribution to a discipline of *aporetics* (from the ancient Greek *aporía*, impassability, contradiction), whose goal consists in teaching us how to live with contradiction and paradox (Rescher, 2001). Plurality, in terms of goals, expertise and logics, pervades organizing (Berti, 2021). Rather than being a sign of dysfunction or inconsistency, contradictions are to be seen as a constitutive feature of any complex system. Paradoxes, rather than being conceits of organization theorists' excessive search for novelty, should be considered a lens or a tool that managers may use to make sense of and manage organization.

This chapter introduces key definitions and ideas developed by organizational paradox scholars, which constitute the currently agreed upon conceptual core of paradox theory. It explains why paradox deserves to be studied and offers a brief history of the evolution of the concept and of the vital scholarly community studying paradox. The chapter also includes a discussion of the origin of paradoxes along with different uses of the concept.

BOX 1.1   THE FEAR OF PARADOX

Paradox has traditionally been viewed as an invitation to irrationality, a facet well explored in the artistic realm by artists such as Escher (2000). Consider Tetenbaum's (1998: 23) description of the dangers of such a perspective: "It is human nature to prefer, to seek out, and even to expect certainty. Paradoxes threaten that world order. A common way to handle this unpleasant state is to 'fix' on one polarity and to see the world as 'either-or' rather than to reconcile the two polarities with 'both-and' thinking." The fear of paradox is possibly rooted in the engineering origins of organization theory (Shenhav, 1995). For classical organizational theorists organizing was an exercise in uncertainty reduction. Organization implied the elimination of uncertainty. Paradox, by contrast, refers to the acceptance of ambiguity and tension. From a classical perspective, paradox is the expression of disorganization, of 'noise' in the organization system.
Management and organization studies is a field that favours the rational and expresses its distaste for the irrational. Nonetheless, it is simultaneously open to fads and fashions (Benders & Van Veen, 2001), as well as to what Gimpl and Dakin (1984) termed the appeal of magic, in the form of spells cast against the uncertainties of futures unknown, such as long-range strategic planning, or learning premised on superstition, perhaps caused by the need for control. Intolerant of ambiguous situations and the uncertainties of futures unknown and their contradictions, managers can invoke 'magical' techniques to gain an illusory sense of control, fulfilling an important psychological function. More realistically, perhaps, recent invocations of agile organizations assume that organizations do need to learn how to improvise and accept their vulnerability in face of change.

WHAT IS PARADOX?

Organizational life is increasingly described as being rife with paradox. Following a well-known definition, paradox refers to "contradictory yet interrelated elements that exist simultaneously and persist over time" (Smith & Lewis, 2011: 386; see also Box 1.1). Paradox marks those processes characterized by interlocking oppositions that cannot be willed away, something well expressed in the name paradoxes were given during the Middle Ages: *insolubilia*. The interlocked nature of oppositions is important as not every tension or contradiction corresponds to a paradox. For example, the make vs. buy decision is a dilemma, not a paradox. The two options are independent. But change and stability are better viewed as paradox: one element defines the absence of the other; change is the opposite of stability, yet neither can be understood without the other, as they compose a duality (see Glossary). As Farjoun (2010) explains, one is understandable only in the presence of the other. Their relation is dynamic; they mutually constitute each another as organizations evolve. It is this interlocked dynamic relationship that constitutes paradox.

BOX 1.2   DEFINITIONS OF PARADOX

There are many definitions of paradox. Here is a sample:
"A paradox is a stretch of reasoning that leads from apparently impeccable premises by apparently straightforward steps of reasoning to an unacceptable conclusion. Usually (though not always) the unacceptability of the conclusion is that it is contradictory" (Goldstein, 1996: 299).
"A paradox is an argument with premises which appear to be true and steps which appear to be valid, which nevertheless ends in a conclusion which is false" (Priest, 1979: 220).
Paradox "denotes contradictory yet inter-related elements-elements that seem logical in isolation but absurd and irrational when appearing simultaneously" (Lewis, 2000: 760).
"Paradox may refer to: 1) claims contrary to common opinion, often suggesting that the statement is incredible, absurd, or fantastic, but sometimes with a favorable connotation as a correction for ignorance; 2) a statement that seems self-contradictory, but which is actually well-founded; 3) a statement that involves a genuine contradiction; 4) in logic a conclusion based on acceptable premises and sound reasoning that nonetheless is self-contradictory" (Bufford, 2006: 531).

Competing demands recur at every organizational level from the strategic apex to the operational base (a topic discussed in Chapter 5). Top managers embed paradoxes in their organization's strategies for exploring and exploiting, organizing the long term and the short term, cooperating and competing, disrupting their organizations while reinforcing their value (Smith, 2014). At the operational level, in the call centre, operators are supposed to deliver courtesy, efficiency and effectiveness, comprising what Clark et al. (2019) call triple trade-offs. The most successful operators are able to synthesize competing demands in a fruitful way, finding synergies between what at first appears incompatible. New leaders are expected to prove themselves quickly while knowing that quick results are an inherently dangerous pursuit (Van Buren & Safferstone, 2009). As Bahcall (2019) put it, managers must equilibrate roles as metaphorical artists and soldiers in their organizations to succeed. Artists create ideas and designs to gain an advantage, while soldiers are drilled to perfect routines. If the organization employs too many soldiers it will repeat the same routines; too many artists will lead to creativity in design, but these diverse designs will need to be applied in the complexity and messiness of the 'battlefield'.

Paradoxical tensions, according to Smith and Lewis (2011) may be exacerbated by tendencies such as digitalization and the globalization of the world economy, creating ever more febrile organizational environments. In the face of these tensions new challenges emerge, such as the need to embrace new digital business models and organizational designs that must necessarily coexist with existing models. Globalization creates awareness of different modes of managing and organizing. For instance, in some settings leaders can be both authoritarian and benevolent, a seemingly paradoxical combination (Cunha et al., 2021). One vivid example is offered by Jared Diamond in his book *Collapse* (2005). This author describes how the decisions of Joaquin Balaguer, the despotic political leader who dominated the political scene in the Dominican Republic in the second half of the 20th century, were instrumental in preserving the nation's environment, especially in comparison to the ecological devastation experienced by the neighbouring Haiti. An equivalent capacity to navigate contradiction has been associated with former Colombia President and Nobel Peace Prize winner, Juan Manuel Santos, whose approach oscillated between acting as a hawk and a dove (Ortiz, 2020).

Evidence shows that successful organizations have learned how to master the art of the paradox. Marvel, for example, has used continuity and renewal, positive and negative emotions to sustain its blockbuster machine (Harrison, Carlsen & Skerlavaj, 2019). Yet, the idea of 'mastering' paradox is treacherous. Organizations change over time because the tensions they face are themselves dynamic. As organizations tackle one tension, they open other tensions. As governments in Southern Europe were forced to embrace financial discipline to balance their accounts, they unbalanced the established equilibria in a number of services, such as healthcare, a process whose consequences became clearer only years after the measures were taken. Once equilibrium was more or less restored, the COVID-19 pandemic forced these (and other governments) into rethinking the efficiency-resilience trade-off. Equilibrium, therefore, is dynamic and precarious, implying cycling back and forth. In cases where none of the phases overwhelms the others, the system can be said to remain in a state of dynamic equilibrium (Bahcall, 2019). Yet this equilibrium is necessarily precarious, as one phase may at some point, for some reason, become dominant.

WHY STUDY PARADOX?

Scholars have embraced the paradox view of organizations for several reasons. Paradoxes are a pervasive presence in organizations. They do not constitute an anomaly but rather something normal, even ordinary. Studying paradox facilitates a departure from dualistic views of organizations, in which more of one force represents less of another, to a view that is more complex but also closer to philosophical views of the world that underline interdependence, with a focus on duality. From a duality perspective, organizational opposites form one another, instead of involving either-or types of challenges. A paradoxical view is therefore an invitation to constitute organizations as tensions that can be generative or debilitating, composed of dualities that offer fresh forms of understanding as well as complementarities between moments of balance and imbalance. The setting of paradox theory, in other words, is a Protean world, one not only with the potential for predictability but also for surprise – just like the 'real world'. Unsurprisingly, managing complex paradoxes successfully with simple recipes is impossible. In spite of the attractiveness of both-and balancing (Smith, Lewis & Tushman, 2016), paradox may sometimes imply temporary either-or imbalance (Bednarek, Chalkias & Jarzabkowski, 2020).

BOX 1.3   PARADOX IN THE ARTS: A SOURCE OF AESTHETIC DELIGHT

Artists have explored the potential of paradox to discuss the human condition and experience from multiple angles, of which we explore three possibilities opened by Kafka, Carroll and Escher.

Kafka. The work of Franz Kafka provides some of the best illustrations of paradox in literature. His books offer vivid accounts of how bureaucracy can become monstrous. In the labyrinthine organizations he describes, humans feel that organizations gain a life of their own that in its inscrutability and perplexity runs against the interests of the general public or, at least, those that are powerless before it. His works, namely the short story *In the Penal Colony*, anticipates the bureaucratic work with which modern organizations created death camps normalizing evil (Clegg et al., 2013; see also Chapter 4 on the dark side of paradox).

Lewis Carroll. As Nicholas Rescher (1960) pointed out, Lewis Carroll's *Alice in Wonderland* and the respective gallery of characters it presents, tests the limits of logic. Wonderland is a very different world, the logic of which differs from any known or depicted reality. The point, however, is that real organizations frequently resemble Wonderland rather more than any known reality in which people are easily capable of believing as many as 'six impossible things before breakfast', especially at away days in which a form of Wonderland becomes imagined into schemes and dreams.

Escher, Parmigianino, Uccello. Visually Escher's subtle transformations and 'impossible objects' offer one of the most attractive depictions of paradox. The worlds of Escher present intriguing transformations: they provide examples of visual paradox. However, the introduction of visual paradoxes is not a 20th-century invention: the 16th-century painter Parmigianino also included in his works "background elements (such as columns) which are inconsistently organized, playing. Although these paintings are not self-referential as are typical verbal paradoxes, they are equivalent to the paradoxical form 'true if and only if false' in that they contain incompatible or circular elements which express a feeling of unease" (Duran, 1993: 239). Similarly, the 15th-century artist Paolo Uccello anticipated Cubism, creating images that "were truer when they were less true to life" (Argan, 1968: 186).

PARADOX IN ORGANIZATION STUDIES: A VERY BRIEF HISTORY

The idea of paradox as a constitutive feature of its subject matter has been historically discounted by management and organization theorists, but the idea is gaining momentum. As pioneering paradox scholars Poole and Van de Ven (1989) point out, most theories of organization try to build internally consistent arguments. Less attention has been paid to the potential for theory building of the same phenomena that focuses on tensions, oppositions and contradictions. Organizations, as noted in the Introduction, have been largely imagined as spaces of order and rationality. Conceiving of them as paradoxical poses a threat to imagined order, a threat that began to emerge in the literature in the 1970s and 1980s.

The 1970s and before: Paradox as aberration. The role of tension in management and economics is possibly as old as the study of these topics. Class conflicts in the Marxist tradition, or the tension between managers and workers in Taylor's (1911) analysis of processes such as soldiering, offer examples of irreconcilable oppositions giving rise to tensions as a topic for management studies. While these old themes in research are well established and reconciled (Braverman, 1975), the study of paradox per se is a more recent phenomenon.

Whenever *apparent* paradoxes were detected in bureaucratic organizations, they were approached as puzzles to be solved. The contradictory evidence showing that more competitive groups are less productive, whereas more competitive individuals are more productive, was explained by Blau (1954) as demonstration of the importance of social cohesiveness and cooperative norms for productivity. Similarly, the paradoxical observation that increases in delegation of authority (decentralization, or reduction of control) are associated with an increase in standardization (which amounts to centralization, or increase in control), is explained by Perrow (1977) as an apparent contradiction caused by a confusion between different forms of control (direct and indirect) and that effective management is achieved by an appropriate mix of different forms of control.

The 1980s: Paradox as phenomenon. The first substantive engagement with interdependent tensions was offered by Benson (1977). His important and still highly influential analysis described organizations as dialectical processes, with tension occurring because of the embeddedness of organizations in social totalities. He defended the thesis that organized social processes are contradictory. Social totalities are systems in which a plurality of interests coexist, necessarily infusing organizing with contradiction and opposition. Phenomena such as organizational politics and resistance to change are not organizational anomalies but a necessary expression of this plurality. The dialectical view offered by Benson (1977) is still bearing fruit in several works analysing the process through which tension introduces novelty into organizational systems (Clegg & Cunha, 2017; Farjoun, 2019). The relationship between dialectics and paradox has been subject to recent scrutiny (Hargrave, 2021; Hargrave & Van de Ven, 2017). Overall, the dialectical perspective helps to explain why persistent paradox does not produce 'stuckedness' (Vignehsa, 2014) in the form of paralysing tensions that are never resolved. Contradictions framed as paradoxical potentially may be transformed through synthesis, despite being persistently imperilled by forces outside managerial control.

Among the pioneers to explicitly explore paradox as an organizationally relevant concept were Quinn and Cameron (1988) and Poole and Van de Ven (1989). These authors discussed paradox not as noise to be removed but as a characteristic of organization – a lens with which to explore contradiction. Poole and Van de Ven justified the metatheoretical potential of paradox through focusing on tension and opposition to expand other theories of organizations. While phenomena such as organizational change and institutionalization processes do not have to be approached from a paradox perspective when analysed from the point of view of the contradictions they necessarily trigger, some of their attributes become more transparent. If the tension between existing power structures and emergent power relations are ignored, change becomes more difficult to explain. As Poole and Van de Ven (1989) explain, tensions and contradictions constitute one possible source of change that can be analysed along with other sources.

The idea that paradox was not a sign of dysfunction but rather a manifestation of organizational complexity was proposed by Quinn and Cameron (1988). Cameron (1986) discussed the idea of organizational effectiveness as paradox; with the competing values model (Cameron et al., 2014) he presented organizational culture as a form of balancing competing cultural orientations. Where organizational culture is dominated by a singular sense of what is valuable it will potentially create an unbalanced organization. The push-pull between different values is necessary to nurture contradictory but necessary attributes, such as internal solidarity, a focus on metrics and results, rule clarity and a measure of innovation. When one value dominates and overrides the others the system becomes compromised. More recently, Cameron presented positive organizational scholarship as a paradoxical journey (Cameron, 2008), an idea subsequently expanded by Cunha, Rego, Simpson and Clegg (2020), as well as in Chapter 3 of this book.

Smith and Berg (1987), in exploring the tensions inherent to teamworking, pioneered the study of teams as paradoxical. Inspired by psychodynamic theory, they noted the inherent paradoxicality of group life. Teams are simultaneously spaces in which people expect a measure of integration and differentiation, aiming to satisfy their needs of belonging without compromising unique individuality. Also inspired by a psychodynamic perspective, Kets de Vries (1995) explored paradoxes of organizations and leadership to show that beneath the façade of rationality, organizations and their leaders express a number of themes that would remain inexplicable if representing organizations as strictly rational phenomena. These efforts can be critical to understanding how teams manage to articulate a number of simultaneously occurring paradoxes (Silva et al., 2014) while creating and recreating a viable team identity. As Murnighan and Conlon (1991) revealed, while these tensions may be implicit or explicit, they need to be articulated for the team to perform at a high level. The pioneering work of Smith and Berg resonates with more recent research by Edmondson and Lei (2014) on how successful teams balance psychological safety and accountability. These pioneering paradox scholars saw contradiction and opposition not as a categorization mistake or an aberration, but as 'real' phenomena, ordinary implications of organizing plurality.

The 1990s: Paradox as signal of complexity. The adoption of a complexity perspective by authors such as Stacey (Stacey et al., 2002) and Eisenhardt (2000), and the exploration of organization as process by scholars such as Tsoukas and Chia (2002), offered a new perspective on paradox as an organizational phenomenon. Paradox was being approached obliquely, as an outcome of the complexity of organizations. Organizational processes are recognized as being complex, such that, to preserve vitality, organizations need to remain at the 'edge of chaos', the interstices in which order and disorder collide and coexist. Eisenhardt explained how organizations engage in high degrees of complexity to adapt to markets that shift relentlessly (Brown & Eisenhardt, 1997, 1998). Eisenhardt's work described organizations as needing to define simple rules in order to adjust to complex environments. The notion of simple rules as heuristics that help to cope with what can otherwise be paralysing complexity was further developed by Sull and Eisenhardt (2015) as a requirement for remaining organized without becoming rigid (excessively structured) or disorganized (insufficiently structured).

Robert Cooper (1986) developed the idea that it is better to conceptualize organizations as processes that exist in relation with other organizations rather than assuming that they are self-sufficient machines. Cooper's work on the tension between organization and disorganization anticipated several future research agendas. A debate was launched in the 1990s concerning the need to complexify (Tsoukas, 2017) or to simplify (Sull & Eisenhardt, 2015) organizations, if they are to thrive in hypercompetitive economies. Other important developments in a paradox theory of organizations at this time included Westenholz's (1993) embrace of paradoxical modes of thinking. Overall, the 1990s viewed paradoxes as means for understanding the embeddedness of organizations in incessantly changing and complex environments.

Another central contribution to the study of paradox as an expression of complexity is offered by the work of the German sociologist, Niklas Luhmann. Considering organizations as social systems that must mark their difference from their environments, they engage in a process of selection that reduces environmental complexity (Luhmann, 1995a). Such selection processes generate a first paradox: while organizing simplifies reality to enable action, at the same time it generates new contingencies, information and differences, deriving either from "an increase in differentiation or … a change in the form of differentiation" implicated in organizing (Luhmann, 1995a: 21). Moreover, organizations can be considered as "systems that consist of decisions and that produce the decisions of which they consist, through the decisions of which they consist" (Luhmann, 1992: 166, cit. in Seidl & Mormann 2014: 137). These decisions are intrinsically paradoxical, in that they both imply and exclude the possibility of alternatives (Cooren & Seidl, 2020). To hide these contradictions, organizations respond with attempts to 'deparadoxify' (Luhmann 1995b: 46), by shifting attention from the content of the decision to its premises (i.e. the logic followed), or by attributing it to a decision maker, thus emphasizing their motivations. Therefore, organizational decisions cannot be 'simple' choices if only because not considering complicating aspects, such as human motivations and chains of premises, would reveal their intrinsic paradoxicality (Luhmann, 2018).

A third organizational paradox described by Luhmann derives from communication, another essential component of social systems. Communication requires, in addition to information and utterance, also understanding; thus, the listener is the one who determines the meaning of the communication and decides whether to accept or reject it in the context of other communications (Luhmann, 1986). The process of understanding is difficult to observe and predict, which undermines the structure of expectations on which social systems are based (Luhmann, 1995a). To deal with this problem, social systems use actions as a connecting device. This is because "actions appear self-defined and do not presuppose other actions" (Seidl, 2004: 12), which enables organizations to separate actions and to attribute them to specific agents. However, this simplification strategy increases separation of actions and agencies, paradoxically increasing complexity in the system. In other words, in organizations individual members are viewed only as vehicles for performances, producers of tangible deliverables; the other aspects that make human experience meaningful (intentions, emotions, interpretations et cetera) are instead ignored (with the intent of simplifying things). Yet, this forced reduction of complexity triggers tensions, conflicts and contradictions that feed complexity back into organizational dynamics.

The 2000s: Paradox as opportunity. The new millennium brought a new level of attention to paradox theory and practice, implying that good management may entail working with paradox (Fiol, 2002). In the early years of the decade, one of the authors of this book organized an initial volume dedicated to management and organizational paradoxes (Clegg, 2002) and Marianne Lewis made a number of pivotal contributions. She offered a 'comprehensive guide' to the field (Lewis, 2000), also pioneering the examination of the potential of paradox for business education (Lewis & Delher, 2000). In the following years she explored several facets of paradox in organizations including the paradoxes of innovation (Andriopoulos & Lewis, 2009), leadership (Lewis et al., 2014) and governance (Sundaramurthy & Lewis, 2003). Lewis later collaborated with Wendy Smith in developing a view that paradox is not a lens with which to explore some other phenomenon but an important organizational phenomenon in its own right.

The article by Smith and Lewis (2011), 'Toward a theory of paradox: a dynamic equilibrium model of organizing', consolidated the parameters of a paradox perspective on organizations. It presented paradox as a stimulus of processes potentially creating dynamic equilibrium for organizations. Paradoxes could stimulate virtuous circles from which cycles of belonging, performing, learning and organizing could be generated as these paradoxes coevolve (Jarzabkowski et al., 2013). Equally, the response to paradoxes might be a vicious cycle of alienating, stalling, ignoring and disorganizing. Smith et al. (2016) subsequently explored paradox as a managerial tool, confronting managers with opportunities to gain value from organizational tensions. Doing so, they suggest, entails not making an either-or choice but one that promotes what they refer to as a 'both-and' approach. Accordingly, paradoxes must be approached not as something to overcome but as a normal state of affairs. In their normalcy, paradoxes in competitive landscapes that are ambiguous and rich in tension become a potential source of temporary advantage when they are embraced rather than rejected.

The 2000s saw paradox become a more widely adopted theoretical lens, in part because of parallel developments in organization theory. James March's work was significant. March's contributions to the study of organizations are major and long-lasting; through his work both the systematization and the poetization of organizations has thrived; the former through his *Handbook* (March, 1965 [2013]) and textbooks (March & Simon, 1958), the latter through his playfulness in articles (March, 2006a, 2006b). Of his later works, perhaps none gained more traction (and certainly citations) than his analysis of the tension between exploration and exploitation in organizations (March, 1991). The paradoxes in his analysis of these tensions are evident. To survive, organizations need to find a way of maintaining both exploration and exploitation in tension rather than becoming fixated on one or the other: they must embrace both. If they do not, organizations risk being myopic. To avoid myopia, mixing the bodily metaphors, organizations must be ambidextrous or, staying with the optical metaphor, they need 20/20 binocular vision, focused on both exploration and exploitation.

Successful organizations cultivate ambidexterity (O'Reilly III & Tushman, 2013). Managers in ambidextrous organizations work less at wholly controlling rationality but also strive to release imaginative potential. Leaders need to be able to nourish both poets and plumbers (March & Weil, 2009). Too much poetry becomes delusional; too much plumbing and the organization will merely repeat itself. Therefore, leading is a dual task, one that implies both pragmatism as well as the search for beauty. March's earlier writings on topics such as foolishness contributed towards questioning the assumption that seeing the irrational side of organizing is itself irrational. He showed that the theoretical reduction of organizations to their rational side constituted a gross simplification of the complexity of organizations that involve opposite elements in a state of coexistence. Rationally, however, the notion of ambidexterity serves to keep the plumbers and the poets apart, something that characterized the distinction between March's poetry and contributions to science (Chytry, 2003). Suffice to say, March's contributions in the 2000s were critical for normalizing the idea that organizations can be considered paradoxical in a positive way. March was the organization theorist that brought the idea of paradox out of the dark and into the light as a central theme in explaining the functioning of organizations.

The 2010s: Expanding paradox theory. A hallmark of institutionalization in the realm of ideas is increasing specialization. Paradox theory was considerably institutionalized in the second decade of the 21st century. In the 2010s, important literature reviews were produced (Putnam et al., 2016; Schad et al., 2016); a paradox theory handbook was launched (Lewis et al., 2017); a specialised anthology published (Farjoun et al., 2018); special issues organized (Smith et al., 2017; Bednarek et al., 2021; Lindgreen & Maon, 2019;

Waldman et al., 2019); as well as a standing stream maintained in the annual colloquium of EGOS. Putnam et al. (2016) observed the number of papers published increasing, reflecting a movement gaining aficionados. Intellectual investments were being made in a bet that they would yield interest and build capital. In the process, *opposition*, *interdependence* and *persistence* became the standard definition of what constituted a paradox. A community of scholarly practice was coalescing around the banner of paradox, nurtured via regular symposia attended by a cohesive group of scholars, including the movement's leading intellectual apostles (Wendy Smith and Marianne Lewis).

BOX 1.4   CREATING A SCHOLARLY COMMUNITY: A COMMENTARY BY WENDY SMITH

The early 2000s was both an exciting and a lonely time to write about paradox. I encountered insight about paradox as a doctoral student, while studying how top management teams manage change and innovation. This lens seemed like a perfect framework to help inform my thinking about the tensions these leaders encountered between exploration and exploitation. Luminaries in organizational theory had written key pieces to advance scholarship on paradox, setting the stage for future work to build on. Yet these pieces remained scant. In fact, many of these same scholars invested in advancing paradox theory offered caution. Paradox scholarship remained peripheral in the field, and therefore challenging to publish in top journals. Two things happened that motivated me to continue to publish in the field. First, Marianne Lewis published her article in the *Academy of Management Review* (2000), which won the best paper award that year. I asked her for advice, and we met at the Academy of Management in 2004. Our energizing conversation started an ongoing dialogue that continue to be a tremendous collaboration. Second, I joined the Strategy-as-Practice track of EGOS in Amsterdam in 2008, where I met Ann Langley, Paula Jarzabkowski and other colleagues committed to the power of a paradox lens. Paula, Marianne and I submitted a sub-track on paradox scholarship for EGOS 2010 in Portugal. We were overwhelmed by the response to the call for papers – colleagues around the world interested in applying a paradox lens to a myriad of phenomena at various levels of analysis responded. Energized by the conversations and connections at the sub-track, the scholars there decided to continue to organize this community both online through a newsletter and social media, as well as through conference connections at EGOS, Academy of Management and other venues. These efforts sparked continued and expanded interest, connecting collaborators, while also advancing initiatives for special issues, handbooks, special conferences on paradox.

Together this work advanced our insights about paradox, while building community and connection along the way.

This new maturity was expressed in a number of new angles. A central debate focused on the ontological and epistemological dimensions of paradox. It became accepted that paradoxes are ontologically inherent and epistemologically socially constructed, even if different authors gave more emphasis in highlighting one or the other facet. These two dimensions were often assumed rather than being positioned as topics for discussion. Towards the end of the decade scholars started to problematize the analytically constitutive features of the topic, invoking quantum theory (Hahn & Knight, 2019), the role of supporting actors in interpreting paradox (Pradies et al., 2020) and micro-macro links (Schad & Bansal, 2018). These discussions increasingly revealed the nested nature of paradox and a concern with analysing paradox critically.

Some research explored the limits of 'both-anding', assuming that in some cases competing demands may need to be viewed as trade-offs or dilemmas. When paradoxes are regarded as irresolvable dilemmas they can stimulate management by impressions that conceal the underlying tensions, as exemplified by the case of Volkswagen's 'dieselgate' scandal (Gaim, Clegg & Cunha, 2019). In Wolfsburg, a façade masking a false mastery of paradox was constructed to manage impressions rather than emissions (see Chapter 4 for more details). Managing politically by deceit trumped managing paradoxes pragmatically. Berti and Simpson (2019) and Cuganesan (2017) also researched paradox from a power and politics perspective, noting that paradoxes' contradictions may create not so much politically virtuous cycles as ones that lose meaning and become illogical (Berti, 2021). Avoiding a Panglossian view of paradox, seeing all paradoxes as good (Berti, 2021), a more realist account of existential dilemmas in managing paradoxes was provided.

In summary, the trajectory of paradox scholarship by organization theorists transformed paradox from being seen as a sign of dysfunction, an incongruity, to a situational source of advantage, depending on the strategies and politics that represent and engage with paradox. Paradoxes are neither good nor bad; as opportunities they can lie fallow, be harvested or left to rot in situ. The politics of strategy for paradoxes pivots on deciding when and how to do which of these options in organizing imagined futures.

The 2020s: Exploring metatheoretical potential? Metatheory is based on a set of shared underlying assumptions, not confined to specific contexts, variables or methods underlying a theory. The concept describes a constellation of commitments to theoretical beliefs, values and techniques shared by a relevant scientific community. Paradox has lately been presented as a metatheory informing and enriching different theoretical streams capable of integrating a diversity of phenomena and interpretations within one broad framework (Abrams & Hogg, 2004; Ritzer, 1990). Being a 'true' metatheory requires more than methodological variety: it implies providing an overarching perspective that can incorporate and inspire multiple approaches. A strong form of metatheory including methods, objects of interest and an exemplary body of knowledge is usually referred to as a paradigm (Ritzer, 1975), providing identity for a specific scholarly community.

Paradox may not yet be a paradigm, but it certainly constitutes an over-arching perspective, complementing existing theories by elaborating the role of contradiction, tension and opposition in different organizational processes. Poole and Van de Ven (1989) point out that most paradox researchers try to build internally consistent theories rather than auxiliary hypotheses. The search for consistency has resulted in less attention being paid to the potential for theory building related to *phenomena* characterized by tensions, oppositions and contradictions. Paradox theory functions as a metatheoretical perspective offering a broader conceptual framework which can bridge and interrelate multiple organizational theories that purposefully examine and surface tensions, as a heuristic device. Hence, it does not compete with other theories striving for paradigmatic dominance such as contingency, resource dependence, dynamic capabilities, neo-institutionalist theories, positioned as yet another analytical structure studying one particular set of phenomena (Shapira, 2011).

The boundary conditions for paradox scholarship exclude representations of phenomena that do not focus on tensions. Conceptual coherence is to be achieved by constructing a set of complementary and interrelated concepts that encompass different constitutions, manifestations and constructions of organizational paradox. The necessity of a variety of alternative foci – each coherent with a different onto-epistemological orientation – derives from the conceptual core of the theory, as defined by Lewis and Smith (2014): the existence of a dynamic duality between ontologically substantive tensions and their cognitively, socially (and politically) constructed manifestation as paradoxes.

In line with the idea that a paradox lens can be fruitfully employed not just to examine specific phenomena, but also to account for a whole range of complex social dynamics, Clegg, Cunha and Berti (2020) have proposed a conceptual model explicating the dynamics that regulate theory selection and retention in management and organization studies. They attribute the sustainability of a research programmes (e.g. contingency, institutional, resource-based perspectives) to the capacity of the research movement promoting it effectively to navigate paradoxical tensions that derive from efforts to organize the socio-material elements (grammars, thought styles, material artefacts and empirical craft) that underpin theorizing (Clegg et al., 2020).

ARE PARADOXES MATERIALLY REAL OR SOCIALLY CONSTRUCTED?

An ongoing debate in the paradox literature refers to the ontology of paradox. The central question in this debate is: are paradoxes materially real or are they socially constructed? There are good reasons to defend the merits of both perspectives. Interdependent oppositions that persist as organizing efforts unfold need to be constructed *as paradoxes*, which does not always happen, either on the part of managers or researchers. People may live with competing demands without constructing them as paradoxical (Child, 2019). From the materialist perspective, which we review next, paradoxes are real in their effects even when they are not socially constructed as so being.

The materialist perspective. The materialist perspective treats paradox as belonging to the domain of the real, as a phenomenon with causal powers that will become manifest, irrespective of their cognition as such by actors. Realist approaches to paradox are grounded on the assumption that there is a material world independent of social constructions (Kilduff, Mehra & Dunn, 2011). Paradoxes, in this regard, have real properties. Sometimes these realities are visible and graspable; other times they are 'unactualized propensities' (Ramoglou & Tsang, 2016: 410) with a material base that exists in reality, albeit one that may be neither evident nor grasped. In such a grasp of paradoxes the role of organization decision makers is to be alert to the contradictions inherent in the real and invest in their recognition (Knight & Paroutis, 2017; Tuckermann, 2018) as a source of competitive advantage.

From a materialist perspective, paradoxes originate in the realm of the real (Bhaskar, 1975) and exist regardless of their observation as such. When social totalities produce manifest contradictions between current and alternative possibilities (Benson, 1977) paradoxes may gain attention. Contradictions materialize at some point and become expressive, for example, in class conflicts or gender relations. From this perspective, the roots of paradox belong to the tangible world of materialities composed of contradictory elements. Any form of structurational goal conflict would be considered likely to produce paradoxes resulting from frictions occurring when latent causal powers or propensities become manifest. When treated as real, paradox is anchored in the world of phenomenal things: bodies and their relations with each other and with the actants of organizations, the materialities and structures framing them. As persistent processes, paradoxes may be latent and take place in the absence of clear cause-effect chains. For instance, gender relations were of little cognitive concern for management theorists in the era of the 'organization man' (Whyte, 1956) although class relations were recognized as being organized largely through pattern bargaining by organized labour (Levinson, 1960). Today, the

situation is reversed as liberal political economy has reduced the salient identity of class relations and made gender relations an enhanced identity concern.

Contradictions are an inherent feature of complex systems, as discussed by
authors in the tradition of systems theory (Boulding, 1956; Katz & Kahn, 1978;
Stacey, 1996). Systems complexity is seen as real-constitutive and the conflicting nature of those systems that create paradox is stressed. These systems are
themselves composed of complex agents (Simon, 1996) whose competing
goals necessarily produce divergence and contradictions that need to be
tackled simultaneously; for example, change and stability (Farjoun, 2010) and
exploration and exploitation (March, 1991). Tensions between these forces
are structurally rooted as inherent features of systems that emerge from the
complexity of the system itself (Schad & Bansal, 2018). The lack of balance
in the management of tensions sometimes becomes manifest in processes
such as lack or excess of change (Langley et al., 2013), too little or too much
innovation (Martin, 2009) or competing goals and worldviews originating in
different organization silos or thought worlds (Leonard-Barton, 1992). From
a paradox perspective these are all manifestations of organizational imbalance.

Paradoxes, as processes, are inherently temporal, unfolding, coming to be
and passing away. While managers may express "little engagement with the
future as fundamentally open" (Berg Johansen & De Cock, 2018: 187), being
unaware of latent paradoxes assuming manifest shape over time, it is likely
because most of the systems to which they are held accountable have limited
temporality. Institutionalized accounting schemes are tightly time prescribed.
When processes are bracketed over short periods of time, as they often are,
momentary paradoxes might emerge (Berg Johansen & De Cock, 2018).
Tensions and contradictions unfolding over significant intervals can be difficult to detect, even when their material roots are present, as appears to be the
case with some democratic politics, such as the 2016 Brexit Referendum in the
UK. The referendum concentrated multiple senses of tension and contradiction
into a popular vote of perceived English subaltern protest, an electoral howl of
outrage at being marginalized too much for too long, while in Scotland the tensions and contradictions coalesced around Brexit in quite different social constructions of national identity. People experiencing the effects of paradoxes do
not necessarily grasp their materially deep mechanisms. When analysis zooms
out to apprehend patterns it is often after the event (Schad & Bansal, 2018).
Ways of seeing that are habitually grounded in the routines of the present and
its recent past often cannot discern distinctive features that become apparent in
analytical retrospect after current events have faded.

Dealing with paradox implies awareness of the role of time and of temporal
scale (Bansal, Kim & Wood, 2018), the unfolding of being in the potentiality
of becoming. The time scale of paradox renders inter-pole tensions difficult to
perceive. Approaching paradoxes as temporal experiences in which that which

is not immediately discernible, that which is latent, becomes manifest, implies a rare skill to render long-term projections concrete, a demanding exercise (Bansal, Kim & Wood, 2018). More probable is that as organizations converge towards institutionalization and reinforce existing solutions, the tendency is to attend largely to just one of the demands, that which is most apparently immediate. Choices such as this, prioritizing one of two options, such as exploration or exploitation, exacerbate the need for the other (Sundaramurthy & Lewis, 2003).

Paradoxes are inherent and cannot be ultimately *solved* (Putnam, Fairhurst & Banghart, 2016); managing paradoxes implies what Andriopoulos and Lewis (2010: 106) denote as 'tapping their energy'. Paradoxes seen in these terms express the ontological quality of organizing, reflecting the deep structure of organizing as inherently political, pervaded by pluralism and antagonism. Because "pluralism is inherent to organization" (Clegg, 1994: 164), organizing implies tension. To summarize, paradox *can* be approached as materially real.

The constructivist perspective. From a social constructivist perspective intersubjectively contradictions perceived in reality may or may not categorize them as paradoxical: taken-for-granted realities are produced via intersubjective interaction (Fairhurst & Grant, 2010). Here actors 'construct' their reality according to the 'psychological frameworks' they have 'evolved to make sense of' phenomena, rather than 'perceiving' some objective reality (Eden et al., 1981: 40). A valid interpretation of complex environments might be to anchor these realities in contradiction and tension. From an interpretivist, social construction perspective, reality is not some objective truth waiting to be discovered but an outcome of discourse and social interaction, leading to the coexistence of multiple realities in contests for legitimacy. Paradox is an 'in the eye of the beholder' type of phenomenon (Fairhurst & Grant, 2010): language is formative of a sense of reality rather than corresponding to it; the representations used to frame reality shape the way phenomena are constructed. From this perspective, paradox's detection is attributional: people stamp paradoxical qualities on the complex realities with which they engage. Reality itself is not paradoxical unless represented as such, and where some see a paradox, others might see 'normalcy'.

Paradoxes, seen as social constructions, are a product of human practice and communication, rather than of material realities outside the realm of cognition, a central idea in the theorizing of authors such as Putnam et al. (2016) who stress how actors construct paradoxes communicatively in practice. Paradoxes are not produced by isolated individuals but through interactions made possible by public language shared, developed and legitimated by social relations (Hengst et al., 2020). In this view, a paradox is not revealed and made manageable unless it is *constructed* (Tuckermann, 2018) *as such* through practice.

Paradoxes are embedded in social contexts, with actors making sense of them through socially collective construction.

BOX 1.5 PARADOX, CULTURE AND INTERPRETATION

In some cultures, some paradoxes may be perceived as less paradoxical than others, because they have become almost second nature, culturally accepted. For instance, a study of Chinese leaders indicated that a Chinese style of developmental leadership integrates authoritarian and benevolent features (Wang, 2019). This combination, unorthodox in other cultures, may be perceived as normal in China. Therefore, what others consider as involving a measure of tension and conflict may, in the case of Chinese leaders, be normal rather than contradictory. What is contradictory here, may be normal there.

Paradoxes also become manifest at more micro levels, without people necessarily constructing tensions as paradoxical or dangerous. As Bateson et al. (1956) explained, people may engage in relationships marked by communication patterns that lock individuals in problematic dynamics, such as double binds. In the double bind, two or more people regularly engage in communication patterns marked by injunctions that conflict with one another, such as 'You need to be creative!' and 'I will not tolerate mistakes.' In some contexts, such as those of power imbalances, subjects cannot escape these dynamics. The absurdity of the situation can be normalized as just another day at the office. Its effects, however, can be debilitating as individuals may not be able to escape this vicious circle that ends up creating Kafkaesque forms of organization (Clegg et al., 2016).

To summarize the social constructivist perspective, paradoxes are intersubjective accomplishments (Sharma & Bansal, 2017) that are "talked into existence" (Lindberg, Rantatalo & Hällgren, 2017: 175). The fact that, from a materialist perspective, they might be real does not necessarily render them transparent or explicit (Metcalf, 1940). In terms of social constructions, organizational structures will often be designed to address one element of a dialectical intertwining of paradoxical poles. For instance, they might focus on exploitation of what is known, secure in the here-and-now, while neglecting investment in exploration of innovation for the future. To aggravate the difficulty, it is even possible that, in some cases, the here-and-now focus is sufficiently successful as to override concerns about exploring for the future. The presumed 'resolution' of paradox, working well in the short run, leads to the inference that there is no paradox at all. For this reason, the social construction of a phenomenon as paradoxical should be taken as a deliberate and effortful endeavour.

Integrative views: the case of performativity. By contrast to dualist approaches, performativity denotes realities and their representations as simultaneously enacted or performed as a result of the interweaving of the social and the material. From this perspective, discourse and materiality are perceived as analytically inseparable and mutually entangled, neither having a privileged status over the other: "words constitute reality and affect organizational outcomes by creating a shared sense of reality that brings phenomena into being" (Lockwood, Giorgi & Glynn, 2019: 23). A performativity perspective "shifts the focus from linguistic representations to discursive practices" (Barad, 2003: 807), helping to bridge the worlds of theory and practice, explaining the human/social and non-human/material interventions in the emergence of paradox.

The performative view explores how paradoxes are turned into reality through practice and how practice reinforces the reality of paradoxes. Meaning and matter are held together via the enmeshment of language, cognition and place, with practice mediating the relationship between the discursive and the material, which coexist as enmeshed facets of reality. Performing is an exercise in relational enactment through practice (Law, 2008). By taking practice as the primary building block of social reality (Feldman & Orlikowski, 2011), paradox becomes seen as "something people do, rather than something that organizations have" (Guérard, Langley & Seidl, 2013: 574). Such a notion helps with seeing how paradox is *done* as a process that people enact, rather than assuming it to be either already formed as a thing that people discover or as a construction of language and intersubjectivity. Practice brings paradox to reality via the mutual entanglement of words and deeds, in incessant recursive cycles in which contradictions are categorically framed and established categories are fulfilled.

USES OF PARADOX IN ORGANIZATION STUDIES

Paradox has been used in the literature in different ways (see Figure 1.1 and Table 1.1). In this section we organize these uses around three views: paradoxes viewed as descriptive, normative and instrumental. Descriptively, paradox is used to depict specific organizational phenomena; instrumentally, practitioners cope with paradoxes through particular paradoxical mindsets and agency and cognitive, structural and practical responses; normatively, paradox signifies the pros (and cons), both for theoreticians and strategists, of adopting a paradoxical frame of reference for making sense of reality. The perspectives offered by these three views are not incompatible, which means different actors can make use of more than one for different purposes. For example, the nurturing of a paradox lens can help organizational members discover prescriptive uses of the idea. As Lüscher and Lewis (2008) put it, paradox can change from label to lens and prescriptive uses can be derived from the lens.

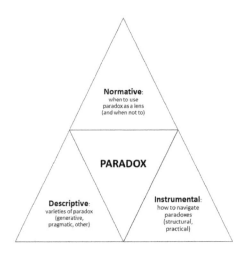

Source: Adapted from a figure proposed by Hahn et al., 2018.

Figure 1.1   Descriptive, normative and instrumental views of paradox

The descriptive view. This perspective aims to theorize the different types of paradoxes that exist 'out there', the operation of paradox (what triggers it, how it unfolds) and its consequences (circles, synergies). The descriptive role of theory consists in studying paradox to understand what it is and how it happens. This view resulted in important contributions that help to make sense of paradox as a phenomenon.

Work in this strand explains the origins of paradoxes as well as the process associated with managing, or not, paradox in organizations. It has helped with classifying different types of paradoxes along typological lines, such as those presented by Smith and Lewis (2011) and Berti and Simpson (2020). Smith and Lewis (2011) discussed four types of paradoxes, introducing nuance in the discussion of paradoxes. Berti and Simpson (2020) classified paradoxes with a logic that is sensitive to power dynamics, showing that paradoxes are not equal in their import and impact but also that some paradoxes can be debilitating. Pragmatic paradoxes, as they explained, can actually confront organizational members with impossible choices. In combination, work in this stream is helping to map the complexities and nuances of the paradox landscape.

The normative view. Approaching paradox as an idea rather than as a thing (as in the previous case), the normative view extols the potency of paradoxical thinking in addressing complex organizational issues. Normative approaches stress the intrinsic value of paradoxical perspectives as a norm with which to tackle complex problems. As a lens, paradox offers a way of seeing that illuminates aspects of organizations and of organizational functioning obscured by other approaches to organizations. Seeing through paradox accentuates dimensions of organizing not necessarily considered in other perspectives, such as tension, contradiction and opposition. These aspects are seen as an inevitable part of organizing. In other words, regardless of the organizational process under consideration, it will inevitably be marked by these attributes. The boundary conditions limiting the idea of paradox are defined as complementary tensions in opposition. A normative paradoxical perspective helps with understanding cases in which forces that oppose one another also define one another (i.e. are interdependent). In cases in which tensions are independent, it is of little or no use.

The instrumental view. Instrumental approaches to paradox theory lead to prescriptive models for application, helping to change organizations, establishing connections between tensions and organizational outcomes, and thereby managing tensions for organizational advantage. To some extent the instrumental view derives from the normative but more as a tool rather than as an orienting idea. Paradox, as a possible source of competitive advantage, consists in the capacity for seeing and intervening in a world aware that dualistic thinking limits the ability to capture the ambiguities of experience. Instrumentally, paradox constitutes an invitation to intervene in a world inherently composed of opposites in tension, freeing organizations from the tyranny of 'either'-'or' choices (Collins & Porras, 2005). By loosening such a conceptual straitjacket, organizations may help their members redefine organizations as spaces where opposite goals may be achieved – a need that becomes more relevant as organizations are urged to find synergies between different stakeholders with divergent needs (Tantalo & Priem, 2016) in order to tackle grand challenges (Schad & Smith, 2019). By applying a both-and type of reasoning to organizational and societal challenges, managers aim to find novel viable synergies to tackle important issues. Instrumentally paradox has been presented as a way of dealing with the world through an integrative mindset, one that rejects the simplicity of dualism. Some instrumental views of paradox have been advanced, including Johnson's polarity map (Johnson, 2014) and Smith, Lewis and Tushman's (2016) 'both-and leadership', presented as mechanisms for extracting synergies out of paradoxical tensions.

Table 1.1   *Uses of paradox in organization studies*

	Descriptive	Normative	Instrumental
Goals	To represent paradox as it happens in the 'real world'	To define when to use paradox and when not to do so	To guide intervention
Expressions	Typologies, process models	Conceptual clarifications	Tools, practical indications
Target	Mainly academics	Mainly academics	Mainly practitioners and consultants
Limitations	May create perception of paradox as too abstract	May create hard-to-define boundaries between contiguous concepts	May transmit the idea that paradoxes can be controlled
Representative work	Smith & Lewis (2011) Berti & Simpson (2020)	Lüscher & Lewis (2008) Smith, Lewis & Tushman (2016)	Collins & Porras (2005) Johnson (2014)

CONCLUSION

Once upon a time, paradox was perceived as an organizational disease, a sign of malfunction. No more. In contemporary times organizations are commonly described as 'rife with paradox' because "ontologically, organizations are multidimensional, socially constructed realities where different aspects can coexist in complementary, conflicting, hence paradoxical ways" (Morgan, 2011: 467). Initially, as we reviewed the field for this chapter, paradox was represented as a something to be 'solved', to be neutralized. Subsequently, managing paradox became a talisman of success with which to take advantage of the synergies contained in tension and opposition. The foe became a friend. Yet, even when seen as normal, as a part of what organizing implies, paradox can be hard to tackle. The tensions that paradoxes reveal lead as easily to the erection of psychological and social defences against these as to bold embraces in managing them. Some tensions may simply be repressed, forcing people to pretend that they do not exist. Mikkelsen and Wahlin (2020), researching diversity management in the local branch of a global retail chain, found this to be the case. A dominant narrative of diversity impeded people from critically expressing their views so that in the name of diversity, diverse opinions were silenced! These tensions reflect the nuance of paradox, including its absurd dimension, which is where we begin the next chapter. Paradox may be part of the manager's toolkit – but still be difficult to master.

2. How to deal with paradoxes: the role of responses in the construction of paradoxical tension

A fundamental characteristic of paradox is its recursive character: action taken in reaction to the contradictory situation experienced by an actor is not likely to 'solve' the problem. Rather, trying to solve the problem is similar to someone attempting to extricate a tangle by pulling hard on one end. Likewise, efforts to deal with a paradoxical challenge often result in 'tightening the knot', making the situation even more intractable. Indeed, actors' responses to organizational paradoxes are constitutive of their ongoing social construction. In other words, today's paradoxes are often the consequences of responses to contradictions experienced in the past.

Paradox studies have described a wide range of possible responses. One of the most comprehensive catalogues, compiled by Jarzabkowski and Lê (2017), lists 12 possible types of responses: splitting, regression, repression, projection, reaction formation, ambivalence, acceptance, confrontation, transcendence, suppressing, opposing, adjusting. These can be considered as variations on three major themes, or categories of responses: either-or, both-and, and more-than (Putnam, Fairhurst & Banghart, 2016).

The first strategy (either-or) is based on an implicit attempt to preserve one of the cornerstones of Aristotelian logic, the principle of non-contradiction, the idea that opposite assertions cannot be true at the same time. In the face of contradictory demands, a natural reaction is to treat the situation as absurd (Lewis, 2000), which leads to denying the existence of the contradiction, treating it as a mistake that needs to be fixed (Vince & Broussine, 1996). One way of fixing the problem is to subordinate one of the contradictions to the other (Seo, Putnam & Bartunek, 2004). Similarly, agents can choose to highlight distinctiveness and opposition, rather than acknowledge interconnectedness between poles, which often leads to increased tensions (Putnam, Fairhurst & Banghart, 2016). Such an either-or approach was dominant before the introduction and legitimization of a paradox perspective in organization studies (Putnam, 1986; Smith & Berg, 1987).

A second approach focuses on acknowledging the inseparability and interdependence of opposite demands through a both-and strategy (Putnam,

Fairhurst & Banghart, 2016). Responses are in this case accept the need for finding synergies or for accommodating contrasting demands that cannot be ignored or repressed. Doing so requires developing cognitive (Keller & Chen, 2017; Miron-Spektor, Gino & Argote, 2011) and emotional (Pradies et al., 2020; Smith & Lewis, 2011) abilities for thinking paradoxically, which does not come easily. Such a "paradoxical mindset", defined as "the extent to which individuals feel comfortable with and energized by tensions" (Miron-Spektor et al., 2018: 38) is not just an individual trait; its emergence is facilitated by embeddedness in specific cultures (Keller, Loewenstein & Yan, 2017; Li, 2016) and social networks (Keller, Wong & Liou, 2020). The both-and solution can include moving back and forth between differentiating and integrating (Smith, 2014); oscillation between dilemmatic requirements (Lüscher & Lewis, 2008); allowing the interplay of opposites (Clegg, Cunha & Cunha, 2002) as well as achieving a synergistic balance (Andriopoulos & Lewis, 2009).

The third possible strategy is treating the opposition as relative to a specific frame of reference or context and considering the possibility that what seems irreconcilable and dissonant could just be a local manifestation of a complex form of harmony. The idea that contradictions can be transcended or synthesized at a higher level of abstraction leads to consideration of the possibility of 'more-than' responses to paradox (Putnam, Fairhurst & Banghart, 2016). 'Transcendence' in this case facilitates engaging tensions to open up undiscovered possibilities, acting as an epistemological device enabling exploration of new organizing forms.

These three strategies can be seen as part of a continuum, the continuum includes approaches that respond to paradoxical tensions through simplification (i.e. trying to untangle the interrelationship between opposites, separating them or defining priorities, as in the case of either-or strategies). It also involves a contrary approach that proposes navigating the challenge by complexifying the frame of reference. Doing this can be achieved by accepting the normality of the contradiction (both-and strategies) or by reconsidering the original frame of reference (more-than strategies). In the next section we consider how these alternative categories of responses have been assessed by paradox scholarship according to their viability and implications.

GOOD *VERSUS* BAD RESPONSES?

Within the canon of organizational paradox theory, this typology is not just a descriptive representation of possible responses to organizational tensions and contradictions. Rather its intent is ultimately prescriptive, distinguishing between useful and problematic reactions. As noted by Jarzabkowski and Lê (2017: 436), "responses are generally clustered according to largely negative or positive implications". Hence, either-or responses are normatively presented as intrinsically undesirable, expression of a defensive/reactive attitude that is bound to entrench the experienced contradiction, instead of leveraging its generative potential. Conversely, responses that proactively embrace the contradiction, and that aim to work through it, are promoted as necessary to relieve tensions and as also having the potential to generate positive change and innovation (Smith & Lewis, 2011).

The idea that tensions are not occasional flaws in the edifice of organizing but unavoidable constituents of collective social action is indeed one of the most important contributions of paradox theory. From this, it follows that it is important to send a strong message to academics and practitioners that it is often necessary to live with tensions rather than trying to overcome them. At the same time, it is important to avoid falling into a simplicity trap, offering a single one best way to deal with the wide range of organizational tensions that can be experienced (Cunha & Putnam, 2019). Normatively prescribing one set of correct responses would, ironically, betray the very principles that inspire paradox scholarship.

First, paradoxical tensions should be treated not only as problems to be solved: contradictory demands pose significant challenges to organizational actors, which can become insurmountable if they are not adequately equipped with the freedom and power to respond (Berti & Simpson, 2019). Yet, given that paradox is endemic to organizing (Lewis, 2000), ongoing responses are required (Abdallah, Denis & Langley, 2011). The issue is not so much that of choosing and implementing the correct response but rather adapting to or even transforming contingent requirements and constraints, considering that solutions can become part of the problem (Farson, 1996).

For instance, a common challenge in transformation programmes is that of dealing with resistance to change. Yet, this resistance is not just an expression of fear of transformation, vested interests in the preservation of the status quo, or lack of communication. If organizational agents individually and collectively had no capacity to resist to change, organizations would display no inertia, defined as "tendency to routinely repeat past actions and patterns of activities" (Jansen, 2004: 276). Yet structural inertia does not just cause slowness in strategic response: it also increases the reproducibility of structures (Hannan & Freeman, 1984) and facilitates avoiding the risk of falling for momentary fads (Yi, Knudsen & Becker, 2016). During change initiatives it is important to account both for the need to preserve positive traits and to modify undesirable ones: in other words, we want individuals both to embrace and to resist change. Such an observation seems to support the intrinsic superiority of a 'both-and' response to this 'learning' paradox (Smith & Lewis, 2011); however, during a transformation initiative it would be most impractical to communicate to the staff of an organization that they need both to resist and not resist the proposed changes. In practice, it is necessary to implement a repertoire of responses (including either-or ones) depending on the situation.

Second, responses to paradox are not inherently good or bad (Jarzabkowski & Lê, 2017). As discussed in the previous chapter, contradictions are inherent to organizing processes; while often latent, they can become salient as a consequence of external pressures (sudden change or resource scarcity) and/or because of the measurement apparatuses (including management control systems, policies, reward systems, management practices, etc.) adopted by an organization (Hahn & Knight, 2019). Responses to paradox are not just the expression of individual preferences and cognitive frames but are also codified and enabled by social dynamics (Jarzabkowski & Lê, 2017). Codified responses, routinized in organizational practices (Jay, 2013; Papachroni & Heracleous, 2020; Smets et al., 2015), contribute to the construction and reproduction of organizing apparatuses. Hence, all responses to paradox contribute to the reproduction of paradoxes. The implication of this observation is that, rather than trying to determine the appropriateness of a category of responses, it is necessary empirically to assess whether the recursive relationship between paradox and response allows achieving and maintaining a sustainable balance between investments and returns, actions and consequences.

Many organizations have managed to subsist for a long time, despite their apparent 'denial' of the paradoxical tension between exploitation and exploration. Take, for instance, the case of Japanese pluricentenarian companies (*Shinise*), whose survival has been explained through their commitment to values of continuity, craftmanship, cooperation and family ownership (Sasaki, Ravasi & Micelotta, 2019). Indeed successful family firms have outlived and outperformed many corporations by adopting non-paradoxical strategies, based on clarity of mission, continuity, traditional ownership, and focus on preserving strong relationships (Miller & Le Breton-Miller, 2005). In these cases firms achieve longevity by finding an 'optimal' solution to the exploitation/exploration tensions that privileges the former over the latter (Riviezzo et al., 2015). It is therefore necessary to acknowledge that responses to paradox should be assessed longitudinally and situationally, as moves in a complex, recursive and open game aimed at navigating tensions. Mapping different responses to paradox should be considered as a descriptive exercise, oriented to developing an ever-richer repertoire of possible solutions, the usefulness of which should be considered situationally.

MAPPING PARADOX RESPONSES

While we acknowledge the utility of the tripartite distinction between either-or, both-and and more-than response strategies proposed by Putnam, Fairhurst and Banghart (2016), we propose complementing them with another analytic dimension. We do so in order the better to capture different nuances while avoiding the simplistic good-bad response dichotomy and proposing alternative perspectives. This second dimension aims to describe different attitudes towards paradoxical challenges. *Avoidance* refers to approaches that aim to remove the challenge caused by interdependent contradictions, or that acknowledge that it is not possible to avoid the disruption caused by the experience of these contradictions. By contrast, according to a *balance* perspective it is possible to maintain the opposite forces in a dynamic equilibrium through continuous purposeful adjustments, akin to a tightrope walker (Schad et al., 2016). A third possibility is to consider that the paradoxical challenge can be *resolved* through effective responses. Such resolution does not imply that the underlying paradox will be eliminated so much as 'tamed', preserving long-term sustainability of the organizational system (Smith & Lewis, 2011). Finally, the most positive view of paradoxical challenge is the idea that paradox constitutes a vital force that can be *leveraged*, harnessing it as a creative source of innovation and insight.

These four perspectives can be situated in a continuum, depending on whether paradox is treated as a threat or as an opportunity. Crossing this dimension with the three types of paradox management strategies that were described before, we obtain coordinates that can be used to map the many possible responses to paradoxical tensions that have been empirically described (or conceptually proposed) in the literature, relating them to each other (Figure 2.1).

A first group of responses are those that view paradox as a threat to avoid and propose using either-or strategies to cope with it. Some of these strategies seem more instinctive that purposeful, as in the case of denial, or "refusing to accept an unpleasant reality" (Vince & Broussine, 1996: 5). Evading the tension achieves this, such as when an actor escapes from a problem to avoid the tension (Cunha et al., 2019a). Doing this is a defence mechanism, a form of repression that often backfires, because attempts to pull contradiction apart can generate self-referential effects that bind actors (Smith & Berg, 1987), exacerbating experience of the contradiction (Tracy, 2004). In the same class can be included responses based on suppression: in this case, responses to paradox incorporate a political dimension, as the primacy of one of the opposing poles (at the expense of others) is affirmed and supported by an implicit or explicit exercise of power (Jarzabkowski, Lê & Van de Ven, 2013). A third type of response that can be assimilated to the previous two is the situation of false mastery of paradox described by Gaim, Clegg and Cunha (2019) in their study of the Volkswagen emissions scandal. In this case the top management choice of boldly embracing paradox by dictating the unattainable goal to designing an engine combining low emissions and low production with high performances turned out to be an exercise in impression management. The

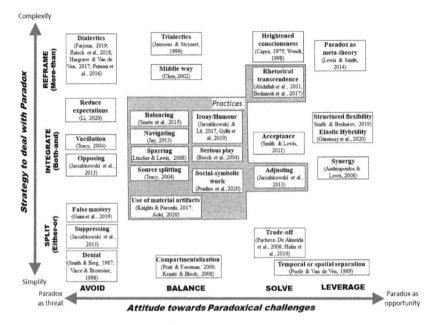

Figure 2.1   A typology of paradox responses

idea of false mastery reveals that in formulating responses to paradox it is not just a matter of a 'can do' attitude but also requires dealing materially with contradictions. Actors that are ordered to pursue contradictory goals without being given the possibility to do so will experience the demand as a pragmatic paradox, a self-contradictory and un-negotiable request that will only produce pathological effects (Berti & Simpson, 2019, 2020).

An avoidance attitude can also be combined with a both-and response strategy, as in the case of responses based on vacillation between poles, situations in which an actor copes with contradictory requirements by "switching between opposing organizational norms depending on the time, person being worked with, or the topic/context" (Tracy, 2004: 130). This requires being flexible and accommodating in some circumstances and rigid and punctilious in others. Actors adopting this response are aware of the need to comply with both contradictory requests but do that in a reactive manner, depending on the pressures they receive. Hence this approach can be problematic, as the organization becomes stuck in "a perpetual oscillation between poles without moving forward" (Putnam, Fairhurst & Banghart, 2016: 126). A similar situation can become apparent when different parties support opposing poles, both being determined to assert their own needs in a balance of power. In such a situation the antagonists become locked in a head-on opposition (Jarzabkowski, Lê & Van de Ven, 2013). The resulting both-and response, in this case as in the previous cases, is defensive and reactive, unlikely to lead to a generative outcome.

The possibility of combining a reframing strategy with a construal of paradoxical contradictions as a source of conflict appears remote in the context of paradox theory. One possibility is suggested by Li (2020), who considered reducing expectations as a way of easing tensions experienced in the case of intractable paradoxes, thus making them more manageable. This proposal is based on the idea that responses to paradoxical situations are not just shaped by mindsets and agency, but also by "the asymmetry between one's capacity and expectation" (Li, 2020: 8).

The upper-left corner of our proposed map is occupied by a class of responses that are inspired by the conceptual framework of dialectics (Benson, 1977; Clegg & Cunha, 2017; Putnam, Fairhurst & Banghart, 2016), one that is both similar and distinct from a paradox perspective. The notion of dialectics originates in Hegel's philosophy, wherein historical transformation is seen as a combination of destruction and combination. In such a process of 'sublation' [*Aufhebung*] new and richer constructs are created through the synthesis and transcendence of contrasting ideas (Hegel, 1812 [2010]). "Sublation [...] has the dual meaning of overcoming and preserving" (Raisch, Hargrave & Van De Ven, 2018: 26). While a dialectical perspective has in common with paradox the idea that tensions are unavoidable and not intrinsically harmful (Tracy, 2004), it is set apart by its emphasis on the role of resistance and conflict in transformation (Hargrave & Van de Ven, 2017). The reframing, and radical transformation of the status quo, happens through a struggle (Clegg & Cunha, 2017) which generates a synthesis that is not an endgame but that will activate further tensions, in a process fuelling constant learning and transformation (Hargrave, 2021). An exemplification is provided by gender identity struggles in organizations, where resistance to oppressive gender roles can paradoxically reinforce gender distinctions while, at the same time, failure to transform unfair conditions reinvigorates resistance to male dominance (Putnam & Ashcraft, 2017).

If the attitude towards paradoxical challenge is less focus on discord and opposition, considering instead the possibility of finding a sustainable balance between divergent requirements, a new group of responses emerges. First, balance can be achieved by recurring to 'splitting', either-or strategies, such as compartmentalization, a choice to preserve multiple contradictory requirements without trying to attain any synergy among them (Pratt & Foreman, 2000). When actors have to accommodate competing institutional logics (Kraatz & Block, 2008) this also happens. An example is provided by Reay and Hinings (2009), showing how health professionals keep decisions attending to different logics strictly separate when dealing with contradictory demands to comply both with medical professionalism and business-like norms. The strategy ends up reinforcing splits between organizations involved in the same ecosystem but with a focus on different priorities.

When actors are willing to seek balance and embrace an integrative (both-and) response, they will seek ways to "work through paradox on an ongoing basis" (Lüscher & Lewis, 2008). In doing this, they develop inter-dependent micro-practices that enable engagement with tensions while maintaining equilibrium. At the same time they also capture and preserve collective tacit knowledge about how to deal with the paradox (Jarzabkowski, Bednarek & Lê, 2018). Multiple paradox navigating practices have been described. In their ethnographic study of Lloyd's of London, Smets et al. (2015) describe dynamic balancing to deal with coexisting logics, based on three mechanisms: segmenting (separating streams of work attending to different logics), bridging (how to integrate differences), and demarcating (counteracting tendency to privilege one logic over another). The metaphor of navigating has also been employed to describe how actors must use sensemaking to find creative routes while avoiding becoming stuck in the contradictions that lurk under the surface (Jay, 2013). Searching for balanced, integrative solutions does not eschew the possibility of conflict, which is however restrained and harnessed to the purpose of synergic results. An example of this is the use of sparring sessions in which participants discuss the tension they experience in a process of reflective questioning (Cuganesan, 2017; Lüscher & Lewis, 2008), creating a "workable certainty" in face of paradox (Lüscher & Lewis, 2008: 230). Another form of role playing that can be used to deal with contradictory demands is source splitting, a strategy in which actors perform opposite roles in coordinated fashion, as in the 'good cop/bad cop' routine (Tracy, 2004).

The use of humour and irony is often associated with the experience of paradox and contradictions (Hatch, 1997; Hatch & Erhlich, 1993). These are not just a safety valve helping to deal emotionally with the absurdity of the situation. Humour acts as a micro-practice actors employ collectively to make sense of the situation, enabling them to come up with extemporary responses to paradox that can be more or less successful (Jarzabkowski & Lê, 2017). Irony can also be used as a discursive device to give voice to different poles, helping their balancing (energizing and embracing them in turn), which is instrumental in advancing discussion and treatment of paradox (Gylfe, Franck & Vaara, 2019). The ironical approach to tensions is based on acknowledgement that contradictions cannot always be resolved through deliberate cognitive processes. Rather, emotions, creativity, mocking of rules and challenges to normal behavioural boundaries can be employed, as a form of serious play (Beech et al., 2004), to accommodate paradox.

Considering the role of practices in the ongoing management of tensions also draws attention to the role of material artefacts in coping with paradox.

Practices always implicate materiality, in the guise of tools and practitioners' bodies (Gherardi, 2012). Artefacts can act as sensemaking cues raising the salience of contradiction for different organization members, inducing them to focus attention on different requirements at the same time (Knight & Paroutis, 2017). In his study of continuous improvement in a Chinese company, Aoki (2020) has shown how various artefacts (boxes, labels, shopfloor layout, graphs, etc.) are used to trigger social interaction, making paradox salient and creating contexts for formulating responses to them. Another aspect of practices that can be leveraged to help working through paradox is social symbolic work, that concerns the reproduction of social relations and shared beliefs imbued with meaning, which has been shown to be instrumental in turning vicious into virtuous cycles (Pradies et al., 2020).

Some authors have also considered the possibility of employing reframing (more-than) strategies in the attempt to preserve equilibrium in face of organizational tensions. An example is pursuing middle-way strategies (Chen, 2002). This notion, deriving from Chinese philosophy and captured in the Yin-Yang symbol, draws attention to the interdependent nature of paradoxical poles and resolving oppositions dynamically through "an active 'harmonious integration' of opposites rather than a reactive compromise between them" (Chen, 2002: 183). A Western parallel can be found in the notion of trialectics, a form of higher-order thinking based on a shift of perspective that allows consideration of complementarity and interdependence and that, differently from dialectics, sees the relationship between opposites not as solved through conflict but as balanced in equilibrium (Janssens & Steyaert, 1999).

Despite the tenet that paradoxes should be sustained, a remarkable number of contributions to paradox scholarship appear intent on identifying responses that 'solve' paradoxical knots, in the sense of disentangling them so that the tensions can become 'tamed' and used for managerial purposes (Cunha & Putnam, 2019). When this perspective is associated with an either-or type of response tensions are typically construed as trade-off choices, "compromise situations when a sacrifice is made in one area to obtain benefits in another" (Byggeth & Hochschorner, 2006: 1420). The idea of the trade-off is central to several disciplines, from the life sciences, such as biology and ecology (Stearns, 1989), to social sciences, such as economics (Skousen & Taylor, 1997) and human communication (Watzlawick, Jackson & Bavelas, 1967). For example, cultural diversity fosters creative problem solving at the cost, it is reported, of decreased coordination and efficiency (Corritore, Goldberg & Srivastava, 2020). In this sense trade-offs are not just the outcome of a non-paradoxical mindset (Miron-Spektor et al., 2018) but an inherent characteristic of situations in which "it is impossible to achieve two or more desirable objectives simultaneously; rather decision makers need to weigh a loss in at least one dimension against a gain in the other dimension" (Hahn et al., 2010: 219). Even if trade-offs have been frequently associated with dilemmas, "either/or choices in which one alternative must be selected" (Putnam, Fairhurst & Banghart, 2016: 73), they do not always imply mutual exclusivity. Rather, because of the inverse relationship between necessary or desirable elements, a choice in relation to their balance is required. Biology offers the best illustration: since some somatic responses cannot increase without a decrease in another (running faster requires lighter bones, so a faster animal will be less strong), multiple different ways to balance conflicting functional demands are possible, each fitting a specific ecological niche (Garland, 2014). Similarly, in an organizational context, the management of the trade-off between commitment versus flexibility in investments can lead to a range of alternative strategic positioning choices (Pacheco de Almeida, Henderson & Cool, 2008).

In their influential paper on dynamic equilibrium in organizing, Smith and Lewis (2011) offer normative prescriptions for the optimal management of paradoxical tensions based on the principle of acceptance. They argue that only the use of "dynamic, purposeful, and ongoing strategies of acceptance and resolution (iterating between splitting and integration) fosters sustainability" (Smith & Lewis, 2011: 394). They explicitly refer to this pro-active management strategy as the one that will lead to "paradoxical resolution" (Smith & Lewis, 2011: 389). Their strategic guidelines for resolving paradox through integrative responses can be implemented by adjusting work practices in order to support both sides of the paradox, for example through intensive interworking between divisions, negotiating compromises between divergent requirements (Jarzabkowski et al., 2013).

The class of responses most often associated with an idea of paradox resolution are those requiring a complete reframing of the context. Opposing poles can be re-situated in this way to transcend dualistic thinking and become appreciated holistically, as a bounded component of the same reality (Wendt, 1998). Transcendence can be seen as the outcome of a cognitive process, a form of heightened consciousness "where the realm of thought and language is transcended and all opposites appear as a dynamic unity" (Capra, 1975: 149). Also emotions can be involved in this switch from the particular to the holistic: groups can form a euphoric bond through "*jamming* experiences, instances of fluid behavioral coordination that occur without detailed knowledge of personality" (Eisenberg, 1990: 139). Transcendence in organization is often a more prosaic affair. Defined as "the ability to view both poles of the paradox as necessary and complementary" (Bednarek, Paroutis & Sillince, 2017: 77), it typically involves rhetorical practices through which the situation is discursively reframed in a way to ease oppositional tensions. Since the legitimacy of the actor proposing the rhetorical solution is essential for a discourse of transcendence to take root, reframing requires "leaders who can articulate a vision that transcends contradictions" (Abdallah, Denis & Langley, 2011:

337). Moreover, rhetorical transcendence is not a one-off achievement but an ongoing process of becoming, wherein each temporary synthesis encounters new tensions requiring further transcendence (Bednarek, Paroutis & Sillince, 2017). Indeed, success in reframing is bound to create new tensions, which will cause the original tensions to resurface in new forms (Abdallah, Denis & Langley, 2011).

To complete our mapping of responses to paradox we also need to consider the most 'optimistic' view of organizational paradoxes, understood as opportunities for innovation and transformation. The synergistic potential of multiple logics and requirements, according to the literature, can be harnessed in multiple ways. The most traditional approach, based on an either-or strategy, is the one proposed in Poole and Van de Ven's (1989) seminal contribution. They see spatial and/or temporal separation as effective methods to respond to paradoxes, 'solving' them and leveraging them. Spatial separation refers to handling paradoxes at different organizational levels, while temporal separation means coping which them at different times. If Poole and Van de Ven referred to paradox as epistemological challenges for organizational theorists, several studies have empirically described the application of these structural solutions for managing organizational tensions by allocating them to different units and processes (Beech et al., 2004; Es-Sajjade, Pandza & Volberda, 2020; Stadtler & Van Wassenhove, 2016).

The possibility of leveraging the generative potential of paradox is more often associated with response strategies based on integration. The idea of actively searching for and leveraging synergies in tensions (in contrast with the emphasis on conflict of dialectic view) is a distinctive element of a paradox perspective (Hargrave & Van de Ven, 2017). The idea of organizing contradictory elements in order to produce mutually advantageous outcomes has been strongly advocated by Andriopoulos and Lewis (2009). They show how this result can be achieved through an ongoing process of iterative adaptation, alternating differentiation and integration actions. It is especially in the context of hybrid organizations, blending multiple logics, such as social enterprises and public-private partnerships (Pache & Santos, 2012), that means to effectively channel tensions towards productive results have been described. This requires structured flexibility (Smith & Besharov, 2019), achieved through a combination of cognitive processes (allowing experimentally engaging with alternative logics) and formal structures, acting as 'guardrails' (Soderstrom & Heinze, 2019) that constrain flexibility, maintaining strategic alignment. A combination of structural features and discursive practices has also been described by Gümüsay, Smets and Morris (2020) as a way to achieve elastic hybridity, enabling the organization staff to engage dynamically with competing logics.

The upper-right corner of our conceptual map is meant to accommodate responses that aim to leverage the potential of paradoxes through reframing. In a 'philologic' sense, doing so would mean embracing the true, etymological meaning of the term para-doxa, i.e. transcending common knowledge: for example, pursuing strategies that actively stimulate the emergence of contradictions. The literature has described purposive efforts to make paradox salient in order to make sure that a broader group of organizational members is aware and willing to engage with this saliency (Knight & Paroutis, 2017). However, we are not aware of studies describing organizational decision makers who employed paradoxical strategies in order to stimulate radical innovation, analogously to how psychotherapists sometimes do (Seltzer, 1986). Instead, the possibility of combining a more-than response with the view of paradox as opportunity is represented in the drive spearheaded by Lewis and Smith (2014) to exploit the potential of paradox as a metatheory, i.e. treating it as broad framework based on a set of shared underlying assumptions integrating a diversity of phenomena and interpretations, without being confined to specific contexts, variables or methods (Abrams & Hogg, 2004; Ritzer, 1990). The emphasis echoes much earlier calls for leveraging tensions for theory-building (Poole & Van de Ven, 1989) or as a device for sensemaking (Clegg, Cunha & Cunha, 2002).

CONCLUSION

Perhaps the most significant contribution of paradox theory, beyond providing an account of the tensions that we all experience in the workplace, in the marketplace and in the public arena, resides in its capacity to complexify our understanding of organizations (Tsoukas, 2017), steering organization studies towards a "recursivity-based view" of organizing, looking at the interplay between process and structure and between stability and change (Hernes & Bakken, 2003: 1512). It grasps the fluid nature of phenomena, appreciating the intrinsic incompleteness of any abstract representation of reality.

Responses to paradox are an essential component of recursive processes through which attempts at ordering social interactions reduce equivocality, resulting in tensions that require new attempts at ordering. With our map of responses to organizational tensions we do not intend to provide a normatively exhaustive account of all possible ways to construe and cope with paradoxes. Rather, our intent is to demonstrate the richness of the response repertoire, beyond any dualistic distinction between constructive and harmful ones.

We must also acknowledge an omission. Ambidexterity (Gibson & Birkinshaw, 2004; Raisch et al., 2009; Tushman & O'Reilly III, 1996) does not explicitly feature in our map, because it represents a range of possible responses to a specific category of organizational tensions, learning paradoxes

(Lewis & Dehler, 2000; Smith & Lewis, 2011) that are represented by the opposition between organizational needs for exploration and exploitation (March, 1991). Originally, ambidexterity was associated with the creation of a distinct organizational unit through spatial separation and using senior executive level personnel to integrate them (Tushman & O'Reilly III, 1996). The idea of structural ambidexterity (and of its shortcomings) has been considered in various studies (e.g. Heracleous et al., 2017; Strese et al., 2016). More recent studies have also considered the possibility of the hybrid use of spatial and temporal separation, to be used in conjunction with integrative processes (Andriopoulos & Lewis, 2009). The idea that ambidexterity is not achieved through structural solutions but by means of specific practices has also been explored (Papachroni & Heracleous, 2020).

Rather than justifying the omission of any other manifestation of organizational paradoxes (and the associated responses), we would like to conclude by considering the possibility of other alternative ways to categorize and compare responses to paradox. For instance it is possible to distinguish at which level responses can be identified and studied: micro (individual), meso (organizational), or macro (systemic or institutional) (Putnam, Fairhurst & Banghart, 2016). Another interesting possibility is to consider the different factors that contribute to dynamically forming responses: cognition, emotions, artefacts, routines, degree of agency of the actor, dominant discourses, etc. This latter point also suggests the opportunity to consider responses longitudinally, i.e. considering their evolution and transformation over time.

3. The bright side: paradoxes and positive organizational scholarship

> The desire for a more positive experience is itself a negative experience. And, paradoxically, the acceptance of one's negative experience is itself a positive experience.
> (Manson, 2016)

> Paradoxically, however, positive outcomes also result from negative problems, difficulties, traumas, challenges, and losses. Some of the greatest triumphs, most noble virtues, and highest achievements have resulted from the presence of the negative.
> (Cameron, 2017b: 216)

An essential paradox of life is that, while humans have a natural heliotropic tendency to flourish and thrive with the positive, we also tend to respond more strongly to negative over positive stimuli. So observes Cameron (2017b), who sees this essential paradox as particularly highlighted in the field of organizational studies dedicated to researching and promoting the positive, Positive Organizational Scholarship (POS) (Cameron, Dutton & Quinn, 2003a; Cameron & Spreitzer, 2012; Dutton & Glynn, 2008). As a discipline, POS is concerned with "positive outcomes, processes and attributes of organizations and their members" (Cameron, Dutton & Quinn, 2003b: 4). This positive focus is expanded as into broader subdomains that include "an emphasis on identifying individual and collective strengths (attributes and processes) and discovering how such strengths enable human flourishing (goodness, generativity, growth, and resilience)" (Roberts, 2006: 292), as well as "the states and processes that arise from and result in life-giving dynamics, optimal functioning, and enhanced capabilities" (Dutton & Glynn, 2008: 693). Cameron (2017b: 216) suggests that the key to "extraordinarily effective performance for individuals and for organizations", rather than dwelling within paradoxes as either-or choices, is transcending them. In defining the essential paradox of life as tensions between the positive and the negative, Cameron appears to assume that distinguishing between these two oppositions is always clear-cut. Deeper analysis reveals that cultivating positivity in organizations is an endeavour that can be much more complex than is often acknowledged by POS scholars. We consider that the domain of POS needs to be cross-fertilized through deeper engagement with paradox theory, to realise the potential benefit of both fields (see Cunha et al., 2020).

Paradoxes often present themselves as dilemmas in which choice between options is considered critical, creating negative crisis situations. Peterson and Park (2011: 58) suggest that when lapses in virtue constitute opportunities for moral reformation and redemption (Brooks, 2019), such negative crisis situations may, in fact, be "the crucible of good character". Other situations of choice between various interdependent and conflicting objectives might include corporate sustainability initiatives that must juggle environmental protection *and* social well-being as well as building upon *and* destroying current activities (Hahn et al., 2018). Leadership studies suggest that virtuous objectives will be more readily achieved by leaders imbued with both a stance of virtue along with healthy narcissism (Owens, Wallace & Waldman, 2015) if only because impression management is important for such people. Similarly, a concern with negativity helps leaders avoid unwanted consequences (McNulty & Russell, 2010); being concerned with negative outcomes means that responsible leadership "implies balancing external pressures of conflicting stakeholder interests with leaders' internal tensions of having to lead coherently and consistently with integrity across multiple contexts" (Miska & Mendenhall, 2018: 118; see also Maak & Pless, 2006).

If positivity presents paradoxes, it is because it is far from one-dimensional; in fact, a focus on the positive implies the negative. Without danger there can be no courage; without hardship, resilience is experientially meaningless; without challenge, there can be no optimism in its mastery; without difficulty, there can be no self-efficacy; without risk there can be no prudence; just as without temptation, there can be no temperance. Meaning-making is always relational and binary, being often based on antonymies, i.e. "semantically opposite relations between categories" (Keller & Chen, 2017: 69–70). As Lévi-Strauss (1967) argues, we think about the world in terms of binary opposites and every *culture* can be understood in terms of these. In our contemporary cultures and times, paradox occurs when rational choice is confronted by existential binarism. When managers are confronted with alternative polarities, they are urged to make rational choices, which typically require accentuating the positive and minimizing the negative. Granting the organizational need to manage the negative, endeavours at increasing positivity can create Pollyanna-ish dysfunctionality as opposed to superior functionality (O'Neill, Stanley & O'Reilly, 2011). In this chapter we explore various paradoxical implications of the term 'positive'. The major body of the chapter will be devoted to exploring three types of *paradoxical positivity*, which we define as persistent interrelated oppositions associated with attempts to embrace positive organizational practices, along with approaches for effectively leveraging and transcending them.

A challenge in studying positive paradoxes relates to ambiguity in defining the term 'positive', with its wide range of connotations, applications and porous boundaries (see Table 3.1). According to Cameron (2008: 7), "The concept of 'positive' has created a great deal of controversy and confusion in organizational studies." There is, however, an emerging convergent usage of the term within POS that qualifies concepts such as *deviance, virtue* and *bias* with the adjective 'positive' (Cameron, 2008, 2017b). Positive deviance, the first area of convergence in usage of the term positive, is concerned with spectacular outcomes that significantly exceed normal expectations of performance (Spreitzer & Sonenshein, 2003, 2004). Positive deviance is accordingly not just effective performance but exceptionally effective performance. Virtue, the second area of convergence, is concerned with the eudemonic assumption (from the ancient Greek *eudaimonía*, the search for happiness and human flourishing) of an inclination within human systems towards pursuit of the good for its own intrinsic worth. Virtue accordingly brings a sense of meaning and purpose to organizational activities. Positive or affirmative bias, the third area of convergence, concerns a focus on positive energy, culture, relationships and communication within organizations. This chapter explores paradoxes within each of these three convergence domains, illuminating the fact that attempts at creating positivity will necessarily raise negativity (Table 3.1).

PARADOXES OF POSITIVE DEVIANCE

Positive deviance relates to extraordinary positive outcomes or "exceptional behaviours that depart from the norm of a reference group in honorable ways" (Spreitzer & Sonenshein, 2003: 209), far exceeding normal or average expectations. Positive deviance research seeks to identity the "explanatory processes accounting for such performance" (Cameron, 2008: 8). The paradox of positive deviance is that generally in organizations, as in society, deviance is often viewed in terms of being 'socially deviant', a status that carries stigma (Goldstein, Hazy & Lichtenstein, 2010; Goode, 1991). The assumption is that whatever comprises the mean of a statistical distribution of traits is 'normal'; therefore, it is positively weighted. That which deviates from this is positioned as 'abnormal'. Abnormality is generally seen as something negative to be avoided. Accordingly, when the words *positive* and *deviant* are coupled, incongruence is invoked if only because in ordinary language use these terms do not belong together.

Bias against deviance can be understood by considering the normal distribution bell curve, where the centre represents zero, left of the centre is less than zero, while to the right of the centre presents as more than zero. When efforts are made to shift the bell curve right in purely performance and efficiency terms, it is rare that the sum of human happiness will be improve, given standard definitions of efficiency. Efficiency comprises the capability of a specific application of effort to produce a specific outcome with a minimum amount or quantity of waste, expense or unnecessary effort; where human effort is

Table 3.1 *Three areas of convergent usage of the term 'positive' within POS with descriptions and paradox examples*

Positive domain	Description	Example of paradox
Positive deviance	Spectacular outcomes that significantly exceed normal expectations of performance.	Society generally views deviance in terms of being 'socially deviant', a status that carries stigma. When the words *positive* and *deviant* are coupled, incongruence is invoked if only because in ordinary language use these terms do not belong together. Positive deviance identifies difference as a potential indicator of strength and a starting point for positive change. Positive deviance inspired change initiatives make salient tensions between forces for renewal and those representing the need to retain a stable personal identity and organizational environment, which respectively underlie paradoxes of learning and belonging and of learning and organizing.
Positive virtue	The eudemonic assumption of an inclination within human systems towards pursuit of the good for its own intrinsic worth.	The tensions between the happiness and well-being of the individual and that of the collective constitutes an essential paradox of virtue. An individual who does what is right and virtuous for themselves in following an ethical rule (deontology) may create undesirable consequences for the organizational collective. Conversely, violating an ethical rule and neglecting the needs and expectations of the individual may provide greater benefit to a greater number of people (utilitarianism).
Positive bias	A focus on positive energy, culture, relationships and communication within organizations.	Organizational culture can never be purely positive or negative. Positive things transpire even in predominantly negative cultures, while negative things transpire in apparently positive organizations.

involved this typically means intensification of work so that more is produced in a given time to a specific standard. Much social and organizational effort, whether it be through organizational policies and monitoring or training programmes, is directed towards those on the minus side of the bell curve, particularly the outliers, the negative deviants, in order that they become normal by moving to the centre of the curve. Feedback frequently focuses on identifying limitations or weaknesses that can be corrected or improved so as to converge with benchmarks representing the status quo. In other words, society is constituted as if it were a gravitational force that pulls people towards the centre to reinforce the norm defining the status quo.

POS is concerned with deviance on the right-hand side of the centre that accentuates positive aspects of engagement, not just the performatively efficient. It strives to increase positive well-being, strengthen engagement and high-quality connections on the premise that these positive aspects will feed into efficiencies more generally. Where the focus is on pushing efficiency without regard for these other aspects the results will not always be positive because the intensification of efficiency may come at the expense of these other virtues. Normalizing tendencies are not absent from positive deviance. Normalization strives to bring the deviant back to the norm. The 'tall poppy syndrome', in which those perceived as endeavouring to be better than others are "cut down" (Feather, 1989), is prevalent in equity-matching cultures such as Australia (contrasting with market-matching cultures) (Gannon & Pillai, 2015) and is an example of how even positive deviance can be seen as a socially unacceptable variance from normalcy. Organizationally, the tall poppy syndrome causes people to silence their own voices, including good ideas, in the interest of being viewed as a good team worker as well as being one that protects group morale. Normal consensus is protected at the expense of important conversations that do not occur, significant concerns that are not being raised and new lessons that remain unlearnt (Argyris, 1994). Most people realize that being a whistle-blower is not an identity most organizations cherish having in their midst (Kenny, 2019). Consequently, and paradoxically, when the status quo profess ignorance of socially constructed non-issues and when the organizational unit (dyad, team, board) lacks emotional carrying capacity to inquire further, a consensus of ignorance prevails.

Departing from the normal, even in positive ways, takes courage. Positive scholars see their role partly as being organizational and social change agents (Cameron, 2008). They contribute by pushing the current plus side of a bell curve (existing examples of the extraordinary) making it the future curve centre (Figure 3.1) (Huppert, 2009). The process supporting such shifts is positive deviance sampling. By identifying examples of extraordinary performance where members are flourishing and thriving, and learning from those positive deviants, positive scholars seek to facilitate positive organizational shifts where the extraordinary becomes the new normal, despite general organizational resistance against changes to the status quo, with preferences typically being for maintaining the familiar, organizational stasis. Positive deviance inspired change initiatives thereby make salient tensions between forces for renewal and those representing the need to retain a stable personal identity and organizational environment, which respectively underly paradoxes of learning and belonging and paradoxes of learning and organizing (Smith & Lewis, 2011).

Pascale and Sternin (2005) describe a process for promoting organizational and even societal change using positive deviance sampling, that "upends standard notions of the way change works" (p. 72). In this process, leaders adopt the role of enquirers facilitating a within-community quest for change,

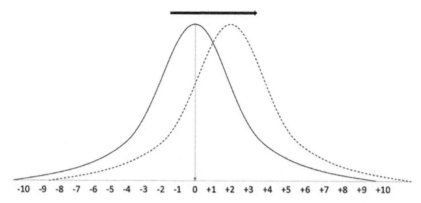

Figure 3.1   *Shifting organizational practices from average (represented as 0) to extraordinary (represented as numbers above) by identifying and learning from positive deviants*

where the community itself takes responsibility for identifying problems and potential solutions. Accordingly, rather than being a process in which leaders identify and disseminate best practices from the outside in, an inside-out approach identifies solutions from positive deviants within the community and spreads them to the rest of the membership. Positive deviance is an asset-based approach involving identifying, tapping and leveraging pre-existing solutions from among those bucking the norm and succeeding against the odds. The contrast is with a traditional deficit-based approach of outsiders importing and imposing best practice solutions that may not be relevant or might well be resisted within the local context. Positive deviance, accordingly, is an approach premised on identifying local solutions to problems, expanding the solution space by discovering new parameters. It is opposed to traditional approaches that generally proceed from problem solving to solution identification where "best practices are applied to problems defined within the context of existing parameters" (Pascale & Sternin, 2005: 74).

BOX 3.1   ORGANIZATIONAL CHANGE THROUGH POSITIVE DEVIANCE SAMPLING, A CASE STUDY FROM GOLDMAN SACHS

The following case of Goldman and Sachs, provided by Pascale and Sternin (2005), is an example of positive deviance indicating realistic direction for organizational change.

At the turn of the century Goldman Sachs's 300-strong force of investment advisors working under the Private Wealth Management (PWM) business unit experienced a series of initiatives imposed top-down from a New York headquarters. Top management were concerned the industry was in the midst of a seismic transformation. There was pressure to deliver lower brokerage fees with higher levels of transparency and compliance oversight. Management wanted to transform the investment advisors' role from one heavily dependent on brokerage income to instead focus on for-fee advice. The investment advisors felt that was too much of a departure from a well-proven and successful formula.

At the centre of the impasse was a manager who chose to identify the teams, with similar territories and prospects, that were thriving despite the difficult climate, spearheading a 'sales force effectiveness' enquiry. He sought to identify positively deviant sales teams. After a two-month discovery period five positive practices were identified among the most successful teams. The community of discovery was then expanded by creating five roll-out squads, one for each of the five practices, charged with creating a template that teams could adopt and implement voluntarily on a national basis. These squads later headed up the process once it was time to train others visiting each of 11 regional offices across the country to explain why and how the practices worked. The final phase involved creating a system for measuring progress towards goals. Regional offices were ranked in their implementation of the five practices with the results publicized in a process exclusively reliant on transparency and peer review with no imposition of sanctions for non-adaptation. Rather, teams themselves wanted to be on top rather than at the bottom.

The effect of this positive deviance approach was that over an 18-month period, behaviour and performance shifted, with the PWM unit getting ahead of the competition. Within three years it had gone from generating tumult and only marginal economic returns to becoming a major earnings contributor with average productivity per advisor nearly doubling, team size increasing from average 1.7 to the near-optimal three members per team, with the fee-based model achieving near universal acceptance.

There is a paradox of the positive sometimes to be found in negative deviance. In this section we have discussed positive deviance as representing extraordinary human performance, flourishing and thriving. In a context where the status quo neglects and undermines human dignity and well-being, negative deviance can be positive, a caveat that provides a nice segue into the next subsection on the paradoxes of virtue.

PARADOXES OF VIRTUE

An important area of POS research, according to Cameron (2017b: 218), "relates to the concepts of virtuousness and eudemonism". In POS virtue has been described as referring to "singular attributes that represent moral excellence" (Cameron, 2011: 27) and *virtuousness* is "what individuals aspire to be when they are at their best" (Woo & McDermott, 2019: 2831). The tensions between the happiness and well-being of the individual and that of the collective constitutes an essential paradox of virtue concerns (Halse, Honey & Boughtwood, 2007; Yan, 2009). An individual who does what is right and virtuous for themselves in following an ethical rule (deontology) may create undesirable consequences for the organizational collective. Conversely, violating an ethical rule and neglecting the needs and expectations of the individual may provide greater benefit to a greater number of people (utilitarianism). A classic illustration of this paradox was the Third Reich context in which Gestapo officers could demand to know if Jewish people were hiding inside a house. In such a situation the homeowner must decide whether or not it is moral to lie. For Brenkert (2009) similar challenges constrain the organizational dilemma experienced by Google in China: should it agree to being censored or 'do no evil'? Positivity and negativity are nuanced categories, confronting managers with challenging paradoxes (Joosten et al., 2014). The temporal dimension also informs the process: what if a virtuous action adopted today generates negative consequences in the medium or long term? Below, we consider the limitations of three virtue frameworks: Manichaeism, golden mean and curvilinearity. We do so to establish the added value of a paradox perspective on positivity (Cunha et al., 2020).

Manichaeism applies a binary approach: organizations and their members are confronted with dualistic choices of virtue or non-virtue. From this perspective, good and evil are separate forces. Individually, this occurs when corporate executives are accused either of being criminals or upheld as heroic role models. Likewise, the same situation prevails when one set of values by which people should live is defined as good and all else as bad, as is frequently the case with extreme ideology and religiosity. Categorizations of this sort resonate by rendering what is constituted as either positive and negative using clear-cut and well-defined boundaries. Simplistic explanations, however, ignore indeterminacy, grey areas, where boundaries are blurred (Cunha et al., 2010), wrongdoing is normalized (Palmer, 2012), where even excellent leaders express recognition of their flaws and limitations (Rego, Cunha & Clegg, 2012). Binarism such as this is present in media accounts constructing organizations as heroes and villains, as well as in narratives of "bad apples" (Trevino & Youngblood, 1990).

Manichaeism contributes to popular narratives that position organizations generally and businesses particularly as non-virtuous by default. The tacit position is that 'business ethics' is an oxymoron because business is essentially oriented to exploitation of value from employees (as well as stakeholders in general, such as suppliers, consumers and the natural environment). Marx's (1976) views in *Capital,* focused on the extraction of surplus value from labour, are the best-known version of this approach. The implication of such views is that only the fittest survive by giving up on virtue beyond minimal compliance with the letter of the law. Manichean explanations, frequently based on halo effects and similar generalizations, problematically provide one-dimensional simplification of complex situations and their paradoxes (Jackall, 1988; Wray-Bliss, 2012). In the long term, paradoxes will continue to persist, and their denial will have debilitating effects on organizing processes (Putnam, Fairhurst & Banghart, 2016).

Golden mean is an approach to virtue (Crossan, Mazutis & Seijts, 2013: 570) based on a philosophical position representing virtue as the "desirable mean states between vices of deficiency and vices of excess". According to this view, virtue is the equilibrium; however, even that which is virtuous becomes vicious in excess, when virtuous strengths become potential weaknesses. The optimal level is to be found in the balance. True moral virtue, according to this perspective, lies in the mean between deficiency and excess. For example, "optimal trust" is the golden mean between "overinvestment" and "underinvestment" in trust (Wicks, Berman & Jones, 1999). Similarly, being courageous resides between having too little courage manifesting as inaction and cowardice and too much recklessness and ill-advised risk-taking masquerading as courage (Smith & Kouchaki, 2018). Moreover, virtues tend to cluster: a virtue is rarely independent of other virtues. Being courageous by firing a friend for dishonesty is not independent of humanity; for example, the friend's possible poor health condition might account for the situation. Enacting compassion sometimes requires being courageous (Simpson & Berti, 2020). Achieving the capabilities of being both courageous *and* humane thus requires managing contradictory tensions.

As a dynamic position, the golden mean represents an unstable synthesis of opposites that is impossible to maintain as a permanent process. Somehow, the middle point between extremes must be identified as the precise position of virtue. Further, taking the mean as a guide to virtue is essentially to hold virtue as a compromise. A practice of cowardly blandness that steers a mid-course through available options to achieve average outcomes is institutionalized that does not account for reason and evidence as a basis for action. Broadcasting policies that consider balance as something only achieved when outlandish and unscientific perspectives are contrasted with credible expert views is an example that poses a particular risk in politics that are increasingly divisive and politically populist. For these reasons, the golden mean approach appears insufficient for capturing the contradictory choices confronting decision makers seeking to be virtuous.

Curvilinearity is a quantitative virtue approach holding that, at a certain threshold, the positive effects of positivity will weaken and likely manifest negative effects. Several domains of management (e.g. Pierce & Aguinis, 2013) and business ethics (Miao et al., 2013) explore the notion of curvilinearity. Curvilinearity's consequences are important: where there is too much trust, people may turn a blind eye to misbehaviour; when there is too much confidence it may lead to excessive risk-taking and rule breaking. In contrast to the golden mean conceptualization of virtue, the curvilinear approach is concerned with the consequences that arise for the dependent variable from having too much of a good thing. As an example, a leader who is *strongly* ethical is certainly also virtuous, yet one that is moderately ethical may produce more positive results for the organization (Stouten et al., 2013).

The ratio between the positive and the negative in behaviour, where at a certain threshold increased positivity causes negative outcomes, defines a curvilinear positivity ratio (Fredrickson, 2009). Criticism of the ratio approach tends to centre on the fixed nature of ratio thresholds (Brown, Sokal & Friedman, 2014). Nonetheless, an interplay between positive and negative processes tends to make sense (Fredrickson, 2013: 814). Recognition of the interplay of positive and negative processes is inherent to a paradoxical perspective, as we discuss next.

Paradox acceptance: the three approaches discussed above, to a greater or lesser extent, deny one or the other pole of the paradox. None of the above approaches are sustainable in the long term because paradoxical tensions will persist (Putnam, Fairhurst & Banghart, 2016). A paradox perspective on virtue recognizes that positive and negative elements are constituted by each other, with tensions persistently interacting in a state of mutual interdependence. Viewing virtue through a paradox lens provides a nuanced understanding of virtue being composed of dynamic combinations of synergy and trade-off, in which virtue and vice interpenetrate as dynamic forces in tension rather than as either positive or negative practices to be magnified or suppressed.

Organizational relations of trade-off and synergy are endogenous, with each element containing the seeds of its opposite, composing a duality (Li, 2016). Trade-offs between opposing forces are recognized as a common element of organizational life (Weick, 1992). Synergy is the higher-level leveraging of opposites which sees tension transformed and transcended as complementarity. By applying a paradox lens to six core virtues identified by Peterson and Seligman (2004), we can demonstrate an interplay between positive and negative trade-offs and synergies. The values historically espoused by cultural, faith and secular community institutions across the globe can be analysed by qualitative and statistical factor analysis (see Box 3.2). Peterson and Seligman concluded that these six virtues are "the core characteristics valued by moral philosophers and religious thinkers: wisdom, courage, humanity, justice, temperance, and transcendence" (p. 13). The researchers additionally identified 24 character strengths as distinguishable routes through which these virtues are cultivated and expressed.

BOX 3.2 PARADOXES OF SIX CORE VIRTUES OF POSITIVE PSYCHOLOGY

Six Paradoxical Virtues

Peterson and Seligman (2004) identified six key virtues that they for the most part found ubiquitously across geography, religion and cultural traditions: wisdom, courage, humanity, justice, temperance and transcendence. Below we analyse the tensions inherent in each of these virtues from a paradox perspective specifically from within an organizational context. Central to a paradox perspective is recognition that the positive can become negative and vice versa. Virtue, socially constructed as paradox, accepts an element of duality that takes the co-presence of opposites as required for the emergence of virtue. Our analysis is accordingly an exercise in highlighting the synergy and trade-offs found between polar forces.

Wisdom as organizational paradox comprises a subtle paradoxical tension between knowledge and doubt (Pfeffer & Sutton, 2006). Within the organizational context wisdom is expressed through processes by which members acquire and utilize knowledge according to the needs of a specific context (Schwartz, 2011). Decisions regarded as wise in a particular place or time will be recognized as unwise in other contexts and new technological challenges, such as artificial intelligence, can raise new challenges regarding wisdom (Clegg et al., 2020). Wisdom as paradox is not concerned with strategically spinning one paradoxical pole against the other but rather with engaging in open debate that willingly considers alternative positions to determine the merits of various competing perspectives (McKenna, Rooney & Boal, 2009). For Van Dierendonck and Patterson (2015: 122) wisdom is the capacity of "people who can bridge contradictions, act selfless, integer and sometimes paradoxical with a sense of taking care for the whole". According to Bachman, Habisch, and Dierksmeier (2018) practical wisdom in organizations incorporates tension, contradiction and paradox as a necessary deliberative process. Considerations of the instrumental and ethical, dispositional and situational, as well as organizational and individual, all give rise to contradiction and tension. It is through deliberation on how to balance tensions arising from competing interests, rationalities, emotions, requirements and challenges in organizational practice that practical wisdom is cultivated.

Humanity in organizations is premised on expressing a responsibility of caring for and befriending others, precluding the need to deliberate on the receiver's Otherness, as opposed to one's personal identity and sense of dignity (Pirson, 2019). Such kindness and generosity of heart, however, should be supported by appropriate boundaries rather than being irrational and sentimental (Nussbaum, 2003), as relations of care and compassion are also steeped in relations of power (Simpson, Clegg & Pitsis, 2014b; Simpson, Clegg & Lopez, 2014a; Simpson, Clegg & Freeder, 2013). Research highlights cases of leaders whose care for their people is paradoxically accompanied by strength and toughness (e.g., Zhang et al., 2015). New Zealand Prime Minister Jacinda Ardern is a case in point, widely lauded for her compassionate leadership since her election as New Zealand Prime Minister in 2017. What is immediately fascinating about her leadership is that it is described in paradoxical terms. The *Financial Times* referred to responses to crises such as the Christchurch massacre that saw 51 people murdered by a terrorist as a combination of "solace and steel" (Smythe, 2019). *Vogue* expanded this emotion-metal metaphor by explaining that Ardern is "deeply empathetic, but she has nerves of steel – and can lead in times of chaos and tragedy" (Wickstead, 2019), while *Forbes* reflected on how Ardern "empathised with the victims while remaining a strong leader, how she cared and led at the same time" (Jamet, 2019). *Time Magazine* commented on her response to the COVID-19 pandemic as "a form of leadership that embodies strength and sanity, while also pushing an agenda of compassion and community – or, as she would put it, 'pragmatic idealism'" (Luscombe, 2020). These descriptions of compassion as strength suggest a paradoxical approach of leveraging opposite tensions, rather than oscillating between extremes.

Courage manifests within organizations where the pursuit of valued objectives persists despite significant opposition. Described as a "difficult virtue" (Worline, 2012: 304), courage involves a combination of both caution and bravery. March and Weil (2009) observe that courage and insanity can appear dangerously similar, as in the commitment to crash through or crash. While courageous leaders might be recognized for their extreme bravery, such bravery is not virtuous per se. As argued by Mahoney (1998: 190), "there may be a closer connection than at first appears between courage and caution, or equally paradoxically, proper moral courage may lie in taking due thought and care in all one's actions". Courage without healthy caution is irresponsible. The person endowed with the virtue of courage is both fearful and fearless (Heil, 1996). Such courage not only requires deliberation concerning right action and executing it well but also requires the "skill" of a "special kind of calculated risk taking", that is cultivated "over a period of time, often decades" (Reardon, 2007: 60).

Justice within organizations draws from a design that is based on principle, policy and accountability, ensuring that processes are consistent, rules based and fair. Paradoxically, justice entails a synthesis of safety and accountability (Dekker, 2012): when there is an excess of accountability towards employees or the environment, safety is reduced, organizational viability is undermined; conversely, when there is an excess of safety, organizational accountability is eroded. Similar conflict is found in governance as the tension between dual obligations for protecting citizen freedom and safety (Nguyen-Vo, 2012). A capacity for applying rules as principles that also attend to exceptions is required in managing this tension. Justice further demands paradoxical thinking as its application requires drawing on other virtues such as temperance and humanity. Organizational justice requires being both procedural and caring, blind and observant, responsive to individual needs and idiosyncrasies while also being consistent between individuals (Fu, Flood & Rousseau, 2020). Specifically, within the Human Resource Management (HRM) context, justice focuses on both equality/consistency by treating employees uniformly regarding specific HRM practices, as well as considering individual differences in capabilities and efforts in terms of equity/individual responsiveness. Managing this challenge requires line managers to act as 'paradox navigators' in the implementation of HRM policies. Blind justice applied without considering circumstances, which, while desirable in the abstract, is problematic for concrete daily practice. Justice must therefore be approached as a paradoxical synthesis of general principles, applied blindly according to specific circumstances.

Temperance is manifest organizationally through processes that instil forgiveness, mercy, humility, prudence and self-regulation (Peterson & Seligman, 2004). Humility is illustrative of the paradoxes inherent to this virtue. Humility can be conceived as a capacity for being modest without appearing weak (Owens, Johnson & Mitchell, 2013; Rego et al., 2019), a challenging undertaking: "if leaders wield their power to an excessive degree, they are considered tyrannical; if they are too self-effacing, they are considered weak" (March & Weil, 2009: 54). Organizational members' ability to be tempered communicates an awareness of personal strengths without implying unawareness of the strengths of others. Humility accordingly constitutes a marriage of opposites, the exercise of self-regulation (Crossan, Mazutis & Seijts, 2013) where force is demonstrated by expressing vulnerability.

Transcendence is a quintessential response to paradoxical organizational phenomena implying capacity for being present on dual planes, accepting one thing along with its opposite, framing contrariness as elements of a greater unity (Abdallah, Denis & Langley, 2011). March and Weil (2009) describe transcendence as confronting organizational leaders with needing to act both as poets and as plumbers, elevating the spirit while also repairing damages and maintaining mundane facilities. One capability without the other indicates deficiency. The poet-plumber dual imagery implies that focusing on a bright future should be accompanied by realistic assessments of the present reality. Transcendence can explain leadership that persists towards aspirations that others perceive as utopian (Newark, 2018), possibly highlighting the power of vision. Present and future are two forces that are far too frequently separated, representing the temporally immediate and the temporally distant in distinct ways (Trope & Liberman, 2003), focusing on immediate needs while excluding the needs of the future. Transcendence is accordingly critical for framing significant organizational issues in a manner that is not viewed as overly idealistic (Bansal & Song, 2017), enabling members to be grounded while aspiring for higher ground.

Our analysis of positive virtue using a paradox lens brings new insight and complexity, specifically highlighting the need for paradox acceptance and transcendence to draw power from virtuous qualities. Without transcendence, the paradoxes inherent to virtue cause a lack of balance and discomfort (Vince & Broussine, 1996) as well as paralysis that inhibits action (Smith & Berg, 1987). Virtue is a most fragile process; when approached as paradox, it is even more fragile. Paradox acceptance approaches the positive not by denying the negative but rather accepting positive and negative as a dynamic interplay (Cunha et al., 2020; Putnam, Fairhurst & Banghart, 2016).

PARADOXES OF AFFIRMATIVE BIAS

The third area of convergence with regard to POS is positive or affirmative bias, described by Cameron (2017a: 14) as an approach that emphasizes "positive energy, positive climate, positive relationships, positive communication …" that also "does not exclude consideration of negative factors but, rather, incorporates them in accounting for positive outcomes and the best of the human condition". POS scholar Robert Quinn (2015) describes such an affirmative bias as underpinning a positive organizational culture of abundance. Why do more organizations not leverage an affirmative bias towards creating a positive culture of abundance? Quinn suggests that the major obstacles here are the rigid mental maps with which leaders focus on solving problems and accomplishing tasks. Heightened awareness of organizations as dynamic paradoxes rather than as static entities can expand these limits. There is a tendency to rely on fixed binary categories when making sense of organizational life, despite organizations' complexity, often dissolving logical categories. Accordingly, organizational culture can never be purely positive or negative. Positive things transpire even in predominantly negative cultures, while negative things transpire in apparently positive organizations. Nelson Mandela's wisdom was born from 25 years' refection while imprisoned on Robben Island. Acknowledging shades of positivity and negativity in every organization can mean evaluating the quality of an organization's culture by informally calculating the ratio of the organization's positive and negative behaviours (Fredrickson, 2009, 2013). When patterns of positivity occurring within an organization exceed conventional expectations, a positive organizational culture is often assumed (see the earlier discussion on virtue ratios).

Ten attributes that might provide the foundation of an abundant organizational culture (see Table 3.2, left column) include growth focus, self-organization, creative action, intrinsic motivation, positive cognition, full engagement, individual accountability, decisive action, achievement focus and constructive confrontation. Typically, any organization exemplifying such attributes could be expected to be productive, progressive and staffed by people brimming with enthusiasm and accomplishment. Pausing to reflect more deeply on these ten attributes, however, might additionally raise a number of concerns: an over focus on growth might also bring about waste, while an emphasis on self-organization might precipitate a lack of clear direction and focus. An excess of any positive can become a negative (as discussed in the previous section on virtue and the golden mean). Quinn (2015: 12) explains this tension as follows: "*every* positive characteristic, without a competing positive value or characteristic, can become a negative". The ten attributes in Table 3.2 need to be offset by their opposite attributes of cost control, organizational predictability, procedural compliance, managerial control, objective analysis, life balance, cohesive teamwork, group deliberation, authentic relationships and appreciative expression (see Table 3.2, right column). This second list of attributes acts as a counterbalance to the first: growth is counterbalanced by cost control; self-organization countered by predictability; creativity countered by procedure, motivation contrasted with control, positive cognition contrasted with objective analysis, etc. Positioned side by side in the table, the two lists highlight paradoxical tensions that are not mutually exclusive. Greater power can be leveraged from these attributes when they are paired as existing simultaneously, as growth and control, spontaneity and predictability, creativity and compliance, action and deliberation.

The attributes of the left and right columns are mutually interdependent contrasting tensions. On their own they are logical but in relation to each other they are contradictory, which means they are true paradoxes. When these tensions are successfully integrated the paradox is transcended. The ability to engage with tensions and leverage them for extraordinary performance has

Table 3.2   *Greater power can be leveraged from opposing attributes paired as existing simultaneously*

First pole	Second pole
Growth focus: Investing in the future, seeing possibility	**Cost control:** Efficiency, preservation of assets
Self-organization: Empowerment, spontaneity	**Organizational predictability:** Stability, order
Creative action: Responsive, learning organization	**Procedural compliance:** Routines, policies
Intrinsic motivation: Meaningful, fulfilling work	**Managerial control:** Consistent, dependable performance
Positive contagion: Positive motions, optimism, enthusiasm	**Objective analysis:** Measurement, assessment
Full engagement: Commitment, fully involved, loyal	**Life balance:** Renewal, re-energizing
Individual accountability: Responsibility, excellence	**Cohesive teamwork:** Collaboration, belonging, positive peer pressure
Decisive action: Speed, urgency	**Group deliberation:** Participation, consensus
Achievement focus: Accomplishment, success	**Authentic relationships:** Caring, selfless service
Constructive confrontation: Honesty, challenge	**Appreciative expression:** Praise, celebration of others

been described by Smith and Lewis (2012) as the underpinning of exceptional leadership. This idea is taken further by Quinn who suggests that the basis for an extraordinary culture of abundance is the organizational ability to balance simultaneously an entire system of competing tensions in a manner whereby each attribute remains positive without becoming sufficiently extreme as to become negative. An illustration of this principle is the tension between life-work balance and full work engagement: too much or too little of either is problematic. Quinn provides a demonstration of this idea by adding to the 20 positive attributes listed in the table above, an additional list of 20 corresponding negative attributes (Table 3.3). These 'negative zone' attributes develop from the overemphasis of any single positive tension (middle right or left columns) at the expense of the opposite positive tension through strategies of repression or denial.

A helpful metaphor for the fine-tuned balancing of paradoxical tensions to achieve a positive culture of abundance might be the extraordinarily narrow habitable zone in which the earth orbits the sun, the Goldilocks Zone as astrophysicists refer to it. If it were any closer to the sun, the earth would be burnt and it would be impossible to sustain life, if it were any further distance from the sun, the earth would freeze and the life would be impossible to sustain. The position of the earth in relation to the sun is 'just right', as in the fairy tale of Goldilocks and the three bears. Goldilocks was only satisfied with the chair

Table 3.3   Framework of competing organizational values, with positive and negative zones

Negative zone (from Paradox Denial)	Positive zone (Balanced Paradox Tensions)			Negative zone (from Paradox Denial)
Waste	Growth focus	&	Cost control	Austerity
Confusion	Self-organization	&	Predictability	Rigidity
Chaos	Creative action	&	Procedural compliance	Bureaucracy
Obsession	Intrinsic motivation	&	Managerial control	Micro-management
Delusion	Positive contagion	&	Objective analysis	Cynicism
Exhaustion	Full engagement	&	Life balance	Withdrawal
Conflict	Individual accountability	&	Cohesive teamwork	Group think
Exclusion	Decisive action	&	Group deliberation	Indecisiveness
Selfishness	Achievement focus	&	Authentic relationships	Permissiveness
Abrasiveness	Constructive confrontation	&	Appreciative expression	Conflict avoidance

that was neither too small nor too big; the porridge that was neither too cold nor too hot; the bed that was neither too soft nor too hard. For a paradoxical positive culture of abundance the challenge is of not that of merely simultaneously cultivating opposite positive attributes but also of maintaining the positive zone by not allowing either competing value to dominate.

Leveraging paradoxical tensions to create a positive culture of abundance is a rare leadership capability. Different leaders are gifted with their own unique sets of strengths. Some leaders demonstrate distinctive capabilities in maintaining control, efficiency and productivity but are limited in their abilities to generate cultures of trust, respect, connectivity, learning and growth or to define a higher social purpose. Other leaders have vision but struggle with maintaining a structured organizational system. Finding a positive and abundant culture characterized by both purpose and profit, stability and change, unity and diversity, playfulness and productivity is the ideal. The theory discussed in this chapter suggests that while leveraging such positive paradoxical capabilities is challenging it is nonetheless possible and well worth the effort.

CONCLUSION

The paradoxical tensions of positivity, including those between positive and negative, are explicitly presented as defining POS (Cameron, 2008, 2017b). Despite the paradoxical tensions present in positive constructs and themes, conceptual and practical implications for positive paradoxes remain under-theorized, particularly from the perspective of organizational processes (Langley et al., 2013).

In this chapter we have explored paradoxes within three convergent areas of positivity found within POS research: *positive deviance, positive virtue* and *positive affirmative bias* (Cameron, 2008, 2017b). A paradox perspective has much to offer to the critical analysis of organizational positivity, departing from linearity and dualism towards duality and curvilinearity. Positive scholars have explicitly recognized the importance of avoiding linear thinking (Cameron, 2008, 2017b; Quinn & McGrath, 1985; Quinn, 1988). Extrapolating that the positive is discovered as the opposite of negative is simplistic. From a paradox perspective we gain a non-dualistic view of organizational processes better suited for explaining the complexities of organizational life.

Critiques that hold the positive perspective as overly naïve (Fineman, 2006) can be addressed by adopting a paradox perspective which sees an intertwinement of the positive and the negative, where appreciation of one requires giving consideration to the other. While such dualism is well articulated by POS researchers, particularly those observing negative circumstances as a catalyst for positive approaches (Clair & Dufresne, 2007; Cameron & Lavine, 2006), more simplistic and dualistic POS accounts appear more commonly in one-dimensional academic literature and teaching. A well-articulated paradox perspective can support more robust conceptual understanding of positive organizational practices and phenomena the better to support practitioners facing various organizational challenges, including ethical dilemmas.

Persistence is another significant theoretical window revealed by a positive paradox perspective. Paradoxes are persistent interdependent tensions (Schad, 2017; Schad et al., 2016). Responses to these tensions must recognize that paradoxes are permanent, sometimes latent and at other times salient (Knight & Paroutis, 2017), as opposed to assuming they are temporary and therefore solvable (Smith, 2014). Giving such consideration to temporal factors will enrich POS, for positivity is more accurately conceived of as a process as opposed to a condition. Recognition of paradoxes as persistent tensions surfaces the need for understanding oscillations in positivity that result from persistent trade-offs and synergies, which over time fluctuate, unfolding positive and negative cycles (Masuch, 1985; Tsoukas & Cunha, 2017).

4. The dark side: absurdity and pragmatic paradoxes

> 'No,' said the priest, 'one doesn't have to take everything as the truth, one just has to accept it as necessary.' 'A depressing opinion,' said K. 'It means that the world is founded on untruth.'
> (Kafka, 1925 [2007]: 159)

Probably the most significant contribution of paradox theory to organizational literature is acknowledgement that tensions and contradictions should not be considered momentary lapses, 'creases' in the smooth fabric of organizational rational order. Rather, as unavoidable consequences of organizing, they are pervasive and persistent features of any social context, and as such must be reckoned and coped with, since ignoring or neglecting them produces even more paradoxes and complications (Smith & Lewis, 2011). Recognizing that "persistent contradictions between interdependent elements are pervasive" (Schad et al., 2016: 48) logically leads to the need "to engage with paradox" (Huq, Reay & Chreim, 2017: 514). When it comes to defining *how* to engage, however, most paradox theorists tend to become too enthusiastic about the "enlightening potential" (Lewis, 2000: 763) of all paradoxes. An implicit consensus has emerged in paradox literature around the idea that paradoxes must be appreciated (Knight & Paroutis, 2017), accepted (Miron-Spektor et al., 2018) and finally embraced (Sharma & Bansal, 2017) by organizational actors in order to achieve sustainable performances.

A paradox perspective undeniably helps with identifying opportunities that would be lost if the situation was framed through traditional equilibrium-based lenses (Andriopoulos & Lewis, 2009; Cameron & Quinn, 1988; Heracleous & Wirtz, 2014). However, it is problematic to assume that all "underlying tensions are not only normal but, if harnessed, can be beneficial and powerful" (Smith & Lewis, 2011: 395). First, it exaggerates the consequence of cognitive frames in shaping the experience of tension. By emphasizing paradoxical thinking (Smith & Tushman, 2005), paradoxical frames (Miron-Spektor, Gino & Argote, 2011) and paradoxical mindsets (Keller, Loewenstein & Yan, 2017; Miron-Spektor et al., 2018), the idea is conveyed that all tensions can be tamed and harnessed (Cunha & Putnam, 2019; Fairhurst, 2019). In doing so, trust must be vested in assuming that actors have freedom to respond to paradox. Such trust is easily misplaced. Power relations shape the experience of paradoxes. To assume that powerless individuals, who are paralysed in the face of contradictory demands, are incapable of devising constructive demands, is tantamount to blaming the victims (Berti & Simpson, 2019). Organizational actors have restricted freedom to act; it is the nature of organizational office for this to be the case. Organization constrains agency. Dismissing the role of agency and power in the experience of paradox overlooks that some 'pathological' paradoxes described in the literature are a result of a lack of agency rather than ability. Double binds (Hennestad, 1990; Tracy, 2004) or catch-22 situations (Currie, Lockett & Suhomlinova, 2009) are frequently experienced in organizational life. Assuming that 'both-anding' is always intrinsically preferable to alternative approaches to tensions, such as having to settle for unpleasant but necessary compromise or accepting the existence of an irresolvable conflict of interest, can bring about a deeper form of denial. Such denial can cause vicious circles that are more perverse than those engendered by paradox denial, tempting actors to resort to dysfunctional impression management strategies (Gaim, Clegg & Cunha, 2019; Hahn et al., 2010) or entrenching oppressive conditions (Alvesson & Spicer, 2012; Berti & Simpson, 2019; Willmott, 2013).

Building on these reflections, in this chapter we consider several 'dark sides' of paradox: the role of absurdity in shaping the experience of paradox; the existence of pathological manifestations of paradoxes (pragmatic paradoxes) that derive from lack of agency in responding to contradictions; the negative consequences of embracing paradoxes and of thinking paradoxically; as well as the necessity considering also a dialectical perspective on tensions, highlighting the role of power struggles and the possibility of radical, conflict-driven transformations.

ABSURDITY AND PARADOX

Not all paradoxical experiences are equivalent. For instance, all the following might be described as paradoxes. First, an executive trying to balance competing needs to explore new business prospects while exploiting existing opportunities and avoiding cannibalization of current value-creating assets (March, 1991; Smith & Tushman, 2005); second, a theorist trying to reconcile the apparent inconsistencies and paradoxical demands of an influential conceptual approach (Lado et al., 2006); and, third, an employee subjected to a directive that is both peremptory (hence, non-negotiable) and self-defying, such as 'take initiative!' or 'be proactive' (Cunha et al., 2021). While all these situations fit the definition of paradox as persistent interrelated contradictory tensions (Lewis, 2000; Smith & Lewis, 2011) there are important qualitative differences between them. In the latter situation the order "must be disobeyed to be obeyed" (Watzlawick, Jackson & Bavelas, 1967: 195); as a consequence, agents become trapped "between non-existent alternatives" (Putnam, Fairhurst

& Banghart, 2016: 83), experiencing "untenable absurdity" (Watzlawick, Jackson & Bavelas, 1967: 217).

While absurdity can be instrumental to theorizing (Davis, 1971), flexing our imagination in a way akin to joke-making (Cameron & Quinn, 1988), it is no laughing matter in a real-life context (Cunha et al., 2012). Kafka offered many examples of how the experience of bureaucratic absurdities becomes an intolerable instrument of oppression, as in this quote from *The Trial*:

> 'You're under arrest, aren't you.' 'But how can I be under arrest? And how come it's like this?' 'Now you're starting again,' said the policeman, dipping a piece of buttered bread in the honeypot. 'We don't answer questions like that.' 'You will have to answer them,' said K. 'Here are my identification papers, now show me yours and I certainly want to see the arrest warrant.' 'Oh, my God!' said the policeman. 'In a position like yours, and you think you can start giving orders, do you?' (Kafka, 1925 [2007]: 7)

Analogously, in *The Castle*, the author describes the desperate situation of a father trying to obtain pardon for his family, after his daughter has been unjustly disgraced for disobeying a corrupt officer of the mysterious bureaucracy that governs their village:

> He wasn't so much concerned with winning back her honour as with being forgiven. But to be forgiven he must first establish his guilt, and that very thing was denied him in the offices. (Kafka, 1926 [2009]: 187)

The existence of vicious circles created by conflicting rules generating contradictory expectations (March, Schulz & Zhou, 2000) produces more Kafkaesque than Weberian contemporary bureaucracies (Hodson et al., 2013a, 2013b). The overall complexity of management creates multiple possibilities for the manifestation of absurdity (Farson, 1996), making absurdity a central dimension of organizing (McCabe, 2016). Indeed, organizational members utilize absurdity as a resource to cope, ironically, with the contradictions they face (Jarzabkowski & Lê, 2017; Korczynski, 2011). Organizational leaders can even employ absurdity to make sense of inherent contradictions in their roles (Newark, 2018).

Paradox theory has acknowledged the 'absurd' aspects of paradoxes (Lewis, 2000; Smith & Lewis, 2011) with an important qualification: the coexistence of opposites is described as "*seemingly* absurd" (Lewis, 2000: 761, emphasis added). The idea that the absurd is not an intrinsic feature of reality can be traced back to Albert Camus:

> This world in itself is not reasonable, that is all that can be said. But what is absurd is the confrontation of this irrational and the wild longing for clarity whose call

echoes in the human heart. The absurd depends as much on man as on the world. (Camus, 1955: 26)

For Camus the essential paradox is the irreconcilable dualism between an "appetite for the absolute and for unity and the impossibility of reducing this world to a rational and reasonable principle" (1955: 51). Camus invokes not despair in this realization but a paradoxical justification for life: defending, resisting and taking ownership of such absurdity is what gives life meaning.

BOX 4.1   ABSURD REALITIES
'The hell of Russian bureaucracy', Miriam Elder, *The Guardian*, 24 April 2012

A few weeks ago, I got to a dinner party, promptly hid myself in the host's bedroom for 15 minutes and collapsed into a cascade of tears. The cause? Dry cleaning.

On the face of it, Moscow has most of the trappings of modern, European life. There are cafes, even non-smoking ones, where you can order a flat white. There are websites that will deliver your weekly supplies of hummus, fresh apricots and rich French cheeses. And there are dry cleaners which, in theory, will whisk your clothes away to some unseen locale and steam them spotless in the blink of an eye.

They key phrase here is, of course, "in theory". In practice, daily life in Russia is an endless battle against shopkeepers and waiters steeped in the best traditions of Soviet-era manners (walk into a shop and the first thing you'll hear is: "Girl! What do you want?"); those fresh fruits will probably be black by the time they make it through the city's gridlocked, muddy streets. And dry cleaning – that's a whole other experience altogether.

It goes something like this. You get to the dry cleaner. There's a woman, let's call her Oksana Alexandrovna, sitting behind a low counter, row upon row of clothes in plastic wrap behind her. She's dealing with a customer. This gives you time to reflect. "Russia is amazing," you think. "The changes this place has seen – 25 years ago, would I even be standing in a shop like this? The lady in front of me certainly wouldn't have been handing in a MaxMara dress to clean. A true middle-class experience. In Russia. I'm living it."

By now, about 12 minutes have passed. Oksana Alexandrovna is caressing the woman's clothes. Much paperwork is exchanged. A stamp machine is placed on the counter. You wonder what is happening – but soon enough you will know.

Finally, it is your turn. You put six items of clothing on the counter. Oksana Alexandrovna lets out a sigh. This would be the point where you would normally get your receipt and go. But this is Russia. It's time to get to work. A huge stack of forms emerges. Oksana Alexandrovna takes a cursory glance at your clothes. Then the examination – and the detailed documentation – begins. This black H&M sweater is not a black H&M sweater. It is, in her detailed notes on a paper titled "Receipt-Contract Series KA for the Services of Dry and Wet Cleaning," "a black women's sweater with quarter sleeves made by H&M in Cambodia." Next, there are 20 boxes that could be ticked. Is this sweater soiled? Is it mildly soiled? Very soiled? Perhaps it is corroded? Yellowed? Marred by catches in the thread? All this, and more, is possible. The appropriate boxes are ticked. But that is not all – a further line leaves room for "Other Defects and Notes." By now, you have spent less time wearing the sweater than Oksana Alexandrovna has spent examining it. This process is repeated five more times. Except with that white cardigan that has 11 buttons. Why do you know it has 11 buttons? Because Oksana Alexandrovna has counted each and every button. Twice.

The process is almost over. Oksana Alexandrovna asks you to sign your name. Five times. She firmly stamps each page (for your detailed receipt has now run to two). You clutch the document, hand over 1,500 roubles (£32), say goodbye to that 40 minutes of your life, and go on with your day. If only that were the end of this tale. Some time wasted, nothing more. But five days later, you must pick up said clothes. And that's where the real problems can emerge. In between the dropping-off and the picking-up of the clothes, Russia had a presidential election. Riot police, troops and military trucks poured through Moscow. Protesters took to the streets crying foul, dismayed at the prospect of living another six years under Vladimir Putin. And I lost my dry-cleaning receipt.

This is the horror of horrors. Oksana Alexandrovna was not pleased. This meant more paperwork, more signatures, more stamps. The first thing demanded – my passport. "What does my passport have to do with my dry cleaning?"

"Passport!"

I handed it over. She wrote down every bit of information, making sure to note my registration (every resident of and visitor to Russia must make police aware of their residence, a Soviet holdover that shows no sign of disappearing). Next, I was to write down descriptions of each item of clothing I had handed in. "Five black sweaters and one white one." "Not good enough!" "The white sweater had 11 buttons?" "Please take this more seriously!" More signatures. More stamps. "You've stolen more than an hour of my life!" I yelled. Another passport check. "Give me my clothes!" Forty minutes later, I had them in hand. My nerves were somewhere else entirely.

Possessing paradoxical frames as mental templates encompassing two opposing possibilities (Smith & Tushman, 2005) allows individuals to recognize
their complementarity, positively influencing creativity (Miron-Spektor, Gino
& Argote, 2011) and harnessing the generative potential of paradoxes (Smith
& Lewis, 2011). The importance given to 'mindsets' in shaping the experience
of paradox (Keller, Loewenstein & Yan, 2017; Miron-Spektor et al., 2018;
Zheng, Kark & Meister, 2018) echoes these views. With some conflation,
these 'mindsets' have been attributed to national and organizational cultural
influences (Keller, Loewenstein & Yan, 2017) and used to explain the circumstances under which organizational tensions become a positive influence of
on-job performance and innovation, specifically where individuals accept and
feel energized by tensions (Miron-Spektor et al., 2018).

It is important to stress the role of individual (and collective) attitudes for
the experience of organizational tensions but to do so poses the risk of over-
estimating the power of cognitive representations. An individual may well be
powerless in front of paradoxical demands. Social reality is not the same as
physical reality. Here, meaning and relationships are constitutive of existence,
as much as materiality (Orlikowski & Scott, 2008). Meaning is not given or discovered but constructed and maintained by a collective effort (Garfinkel, 1967;
Goffman, 1959; Schütz, 1974). Organizational members are also enmeshed
in a social network of hierarchical relationships where rationality is treated
as a given (Willmott, 1993), even if it can produce contradictory demands.
Individuals have both to "legitimize their actions by 'logically' accounting
for them, *and* to act in accordance with orders, preserving the unquestionable
rationality of the authority structure" (Berti & Simpson, 2019: 11).

The idea that agents possess definite 'mindsets', expressing a stable identity
and a store of individual knowledge, clashes with the observation that agents
perform multiple identities in the workplace, taking up fragments of dynamic,
socially developed knowledge and practices as they face specific challenges
(Vohnsen, 2015). Absurdity in organizations occasionally derives from inten-
tional malice, intellectual inadequacy or communication breakdowns but more
often than not it arises from the clash of different logics, practices and systems
of knowledge in decision-making and implementation (Vohnsen, 2017).
Talk, decisions and actions are not necessarily aligned (Brunsson, 1989).
Organizational decision makers, subject to contrary societal and institutional
pressures, frequently engage in hypocrisy and façade building (Cho et al.,
2015). While impression management and marketing stunts are accepted as
'normal', organization members are still expected to comply with expectations of technical rationality. Expectations, however, may entail efficiently
implementing a charade, as will be discussed in the Volkswagen case, to be
described later. Being deemed accountable if impossible objectives fail to be
achieved, however, remains a worthy political and organizational ambition. If

the unavoidable emergence of absurdity in organization is not acknowledged and effectively counterbalanced, organizational members can find themselves in situations that are not just 'seemingly' but practically absurd, when they are deprived of any legitimate course of action, so that any choice – including refusing to choose – carries unacceptable consequences. We can refer to these as pragmatic paradoxes.

PRAGMATIC PARADOXES: THE ROLE OF AGENCY AND POWER

The organizational literature offers multiple examples of actors trapped "between non-existent alternatives" (Putnam, Fairhurst & Banghart, 2016: 83). This happens when they are subject to contradictory requests that they are supposed to fulfil simultaneously, such as "Take the initiative/Don't break the rules; Give immediate notice when mistakes occur/You will be punished if you make a mistake; Think long term/Your present behavior will be punished or rewarded; Think of the organization as an entity of responsibility/Don't trespass on others' area; Co-operate/Compete" (Hennestad, 1990: 272). Experience of absurd contradictions does not necessarily stem from direct injunctions but can be implicit to role requirements. Employees can feel trapped between rational and non-rational organizational norms (Wagner, 1978). Employees' innovative and entrepreneurial capabilities can be used as means of control and exploitation (Fleming, 2013); for instance, when flexible work arrangements blur the boundaries between work and home life, employees work without being paid, giving away their 'free time' for free (Putnam, Myers & Gailliard, 2014). Junior employees are exposed to these situations, particularly when they report to multiple 'masters' (Pérezts, Bouilloud & de Gaulejac, 2011). If exposed to workplace bullying they might well find themselves stuck between equally unacceptable alternatives, such as having to face powerful bullies on their own or having to quit their job (Tye-Williams & Krone, 2017).

Managers are not immune to pathological situations. Often, for instance, they are obliged to champion change initiatives that threaten their roles (Dopson & Neumann, 1998) or have subordinates that are both autonomy-seeking and risk-avoiding, making contradictory requests (Ekman, 2012). Structural, historically rooted conditions of disadvantage increase the likelihood of impossible demands becoming manifest. Female employees are often implicitly required to renounce their femininity to be accepted as a peer by male colleagues (Gherardi, 1994). They pay a price for this: female managers have to be authoritative to be taken seriously but "will be perceived as 'bitches' if they act too aggressively" (Oakley, 2000: 324). Moreover, some men still expect female organization members to be simultaneously sexualized and de-sexualized objects (Wendt, 1995).

These pathologies are not exclusive to bureaucratic organizations but have been frequently identified in social and family relationships, being explained as unintended consequences of the dynamics of human communication (Bateson et al., 1956; Watzlawick, Jackson & Bavelas, 1967). When someone is given an order "that must be disobeyed to be obeyed" (Watzlawick, Jackson & Bavelas, 1967: 195), the only reasonable solution is either to discuss or to ignore the demand. If strong relational bonds inhibit either questioning the order or renegotiating the relationship that entrenches pragmatic paradoxes (Bateson, 1972), then a pragmatic paradox will become manifest.

The classic barber's paradox is a case in point: "who shaves the only barber in a village, if the barber shaves all villagers who do not shave themselves?" (Schad, 2017: 32). This intellectual puzzle was used by Bertrand Russell to illustrate the perverse consequences caused by inconsistencies in natural language. These incongruencies are at the basis of most of the logical paradoxes described by ancient philosophers, such as the 'sorite paradox' (when is it that a collection of grains of sand from which grains are removed one at time ceases to be a heap?) or the liar paradox ('this statement is a lie'). Language allows one to formulate grammatically correct and apparently meaningful sentences that – in reality – confuse different logical categories and levels of abstraction. Such paradoxes can be overcome by employing more formal language, with the logical conclusion being that the barber described in the aforementioned story cannot exist (Irvine & Deutsch, 2016). However, we can picture a social situation in which the barber paradox becomes practically and painfully real. Imagine that the barber is a male private ordered by his drill sergeant exclusively to shave only those soldiers who cannot shave themselves (Watzlawick, Jackson & Bavelas, 1967). The cunning enlisted officer (we can picture him as the brutal drill instructor in Kubrick's *Full Metal Jacket*) would place the unfortunate soldier in an impossible predicament: shaving himself (or asking someone else to shave him) would mean disobeying the order; not shaving would cause him to contravene regulations; any attempt to question the order would amount to insubordination. Whatever is done will be wrong and will attract punishment.

In social settings individuals can face contradictions that cannot be handled by any amount of 'paradoxical mindset'. Their occurrence stems from an assumption that actors facing paradoxes lack agency, defined as the capacity to make judgements regarding alternative choices and acting creatively (Berti & Simpson, 2019). Individual agency depends on collocation in a network of power relations; therefore, it is possible to link differences in relation to these to alternative manifestations of pragmatic paradoxes (Berti & Simpson, 2019). Such double binds are paradoxes experienced within the context of relationships in which an actor receives a contradictory request that they are unable to escape "by either metacommunicating (commenting) about it or by withdrawing physically from the scene" (Tracy, 2004: 122). The impossibility of escape attempts brings issues of power and agency that have long been neglected in organizational paradox theory into focus. For instance, the soldier-barber example is premised on coercion, the visible and "direct exercise of power by individuals to achieve certain political ends" (Fleming & Spicer, 2014: 242). Even attempts at trying to navigate contradictions between organizational requirements and personal goals/professional values using ambivalence (Meyerson & Scully, 1995) can be treated as forms of insubordination, while attempts to defuse the situation by metacommunicating can be construed as an affront to managerial authority (Alvesson & Spicer, 2012). Moreover, vicious loops are possible, since "when management do not get the response they expect or want, they will probably increase their signalling and this will increase the degree of ambiguity" (Hennestad, 1990). Vicious cycles ensue that no amount of paradoxical mindset can default.

Manipulation, the indirect, implicit form of power exercised striving to shape "the anticipated outcomes of various behaviors" (Fleming & Spicer, 2014: 243) through setting agendas or determining appropriate topics of discussion, is at the origin of another variety of pragmatic paradoxes: paradoxical predictions (Watzlawick, 1965). Paradoxical predictions are situations in which reaction to a contradiction becomes constitutive of paralysis. An example would be when critical spirit and innovation are suffocated by past successes creating organizational inertia (Miller, 1993). Another example might be when 'best' practice becomes discursively legitimized and objectified to the point that its actual utility in a specific context can neither be assessed nor adapted (Gondo & Amis, 2013).

Domination is the institutionalization of power relations founded on hegemonic values and on systems of relations that are taken for granted as part of a natural order, such as the implicit authority of a corporate hierarchy. Such forms of power relation expect unquestioned obedience (Fleming & Spicer, 2014) that can also generate pragmatic paradoxes, in the form of catch-22 situations (Heller, 1961 [2010]). These become manifest when different norms, implicitly accepted as logical and sensible in the context of a legal-rational bureaucracy, produce clashing requirements, generating an absurd and paralysing impasse. A common occurrence is the situation of an employee lauded for commitment and achievements but denied promotion because s/he lacks managerial experience (an experience that s/he cannot obviously gain in the current role).

Finally, power can also take the form of paradoxical subjectification framing "an actor's very sense of self, including their emotions and identity" (Fleming & Spicer, 2014: 244). In this case pragmatic paradoxes become manifest as "double-think (...) the power of holding two contradictory beliefs in one's mind simultaneously, and accepting both of them ... To tell deliberate lies while genuinely believing in them, to forget any fact that has become inconvenient" (Orwell, 1949: 220). When organizations define autonomy in terms of a relative freedom to express, in multiple ways, their "obedience to the core values of corporate culture" (Willmott, 1993: 527), they limit ways of being an organizational subject to those expressions of doing so that organizational subjectification privileges.

Recognition of pragmatic paradoxes leads to a rejection of a naïve, 'tamed' (Cunha & Putnam, 2019) view of paradox, highlighting the limitations of the dynamic model of organizing; namely, its lack of attention to power relations. The assumption that employees' subjectification in power relations can be exactly predicted and designed implicitly denies the possibility of paradoxical conditions being encountered, a denial that leads to vicious circles. Hence, it is only by removing oppressive conditions (whether deliberate or accidental), and by empowering all organizational members, that pragmatic paradoxes can be overcome. Even if underlying organizational tensions produced by the compresence of multiple goals, logics and interests remain persistent, providing actors with adequate conditions of agency (in addition to helping them acquire paradoxical 'mindsets') is a precondition enabling effective management of paradoxes, turning absurdity into challenging but also productive complexity.

THE RISK OF SEEING PARADOXES EVERYWHERE: MANAGING TRADE-OFFS

The manifestation of absurdity is not the only dark side of organizational paradoxes. Another negative consequence can stem from unproblematically embracing the idea that all tensions should be accepted and framed in a 'both-and' perspective. Paradox theory seems to assume the implicit superiority of such framing over alternative approaches, such as either-or (Smith & Lewis, 2011) or if-then (Lewis & Smith, 2014).

The very appeal of the idea that it is possible to transcend oppositions and to achieve synergistic goals carries an implicit danger of making paradox management a form of wishful thinking. The assumption is that it is always possible to extract value from interdependent tensions. At its worse, it can lead to forms of impression management that destroy value and entrench contradictions. Gaim, Clegg and Cunha (2019) offer a vivid illustration of this in their analysis of the Volkswagen emission scandal. They describe how, by engaging with an impossibly stretched 'paradoxical' goal (producing a fast, cheap and green diesel car in a limited time frame), engineers resorted to a form of impression management, "presenting an illusion of dealing successfully with the tension, rather than actually responding to the tension" (Gaim, Clegg & Cunha, 2019: 6). The engineers did so by devising and installing a defeat device that switched on emission controls only when vehicles were undergoing emission testing (Ewing, 2017).

The case shows that the paradox encountered by Volkswagen staff was not only intrinsic to the contradictory technical requirement (fast, cheap and green); the paradox also referred to the contradictions deriving from their need to 'save face', having previously overestimated their capabilities (or under-estimated the challenge). Cheating (losing face in relation to their sense of a virtuous self) was the only way not to lose face in relation to others. The risks caused by a "false mastery of paradox" and by "persisting in the direction of the impossible" (Gaim, Clegg & Cunha, 2019: 25) led to impression management. For a while, this impression management covered over the gaps between a breakdown in sensemaking between the top management and lower ranks of the organization but at the risk that the paradox between appearance and reality would be exposed. When the risk was realized the organization suffered severe assault on its value and its legitimacy.

The uncritical and problematic preference for 'both-anding' displays the aura of exoticism that paradox theory sometimes seems to affect. The affectation is that innovative solutions can be delivered by borrowing original conceptual frames from traditions that are unfamiliar to Western audiences. Favourite sources include the Chinese philosophy of wisdom, founded on concepts such as: Tao (an understanding of reality as a system of holistically connected and inseparable elements); Ying Yang (the necessary complementary of opposites); and Wu (using intuitive imagination for insight via metaphor) (Li, 1998, 2014, 2016). These adoptions are welcome counterbalances to the Western tendency for analytical separation, reduction to parts and either-or opposition; however, assuming the absolute primacy of these frameworks would, ironically, be inconsistent with paradox thinking. It is by considering *both* the need for synergistic combinations *and* oppositional dialectics that a comprehensively complex approach to organizational challenges can be achieved.

The negative consequences of assuming that all opposition can be integrated are also made evident in the sustainability literature. Hahn et al. (2010) have shown that, despite the prevalence of a 'win-win' discourse in relation to the issue of balancing financial and sustainability goals, in reality it is often not practically possible to do so. There are paradoxical perspectives that promote a Pollyanna-ish belief in being able to have one's cake and eat it. Recognition of the need to sustain and work through tensions between financial, social and environmental imperatives is necessary in fostering innovative solutions, rather than understanding the latter in the limited frame of a 'business case' (Hahn et al., 2018).

One needs to distinguish carefully between the different (albeit coexisting and interdependent) aspects of organizational paradox illustrated in Chapter

1. Paradox can operate as a descriptive theory, useful in studying specific organizational phenomena; it may be used as an instrumental device, helping practitioners to cope with paradoxes (stressing the role of paradoxical mindsets and agency, and of cognitive, structural and practical responses); it can be a normative approach, indicating the pros (and cons), both for theoreticians and strategists, of adopting a paradoxical frame of reference to make sense of reality. Making such distinctions enables one to reconcile the risks of paradoxical thinking. These risks are evident: for instance, treating a trade-off as a potentially generative paradox, with its opportunities, or acknowledging that tensions between different polarities should be sustained, so that it might be possible to turn a trade-off/dilemma into a paradox in future. For instance, the development of cars that perform better and are greener than older models would have been impossible if everyone in the automotive industry had treated the relation between performances and fuel consumption as an inescapable trade-off. Nonetheless, as the Volkswagen case warns, being too optimistic that future technological solutions can preserve the current socio-economic status quo while reducing anthropogenic climate impacts can introduce significant ethical tensions.

In paradox literature, trade-offs are usually seen as the outcome of a specific way of framing tensions. Some ontologically grounded tensions become socially constructed as paradox (Hahn & Knight, 2019; Schad & Bansal, 2018) in situations in which "decision makers need to weigh a loss in at least one dimension against a gain in the other dimension" (Hahn et al., 2010: 219). These situations are characterized as a result of a "trade-off (…) mindset" (Schad et al., 2016: 40), "trade-off thinking" (Cuganesan, 2017: 489) or a "trade-off logic" (Smith et al., 2017: 304). In other disciplines, such as biology and ecology (Stearns, 1989), economics (Skousen & Taylor, 1997) and human communication (Watzlawick, Jackson & Bavelas, 1967), trade-offs are treated as objective, material conditions. In economic terms, trade-offs are typical of Pareto optimality situations, which occur when the "the outcome for one party cannot be improved without reducing the outcome for the other" (Jeffries & Reed, 2000: 875), making win-win situations impossible. A scarce resource can be used in one way or another (e.g. money spent on rent cannot be spent on food); a trait cannot increase without a decrease in another (running faster requires lighter bones, so a faster animal will be less strong), requiring a balance between conflicting functional demands (Garland, 2014).

Some tensions become manifest as inescapable trade-offs: for example, time is a limited resource, so there is an unnegotiable trade-off between sleeping and working. Such zero-sum calculations highlight another limitation of the power of paradoxical mindsets confronting inherent tensions. When facing a trade-off, any gain in one factor must be counterbalanced by a loss/sacrifice in the other. In strategy, there are many such trade-offs. For instance, between abstract generalizability and detail (Bacharach, 1989); between generality, accuracy and simplicity (Weick, 1979); between necessary generalizations and the risk of ignoring specific attributes when making predictions about the future (Ehrig & Schmidt, 2019); between failure to 'optimize' when implementing 'best practices' from elsewhere that cannot be applied to a specific context (Azoulay, Repenning & Zuckerman, 2010). Not acknowledging the existence of such a trade-off can lead to pathological outcomes. Defensiveness and denial in facing paradoxes can lead to negative outcomes (Smith & Lewis, 2011), such as identifying potential synergies which result in impossible expectations that can only be met through deceitful behaviour (Gaim, Clegg & Cunha, 2019). Sometimes individuals can be driven to a pathological and fruitless search for meaning (Tracy, 2004) as they strive to secure synergies.

WHEN PARADOX CAN BECOME A TOOL OF OPPRESSION: INTRODUCING DIALECTICAL APPROACHES

Both the case of the pragmatic paradox and that of the 'false mastery' of paradoxes reveal another dark side of paradoxicality in which contradictions derive from political games and are maintained because they serve vested interests. Double binds can be an expression of tyrannical organizational behaviour, the "tendency to overcontrol others and to treat them in an arbitrary, uncaring, and punitive manner" (Ashforth, 1994: 756). Similarly, doublethink can be strategically employed to maximize exploitation under an illusory impression of self-determination (Willmott, 2013). Employers can seek to persuade those they employ that the only way to negotiate threatening tensions between individual and corporate interests is to self-identify with one's job, by dissolving personal identity into a corporate identity. An example is offered by the relationship between job satisfaction, defined as a "pleasurable emotional state deriving from the appraisal of one's job" (Locke, 1969: 317), and work engagement. The assumption is that a happy worker is a productive worker (Fisher, 2010); however, being satisfied in one's job may well dampen aspirations or drive (Bussing et al., 1999; Grebner, Semmer & Elfering, 2005). Win-win synergies between productivity and personal happiness are not always possible, not only because of the consciousness of the employee. Finding, a trade-off between contentment and balance as a means to an obsessive pursuit of enhanced productivity, performances and rewards, is implicit in neoliberal ideology (Alvesson & Willmott, 2012), in which failure to commit, acculturate and achieve is taken as a moral failing.

The assumption that synergistic solutions can be found has a strong managerialist undertone, harnessing the management of paradox to increase organizational performance (Cunha & Putnam, 2019). If, instead, we consider the perspectives of multiple stakeholders, the reality becomes more nuanced. First, depending on power dynamics, paradoxes can be openly highlighted and discussed or glossed over (Francis & Keegan, 2018). Second, the political neutrality of alternative 'poles' is questionable: "actors will respond by promoting the element they favor and seeking to overcome the contradictory element" (Hargrave & Van de Ven, 2017: 332). For instance, shareholder interests will likely be far more engaged with productivity and profit than individual employee happiness, while for employees, individual happiness is likely to be of more value. For some employees, especially professional workers doing creative work, professional success can be a major source of gratification. Such outcomes cannot be taken for granted, however. Passion for one's work can be exploited by management, as so often happens in the case of academics (Clarke, Knights & Jarvis, 2012), participating in systems of performance surveillance to which they subscribe (Clarke & Knights, 2014).

Incorporating a political lens in our understanding of organizational tensions highlights that accepting and synergistically harnessing paradoxes may reproduce a status quo characterized by inequities and disadvantage. A recent movie by the award-winning director Ken Loach, *Sorry We Missed You*, masterfully depicts the predicament of working-class individuals who become trapped in the contradictions of the discourse of 'entrepreneurialism'. Employment opportunities, earnings and self-determination promised by a delivery job in the gig economy (in the words of a depot manager 'You don't work *for* us – you work *with* us') conceal a multitude of downsides that haunt the protagonist, such as having to buy his own van, being constantly pressed for time, paying sanctions for missing delivery windows, not having sick or personal leaves, et cetera. Working harder and harder to navigate the contradictions (for instance, deciding whether to risk traffic fines and personal safety to fulfil the schedule and receive bonuses) the central character feels as if he is sinking in quicksand: the more he fights, the more he is dragged down. While the story is fictional, it resonates with the experience of many involved in the gig economy. The destructive spiral in which the protagonist is trapped is also manifest in real life, with tragic consequences. Instead of 'accepting' contradictions it is sometimes necessary to resist, using conflict to force resolution (Hargrave & Van de Ven, 2017). A dialectic perspective on tensions understands their development "through conflict process of affirmation, negation, and synthesis" (Farjoun, 2019: 135).

Central to dialectics is a process view of the emergence and dissolution of specific social orders (Benson, 1977). Structure is an ongoing accomplishment, constantly under construction and deconstruction, characterized by dualities within an interdependent totality (Farjoun, 2010). The emphasis on interdependence incorporates a dialectical approach within analysis of paradox in which a central point of divergence is the focus on conflict and power relations (Hargrave & Van de Ven, 2017). Typically, this process is described using the Hegelian idea of dialectics as a struggle between thesis and antithesis that produces a synthesis as the unity of opposites (Putnam, Fairhurst & Banghart, 2016). Yet it is important to stress that this synthesis does not end the process, as it will attract a further antithesis, reactivating the cycle (Clegg & Cunha, 2017). The idea is well captured by the framework of relational dialectics, which examines how meaning becomes constantly constructed and contested through power struggles (Putnam, Fairhurst & Banghart, 2016). In the process, different voices are included and excluded, existing structures and practices are maintained and transformed (Putnam, Fairhurst & Banghart, 2016). "In time most management practices create their own nemesis" (Clegg, Cunha & Cunha, 2002: 491), perhaps best seen in the ways that an emphasis on efficiency and standardization in pursuit of profit but in neglect of statutory regulatory requirements can produce rigidity, demotivation and over-work. A dialectical perspective can account for such situations: organizations may well 'delocalize' to regions where regulatory policies are less stringent, as a way to overcome the contradiction between the logics of efficiency and regulatory compliance. The paradox can be solved (or at least made latent) by forcing one pole to have dominance over the other (financial over regulatory interests).

A dialectical view of tensions helps understanding that social and organizational change does not occur only through incremental processes of paradox management, as suggested by paradox theorists (Smith & Lewis, 2011). Rather, in line with punctuated equilibrium models (Miller & Friesen, 1980; Romanelli & Tushman, 1994), incremental transformation has inertial consequences that can be disrupted by revolutionary transformations. Integrating paradox and dialectical views is therefore necessary both to account for the role of power in revealing and navigating tensions, as well as the potential of contradictions to foster radical change (Hargrave & Van de Ven, 2017).

CONCLUSION

In this chapter we have explored the dark side (or sides) of organizational paradoxes, 'zooming in' on individual experiences of paradox, understood as social phenomena that have material consequences for actors. By doing so, we have stressed the actors' feeling of absurdity, a distinguishing characteristic highlighted in early accounts of paradoxicality (Farson, 1996; Lewis, 2000) that seems to have been overlooked subsequently only to be recently 'rediscovered' (Berti & Simpson, 2019).

We have also shown the dysfunctional consequences of embracing paradoxes and of thinking paradoxically, leading to a false mastery of paradox and the delusion that it is always possible to find synergies in oppositions. Rather, it is useful to consider a dialectical perspective (focusing on power relations and oppositions) in conjunction with analysis of paradox. Doing so, it becomes possible to account for 'resolutions' of contradiction that are based on oppression. One needs to be alert to the possibility that systemic change sometimes implies radical transformation through social opposition and conflict.

Drawing attention to the limitations of 'acceptance' strategies and to the existence of intrinsically pathological paradoxes is not to be intended as a challenge to the conceptual core of paradox theory so much as a 'centrifugal' invitation to expand and reinforce it (Schad, Lewis & Smith, 2019), avoiding oversimplifications. In this way, perhaps, paradox scholarship can acknowledge paradoxes as being both normal and pathological, constructive and destructive, as opportunities to exploit at some times but also as destructive conditions that must be avoided, mitigated or overcome at other times.

5. Nested, multiple and multidimensional paradoxes

At the 30,000-foot level of the corporate suite, plotting digital change is heady, exciting stuff.
(Leonardi, 2020, p. 28)

[w]hat seems paradoxical higher up appears confusing and absurd lower down.
(Czarniawska, 1997: 97)

In 2019 the Business Roundtable (BRT), a non-profit association whose members are chief executive officers of major US companies, issued a manifesto declaring that organizations do not strictly exist to create shareholder value but to respond to the needs of a variety of stakeholders (Harrison, Phillips & Freeman, 2020). While not as famous as Marx and Engels' *Communist Manifesto*, it may well have seemed equally radical to many in business, weaned on Milton Friedman's 'greed is good' philosophy (1970 [2007]). A further manifesto was issued by the World Economic Forum as, "The universal purpose of a company in the Fourth Industrial Revolution", which argued:

> the purpose of a company is to engage all its stakeholders in shared and sustained value creation. In creating such value, a company serves not only its shareholders – employees, customers, suppliers, local communities and society at large. The best way to understand and harmonize the divergent interests of all stakeholders is through a shared commitment to policies and decisions that strengthen the long-term prosperity of a company. (World Economic Forum, 2019: 5)

Such revolutionary stuff, suggesting a need to reinvent capitalism around the idea of purpose, should be situated as a response to increasingly "myopic business behaviour" (Wolf, 2019: 13). Interestingly, now also strategic management scholars (a group that certainly cannot be accused of socialist tendencies) have started critiquing the idea of shareholder primacy, observing that the competitive advantage of firms depends upon the strategic contribution of multiple stakeholders who should therefore participate in firm governance (Kaufman & Englander, 2005) and value appropriation (Barney, 2018).

Regardless of the motivation (ethical or instrumental), it is clear that contemporary organizations must increasingly consider the interests, requirements and logics of multiple stakeholders. As a consequence, organizations need to articulate a number of tensions and/or trade-offs, as each stakeholder brings to the table a plurality of interests that will necessarily collide – no matter how much harmonizing is sought or how strongly one believes in creating 'win-win' situations (Hahn et al., 2010).

In this chapter we discuss the need to examine paradoxes as existing not in isolation from one another but in connection. Multiple interests mean that multiple purposes have to be served. These interests are not shrink-wrapped and separate but embedded and entangled: as Weber (1978) wrote, organizations are characterized by a constellation of interests. Embeddedness means that managing trade-offs will become an important business competence (Kaplan, 2019). As Petriglieri and Petriglieri (2020: 24) point out, where interests tend to be entangled they will also be contested. Contestation breeds tensions as conflict presents different choices that must be faced, such that contestation over conflicting interests traverses different levels and locales in and around organizations. Coalitions of interest will form and fragment, and the foci of issues and non-issues shifts. When organizations formally embrace the purpose of satisfying multiple constituencies of interest, these tensions will become more salient. When approaching organization as a matter of contested, conflicting and entangled interests it is not appropriate to think about single paradoxes occurring around single issues such as change versus stability (Farjoun, 2010). While this approximation may be convenient it is misleading for several reasons. For example, 'change' is a short label for a large class of processes, as is the case for its polar opposite, stability. As such, within any pole, such as change, there are many possible paradoxes, such as between intended and unintended change. To make things more complicated, attempts to tackle tensions around one set of polar opposites will likely "inadvertently" create new tensions (Poole & Van de Ven, 1989: 576). As Tetenbaum (1998) wrote, any "paradox (…) is really a constellation of paradoxes".

The idea of a constellation of paradoxes indexes the idea of a constellation of interests. Existing in relation, being embedded in social relations (Ashby, Riad & Davenport, 2019), contradictions between interests and the resultant tensions that occur in one part of a system will create disturbances in other parts of the system: "it's like squeezing a balloon in one place only to find that it expands elsewhere" (Dodd & Favaro, 2006: 62). Systemic complexity makes causal relations difficult to understand. The consequences of one action may be made visible only later in a different part of the system. Understanding the functioning of a system implies the exploration of space and time in non-Newtonian ways, as complex adaptive systems that are not Newtonian pieces of horology (e.g. Bansal, Kim & Wood, 2018).

If paradoxes are isolated and treated as general abstract categories we risk falling into what Nagel (1986) calls "the view from nowhere", framing them as a-contextual, objective, a-temporal facets of reality. Doing so violates the very reasons that lead paradox to emerge as processual dynamics that happen in space and time. It is often said that there is no text without context, to which we add that there is no *paradoxa* without a *doxa* (see Box 5.1). To understand paradox, we need to consider the *doxa* where contradictions incubate.

BOX 5.1   THE ETYMOLOGY OF PARADOX

The word 'paradox' derives from the juxtaposition of the term para (against, contrary to) with that of doxa (popular opinion, common belief). Paradox thus defines something that challenges some commonly held idea, something that is beyond belief. Paradox thus can be viewed as: (1) something that puts together ideas that are logical when isolated but absurd when held together (Lewis, 2000), but also (2) as an opportunity to extend, challenge or make sense of, received knowledge (Berti, 2021).

As an illustration from the arts, the par excellence domain of paradoxa, consider the emergence of the urban culture of jazz. Jazz became the object of a moral panic during the 1920s (Porter, 2002: 9). The moral panics that grew in the 1920s and 1930s around 'jazz' were barely coded concerns for the contagion of white society by black bodies and black culture. As Lopes (2005: 1468) suggests, from the Jazz Age of the 1920s "the sordid world of jazz and the deviant jazz musician became a common trope in the popular press, pulp fiction, and Hollywood film. Jazz in general served as a trope for the darker side of the American urban experience." Indeed, "The jazz trope that emerged in the late 1930s represented a strange double consciousness of romantic rebellion and potential danger. Jazz deviance – in articulating aspects of race, class, and the urban environment – signified rebellion against dominant norms while affirming these norms in the ultimate tragedy associated with jazz" (Lopes, 2005: 1468). Jazz was described as indecent, pollutive, an "agency of the devil" (Appelrouth, 2005: 1504), yet it became the music of choice for a white hipster and beat intelligentsia. For Black intellectuals such as James Baldwin, "jazz was a metaphor for the struggle of Blacks for survival and self-respect, a struggle ending in tragedy. For the beats, jazz represented rebellion, but this rebellion gave freedom to the beats against straight-laced (sic.) bourgeois culture. For Black authors, no freedom was delivered to their Black protagonists" (Lopes, 2005: 1475).

Going beyond the idea that paradoxes have only two opposite poles, we first look at how paradoxes can be nested or embedded in each other, considering tensions as generated by multiple poles which evolve over time. The forces in tension have varying levels of intensity (Gaim et al., 2020), because of which organization members construct paradoxical experience in different ways

(Jarzabkowski, Bednarek & Lê, 2018: 185). To take an example, given the nested nature of paradoxes (Sheep, Fairhurst & Khazanchi, 2017), contradictions whose intensity is deemed high by the upper echelon of an organization might not be perceived as equally salient by the rank and file (Gaim, Clegg & Cunha, 2019; Knight & Paroutis, 2017). Nestedness has been approached by authors who studied double (Weijers, 1999) or triple (Jennings & Hoffman, 2019) paradoxes, i.e. cases in which paradoxes manifest as multiple tensions at once (such as in the famous triple bottom line). Instead of reifying paradox (Cunha & Putnam, 2019) it is important to adopt a process perspective (Jarzabkowski, Bednarek & Lê, 2018) which regards paradoxes as forever changing as they are engaged. To do so we begin by discussing why paradoxes should be treated as entangled, nested and embedded. It is necessary to consider how organizational paradoxes can be the expression (or at least a partial outcome of) broader paradoxical tensions, between phenomena such as short/long term, centralization/decentralization. Moreover, the nestedness of paradoxes highlights the need to look at them from a diachronic, processual perspective in terms of tensions shaping flows of action.

WHY ARE PARADOXES NESTED AND EMBEDDED?

Paradoxes have often been treated as single forms of tension between two poles – for example exploration and exploitation (March, 1991). In these formulations the poles exist almost as things and as things they belong, analytically, to the same level. They have equivalent properties, such as force or intensity. The dominant conception of the appropriate way to address these tensions historically has been through the influence of thinkers such as Aristotle, Descartes and Newton, through either/or approaches (Lewis, 2000). A thing must be one thing or another; it cannot be akin to Schrödinger's cat – both there and not there.

Paradoxes extend beyond well-defined 'poles' with clear boundaries. In fact, as organizations try to address tensions they create new tensions as changes in one part of a system create changes in other parts of the system (Stacey, Griffin & Shaw, 2000). As Vaill described life in organizations, "everything was interactive … I simply had to learn to understand myself in a spaciotemporal field of relationships, flowing and shitting" (Vaill, 1998: 144). Additionally, decision makers cognitively frame and emotionally feel forces with different levels of intensity depending on their perspectives and interests. These perspectives are framed by the circuits of power through which different actors move in parallel, expressing entangled forms of agency, understood as "the tendency to ascribe conscious intentions to phenomena that are not guided by any such intents" (Rizio & Skali, 2019: 1). In organizations agencies and actants mingle with other agencies and because "organizations consist of embedded groups"

(Barton & Kahn, 2018: 16); this embeddedness will necessarily create tensions and contradictions between agencies characterized by inner paradoxical tensions (Silva et al., 2014). As such, organizations are wholes within wholes, with paradoxes existing within and between these wholes.

As a result, poles may be created where none existed before. For example, the emergence of obesity as a societal issue created a tension for producers of high-fat, high-sugar products. A strategic tension emerged between the social and the business sides of their activity (Pinkse, Hahn & Figge, 2019). This new tension caused a need for reframing activities to protect the business without ignoring the public health debate. A tension was nested in another tension, not because it was 'there' but because as social concerns evolved, they rendered some tensions salient. Once they become more visible (Tuckermann, 2018) they became harder to ignore. Therefore, a new relation is created between one existing practice (production of high-fat, high-sugar products) and a new practice (the need to combat obesity) that was a previous solution (the provision of fast food at low cost). As predicted by Greiner (1998), while a problem is solved the solution will originate new problems in a never-ending process. Paradoxes thus do not exist as two things independent of other things: they result from the entangled, nested and embedded nature of social life, in which processes are in constant interaction, shaping one another in unexpected ways.

CROSS-LEVEL ASSUMPTIONS

Nesting, a term we have used frequently thus far, implies levels; something nests inside something else. There are a number of assumptions that we now render explicit. First, organizational life, as is well known, is hierarchical; it consists of levels. We assume that multiple logics coexist at every organizational level. If multiple logics are the defining attribute of so-called hybrid organizations, then every organization at every level possesses traits of hybridity. Second, we assume that tensions at one level potentially reverberate within and between levels. As a result, tensions co-occur at multiple levels. Third, we consider that such co-occurrence is not necessarily experienced in the same way, as different actors play different roles and do not have the same power or equivalent interests.

Treating paradox as if every organization is a hybrid. The notion of the hybrid organization refers to the fact that organizations embed multiple institutional arrangements with conflicting or contradictory rules and prescriptions for action. Starting in the 1980s, scholars used the term hybridity to make sense of the multiple and conflicting demands of organizing. While competing demands have been seen as a conceptual staple, as pervasive and inherent within all organizations, hybridity scholars depict a more circumscribed phenomenon. Scholars began observing a pervasive experience of multiple demands in organizations. Battilana, Besharov and Mitzinneck (2017) ask whether hybridity is a distinct organizational form or rather a matter of degree within organizations. They note the increased environmental pressures that drive the need for organizations to span categories, legal structures and forms, and suggest that this pressure will only increase over time. Conceptualizing "hybridity as a matter of degree, rather than as a distinct type not only better reflects the empirical reality of many organizations; it also provides an opportunity for research on hybridity to provide insights into the challenges, opportunities, and management strategies that are relevant for a broader set of organizations" (pp. 152–153). Besharov and Smith (2014) conceptualize the degree of hybridity in organizations as a function of the level of compatibility between logics and their respective organizational centrality. This perspective sees hybridity as pervasive within organization, which means that paradox, seen in terms of tensions between different logics, is a necessary characteristic of organizations.

Tensions reverberate. A second assumption is that tensions reverberate. Obviously, tensions at one level are not sealed from tensions at other levels, as actors, actants and organizations reciprocally constitute one another (Michel, 2014). Paradoxes can also 'reverberate', as one paradox may trigger another. Dodd and Favaro point out that "tensions often masquerade as one another" (2006: 64), meaning that appearances are elusive. As such, what happens at a given level potentially has an impact on other levels. For example, when a multinational firm diffuses a new formal value, this value will be translated into actions in different ways in its different subsidiaries. As the value travels and is translated throughout the organization, cascading down to the local operations, it meets the friction caused by local cultures, histories as well as differences between leaders and departments. A single value, for example 'speak up', may mean very different things for sales or R&D, and, as Cunha et al. (2019b) attest, it can mean very different things for teams with different leaders. Paradoxes are informed by their particular context. What is paradoxical in one part of the organization is not necessarily so in different parts of the organization, within the same subsidiary. Many factors, not least including that which is taken to be culturally normal, shape how individuals think about paradox (Keller, Lowenstein & Yan, 2017).

Paradoxes are experienced differently by different actors. The same objective conditions may be perceived by different actors in different ways. For example, within the same organization, 4AD, the record company studied by Cunha et al. (2019b), the tensions felt by the founder were idiosyncratic, precisely because he was the founder. The founder led an organization with an aesthetic vision that was singular and distinctive, one that he had created but that still needed to be balanced with the economic and artistic dimensions of the entire set of artists collected on the label; whereas individual artists were primarily oriented to their specific interests. The paradoxes he faced were thus dependent on the vested interests and the roles of all the participants entangled in the circuits of power that running a record label entailed.

Berti and Simpson (2019) explain that the way people tackle paradoxes depends on their power to be able to do so in their capacity. Some organizational members cannot deal resolutely with paradoxes because of their position in the organization's power circuitry; for instance, they may not have the relational reach and access to resources to be able to initiate much in the way of action. Confronted with paradoxical messages, such agents cannot dismiss an order ('be proactive') on the basis of its contradictory nature even if they interpret it as such. Their relational position in the hierarchy may force them to accept and enact contradictions (see also Chapter 4).

STUDYING PARADOXES AT MULTIPLE LEVELS

Paradoxes have been studied at multiple levels of analysis. Conventionally, distinctions between levels start with the intra-individual level in which micro-level paradoxes are situated; however, even though distinctions premised on 'levels' are conceptually helpful they are also misleading: levels cannot be separated in action. Consider how advances in technology and digital platforms allow the creation of companies such as Uber. As an organization, Uber and other companies in the gig economy create interesting paradoxes: are individual drivers better viewed as entrepreneurs or are they employees without the commitments and obligations that are normally expected and sought for by management in employment relations? Are they exploited or voluntarily self-employed? Do national states legally frame the activity in the same ways?

BOX 5.2   THE NESTED EFFECTS OF THE GIG ECONOMY

The gig economy is often portrayed as the epitome of flexibility. Gig workers are freed from old employment rules and empowered to live their lives as they see fit. This "flexibility fetishism", as Izabella Kaminska calls it, is more complex than it seems. Consider Kaminska's (2019: 9) analysis: "A lifetime in an employee allows a business to absorb low productivity phases because they benefit from over-productive phases. The end result is a virtuous circle where the vitality of youth pays for shortcomings that may emerge later. The end result is a better quality of life for everyone involved." When this social contract is violated by hyper-flexible employers, the burdens of an aging workforce fall upon the state. As such, the state, individual employees-cum-entrepreneurs and platforms are all entangled in multilevel-multidimensional tensional knots with real consequences for individual outcome such as social security, unemployment benefits and health coverage.

Nested paradoxes can also be aligned to political ends, as it is the case of the effects of algorithms and digital platforms in mediating both controls and forms of workplace resistance in the gig economy. While (apparently) workers in the gig economy are less subject to hierarchical controls, as managers are replaced by neutral algorithms, this dehumanization of management 'naturalizes' employer's demands, seen by gig workers as unavoidable hurdles. Energies become funnelled in 'gaming the system' (instead of negotiating better contractual conditions). At the same time, the use of social media and of opaque artificial intelligence systems to measure performances reduces the capacity of gig workers (such as Uber drivers) to build solidarity, as conflict is deflected from the company to other stakeholders (Walker, Fleming & Berti, 2020).

INTRA-INDIVIDUAL PARADOXES

The notion that individuals are paradoxical is poetically expressed in Walt Whitman's verse 'I am large, I contain multitudes', in *Song of Myself*, the source for Bob Dylan's (2020) version. The verse is not only valid biographically and biologically (Yong, 2016) but also psychologically. We all contain multitudes. In terms of the experience of sources of paradox at the intra-individual level, these are manifested by processes forming identities and behavioural tendencies, the roles people play and the logics of action that shape all these.

It is now widely acknowledged that individuals perform more than one identity (Ramarajan, 2014). Performing more than one identity confronts individuals with tensions arising from an identity portfolio: one may be performing as writer or lover, poet or parent, professor or child. For example, Berti, Simpson and Clegg (2018: 181) observe: "the business academic's emerging identity is that of an educator, project leader, networker, self-entrepreneur competing in the academic publishing market" who must "establish a strong brand, and demonstrate a significant 'impact'", while "participating in a political economy based on unpaid contributions of largely privatized authoring, editing, reviewing but also more collaborative conference organizing, industry partnering and consulting". Behaviourally, it is psychodynamically axiomatic (Petriglieri & Petriglieri, 2020) that the self encompasses "two contradictory behavioural tendencies: the tendency toward learning and change and the tendency to protect one's self against the risk of change as a result of learning. The first tendency is self-oriented and critical to the development of self-identity, maturity and autonomy; the second tendency is resistant to change and crucial to the construction of defensive techniques for avoiding anxiety and maintaining security" (Diamond, 1986: 544).

One's identity is diverse, meaning that as people play different roles different manifestations of the self are expressed and performed. Different role demands exist in potential contradiction: being a good parent can collide with being a dedicated employee; being a good writer can collide with being a good teacher when what the student needs is not sparkling prose and a command of language but basic information in order to complete an assignment. This simple example is indicative of the intra-individual paradoxes we all confront. Of course, individuals can try to 'both-and' the paradox, but the paradox is still present, meaning that the psychological tension cannot possibly be solved: it has to be navigated. For instance, an employee who works all the hours that are available may say 'I work this much to provide my children with the best possible education', implicitly tangling up present and future, roles and responsibilities. Roles, whether private and familial or performed at large in public, in organizations, are framed by contexts in which people respond to organizational expectations (Padavic, Ely & Reid, 2020). The organizations may be employers, schools, advertising agencies, sports teams or providers of narcotics and fast food. In addition to between-role demands as parent, poet, et cetera, employment relations can be intrinsically paradoxical. Employment may entail occupying a middle managerial position in which work identities are performed that are inherently paradoxical (Neumann, James & Vince, 2019), articulating tensions between stability and change (Huy, 2001). Even at work, working, doing time, one can be conjuring dreams and schemes as 'escape attempts' (Cohen & Taylor, 2003), into all those other identities one might wish to assume.

Individuals are also exposed to different logics in their respective organizations. Not only do organizations face different logics, such as the logic of care and the logic of efficiency (in healthcare) or the logic of commerce and the logic of art (in the creative sector). Conflicting logics explain why the same work, in animal shelters, can be perceived differently as a function of how people balance the logics of work as job and work as purpose (Schabram & Maitlis, 2017). The case of the founder of 4AD, Ivo Watts Russell, is illustrative of how logics that operate at the level of the organizations have individual-level implications (Cunha et al., 2019b). In this case what started as an artistic endeavour filled with purpose evolved over time and with company success, to be transformed in a more complex commercial venture, one in which the role of economic criteria became more prominent. The coexistence of these two logics created significant psychological tension in the founder, deviating the project from its initial intention, which eventually led the founder to abandon the project. However, even when founders vacate the scene, they may still have an 'enduring presence' (Coman & Casey, 2021).

In facing paradoxes, academic advice to individuals is that they should adopt a "paradoxical mindset" (Miron Spektor et al., 2018; Liu, Xu & Zhang, 2020). These are "mental templates in which the actors recognize and accept the persisting inconsistencies of contradictory forces" (Liu, Xu & Zhang, 2020: 3). Such adoption has been portrayed as a positive attribute that will lead to positive results, such as superior creativity (Liu, Xu & Zhang, 2020). The idea that paradoxical mindsets can be 'adopted' turns them into quasi-choices. If one does not 'have' a paradoxical mindset, on this reckoning, it must be because one decided not to foster adoption. Mindsets of this sort need to be developed such that they can be adopted only in certain conditions. Embracing a paradox mindset in an organization with a penchant for clarity and order may not be well nested. Seen from the vantage point of nestedness, becoming paradox oriented is more than a strictly individual attribute. No matter how paradoxical one chooses to be, expressing this in action is a process with cross-level effects in which organizations support or discourage paradoxical propensities and formal messages often collide with practical actions.

Advising individuals to become paradoxical thinkers can be extremely problematic. Prescriptions such as the following, "individuals could learn to tolerate tensions through challenging life experience" (Liu, Xu & Zhang, 2020: 15), may ring true but their plausibility is questionable. It is because individuals have to endure difficulties that some personal strengths, such as resilience, are necessary. Resilience can help individuals to endure but it is not something that can be adopted. Individuals can be exposed to trying circumstances with the purpose of developing resilience but whether they do or not is a contingent matter (Thornborrow & Brown, 2009). Specific conditions, such as training regimes exposing trainees to tough conditions, as in military training, may strive to nurture resilient skills (Giustiniano et al., 2018). Some fail, however; the experience of adopting the preferred conceptions of their selves as paratroopers, in Thornborrow and Brown's (2009) case, is disciplined both by understandings of what being a paratrooper means and the institutional processes by which paratroopers are made. A paradox opens up between aspiration and actuality as the process strives to build resilience. The paradox is one of tension and ambivalence (Vince & Broussine, 1996). To deal with such tension, context is critical, because paradoxes, as demonstrated by Watzlawick and colleagues (1967), are to a great extent an outpouring of their contextual settings. In some cases, such as in Thornborrow and Brown's account of paratrooper training, the context forces paradoxical choices on aspirants. They want to *be* paratroopers; however, do they want to *become* paratroopers, with all the pain and hardship doing so presumes?

TEAM PARADOXES

Teams are rich in paradoxicality (Smith & Berg, 1987). Their size is typically small enough to preserve an aspiration of individuality which is well captured in De Rond's (2012) defence that there is a 'I' in team. But teams – more than collections of 'I's, aggregates of interpersonal relationships – constitute "dynamic wholes" (Bion, 1946) that exist inside other wholes. The idea that teams are paradoxical was discussed by Smith and Berg (1987) in their influential book *Paradoxes of Group Life*, in which the authors qualify group life as inherently paradoxical, an observation also confirmed in other studies. Silva et al. (2014) empirically explored, in an amateur football team, how the nurturing of a 'team spirit' could be explained as the tackling of a number of paradoxes. These included finding a way of articulating collective and individual identities, and of using both victories and defeats to elevate the team (see Table 5.1). These tensions cannot be solved, only navigated and temporarily balanced, which is what gives them a paradoxical dimension. Edmondson's (2018) work on teams also reveals that great teams are those that manage to find an equilibrium between accountability and psychological safety. These two elements are opposites, but both are necessary to create superior teams, as safety with no accountability will lead to complacency, whereas accountability in the absence of psychological safety will create fear, which will have a negative impact on learning and effectiveness.

When, as is usual, some team members identify more with certain team members than with others, teams contain tension within their boundaries. Team fault lines introduce tensions (Li & Hambrick, 2005) that divide groups and engage leaders in different types of relationships with so-called ingroup and outgroup factions. Differential relationships between leaders and members, as explained by LMX theory, result in further tensions within teams (Graen & Uhl-Bien, 1995). As Murninghan and Conlon (1991) explained with their study of British string quartets, teams that manage to tackle their inner paradoxes tend to outperform other teams that become stuck in dysfunctional dynamics.

Teams also exist in a state of tension with other teams. Teams develop a collective identity over time, such that their interests and worldviews tend to stabilize, a process that may diminish team openness to collaboration with other teams. The process may eventually result in "thought worlds" (Douglas, 1986; Dougherty, 1992) that do not coexist peacefully with other thought worlds. These interpretive barriers may help to create organizational silos in which different 'languages' develop within organizations, diminishing collaboration and confronting managers with substantive problems, including the difficulty for anyone, including top management, to understand the organ-

Table 5.1   Some paradoxical tensions within teams

Paradox	Explanation	Implications
Selfless egoism	Effective team functioning implies the acceptance that the team interest should be above self-interest. But a measure of self-interest is critical for teams to function.	Teams imply the capacity to understand how selfish motivations may reinforce the team.
Results	Good team functioning implies the capacity to learn from victory and defeat.	Teams are more effective when they offer the pride that results from winning but test their psychological safety in the moment of failure.
Conflict	Teams need conflict to avoid groupthink, but conflict can be destructive.	Teams need to learn how to use conflict rather than to avoid it.
Proximity	Teams imply proximity; yet too much proximity can be debilitating as it can constitute an obstacle to individual freedom.	Teams need to practise the "hedgehog effect" (Kets de Vries, 2011): learn to be close without being too close.

Source: Based on Silva et al., 2014.

ization holistically, rather than a set of separate entities (Tett, 2015). To be effective, teams must therefore learn to tackle paradoxes. Some of the studies mentioned suggest that the task is often approached implicitly, i.e. without seeing or framing the tension as paradoxical. Nonetheless, team leaders need to understand the tension and realize that something needs to be done to turn intra- and inter-team tension into a productive force.

ORGANIZATION-LEVEL PARADOXES

Organizations are inherently paradoxical given characteristics such as diversity and plurality. By definition, plurality infuses organizations with a diversity of goals and interests that are ignored when it is assumed that organizations are collectives with one common shared goal. Such aspirations often amount to little more than wishes that remain unfulfilled. As previously discussed, organizations necessarily accommodate a multiplicity of goals because the individuals and teams that compose them have sectional goals as well as specific interests that do not necessarily harmonize. To make organizations more complex, these goals are shifting and dynamic, meaning that a goal that collectively mobilizes at one time may lose the power to do so in another. In addition, as organizations assume that they need to satisfy a constellation of stakeholder interests, matters are made even more complicated as goals and interests conflict with each other. As a result, organizations need to master the art of the trade-off (Kaplan, 2019) and learn to live with multiple logics (Smith & Besharov, 2019) and compromises.

Three dimensions of paradox occur at the organizational level: organizational hybridity, opposite processes, and preparing organizations to tackle paradox as a source of competitive advantage.

Organizations are paradoxical because of their **hybrid nature**, as has already been mentioned. Given the need to respond to different stakeholders, organizations are necessarily faced with the need to equilibrate diverse interests. The clarity brought by a single dominant supra-organizational goal (such as profit in the shareholder view of the firm) is replaced by the need to strike a dynamic a balance between shifting goals (Offe & Wiesenthal, 1980). The notion of shared value (Porter & Kramer, 2011) aims to integrate a plurality of interests under an integrative logic that may dynamically respond to different stakeholders in different moments. Shared value is a noble aspiration. In reality, when different constellations of interest in scarce and shared resources occur such as in a major river system in an arid continent, shared value is difficult to achieve. Sharing the interests of ecology, irrigation of water-intensive crops such as cotton, rural land use, mining, with its demands for water, as well as recreational utilization, across three states, yet still leaving sufficient flow to ensure no salinity when the river system eventually meets the ocean, is extremely difficult, as the case of the Australian Murray-Darling Basin demonstrates (Davies, 2019). The need to balance exploitation of the scarce resource of water amongst many competing interests entails a degree of political complexity and willingness to sacrifice sectional interests that thus far seems unachievable.

In organizations, achieving shared goals is complemented by the need, internally, to promote **opposite processes**: exploration needs to be balanced with exploitation (March, 1991), differentiation with integration (Lawrence & Lorsch, 1967), stability with change (Farjoun, 2010), standardization with innovation (Takeuchi, Osono & Shimizu, 2008). Organizations do not have the luxury of choosing one or the other: they need to be competent in both activities; hence paradoxes arise. It is the realization that management is frequently paradoxical that has stimulated recent attention to how managers can become paradox "savvy" (Waldman & Bowen, 2016) in embracing opposites consistently.

At the organizational level, paradoxes have strategic importance, defining the way organizations tap the power of contradiction and turn it into a temporary source of **advantage** and of virtuous organizational circles. Leaders in this case need to develop a holistic understanding of their organizations, such that paradox becomes a marker of the organization's identity, as in Toyota's combination of Taylorism and innovation (Takeuchi, Osono & Shimizu, 2008) or Southwest Airlines' synthesis of quality and price (Baker, 2013). Consistently achieving paradoxical syntheses of opposites may thus constitute a force of competitive advantage. Conceptualized as the capacity to articulate logics, the notion of organizational hybridity refers to the characteristic of organizations that learn to articulate opposing logics as they conduct their activities. Hybrid organizations have been presented as those that combine financial and social interests, but each time an organization integrates logics, such as those constituted by the interests of customers and shareholders, it is confronted with the need to engage in 'both-anding'.

INTER-ORGANIZATIONAL PARADOXES

Organizations engage in inter-organizational networks, such as alliances. They simultaneously cooperate and compete to create value (Czakon et al., 2020) in a paradoxical coopetitive relation that engages organizations while involving individuals and teams. The process is difficult, with partners sometimes engaging in non-collaborative dynamics, perhaps because of the lack of trust at the level of individual leaders – as illustrated by Renault-Nissan (Campbell, Keohane & Inagaki, 2019) and the events surrounding the arrest and flight of Carlos Ghosn, former CEO, who lost the trust of the board. Coopetition is paradoxical as it involves the capacity to navigate a delicate balance between opposing inclinations (Raza-Ullah, Bengtsson & Kock, 2014; Stadtler & Van Wassenhove, 2016). The logic of coopetition brings tensions and oppositions to the macro level of analysis, making paradox a fundamentally strategic issue. Paradoxes of coopetition refer mainly to decisions around where to collaborate and where to compete. Coopetitive competency is shaped by leaders' previous histories, again showing that cross-level dynamics are fundamental in explaining the management of organizational paradox.

In every sector, to some extent organizations must strike a balance between competitive and collaborative logics to project public legitimacy overall. Regulators arbitrate these projections; even here, balance is critical. Too often "co-operation between companies and watchdogs turns into capture" (Masters, 2019: 13), as has been suggested was the case of Boeing and the US Federal Aviation Administration with the 737 Max crisis (Cassidy, 2020).

SYSTEM-LEVEL PARADOXES

Paradoxes also become manifest at the societal level of systems of actor networks. At the system level, agents interact with other agents and other actants, producing collective dynamics whose complexity is superior to the capacity for understanding and control of any agent. Systems are so complex that they necessarily produce unanticipated effects (Sterman, Repenning & Kofman, 1997) and surprises (Schad & Bansal, 2018). Surprises and unanticipated effects may be explained by macro tensions in terms of systems change. For instance, system-level tensions help to explain the differences in different accounts of organizational change. The two competing accounts are Lamarckian (i.e. the idea that evolution is the product of learning based on experiences which becomes incorporated into action repertoires in forms of values, practices, institutional norms, etc.) and Darwinian (i.e. evolution is the product of random transformation that emerges spontaneously and is then selected by environmental pressures) (Hannan & Freeman, 1984). Both accounts need to be drawn on in an adequate explanation of organizational change. There are various sources of planned change/learning; however, as organizing causes contradictions and paradoxes, the complexity of the system, despite attempts to regulate and 'manage' it, creates chaotic consequences. These generate unplanned variability that is then selected by environmental pressures. 'Decision (sense) makers' then retrospectively create hindsight narratives that 'explain' how the result of this semi-random processes was 'part of the plan'. Organizational- (and inter-organizational-) level paradoxes generate systemic paradoxes in systems of actor networks. Internet pioneer Vint Cerf describes as "ecosystems" those networks able to combine "stability, interoperability and adaptability to change" (cit. in Hill, 2019: 14). In this book's language, this means that the best networks are those able to express paradoxical qualities.

At the system level, actors need to deal with the contradictions introduced in the system by its constituting agents. The study of a healthcare unit in Portugal during the global financial crisis shows how paradoxes were augmented by the multi-organization actors in the decision group formed by the European Commission (EC), the European Central Bank (ECB) and the International Monetary Fund (IMF), known as the Troika. The Troika's decisions confronted managers and personnel at every organizational level with tensions that could not be solved (Cunha et al., 2018a). For example, the Troika emphasized economic discipline and efficiency, which made sense at a macro level, but patients expected a service, not its absence in the name of efficiency. To make the picture more nuanced, different political parties defended diverse positions, in line with their programmatic positions. The Troika's decisions, as a meta-organization (Ahrne & Brunsson, 2005), produced several tensions that rippled throughout the system, down to the level of patient-facing professionals. The decisions made by meta-organizational actors had an impact on individuals at the very end of the process of their implementation. Different poles were involved but they were relatively autonomous. Efficiency at a macro level was far from care at a patient level. Actors at different levels mutually participated in the construction of paradoxes that became manifest at different levels in very different ways.

CLOSING THE LOOP: MICROPROCESSES AND MICRO-MACRO LINKAGES

We now discuss two processes that challenge levels. We do so to attenuate the very concept of levels of analysis. Paradoxes are often presented in highly salient terms as tensions and expressions of the extraordinary. The idea of microprocesses suggests something different: that tensions and paradoxes also exist as the repetition of trivial operations. These are instances of performative forms of repetition that are possibly too mundane to be categorized as paradoxes (Aroles & McLean, 2016). Yet paradoxical they may be, in all their infra-ordinary mundanity (Cunha & Clegg, 2019). Paradox afflicts not only senior executives but also regular employees as they make things happen. Minor expressions of paradox may crop up throughout the organization without being paid attention. One of the most famous examples in organization theory was chronicled by Crozier (1964) in a French tobacco monopoly firm. Production workers were paid on a piece rate dependent on the smooth operation of the production line. The line was not always reliable and was made less so by deliberate sabotage by maintenance workers as a source of local resistance and promotion of their limited power. They were not paid on a piece rate. The piece rate introduced a paradox: the interests of the piece workers was in having the line moving; on occasion the interests of the maintenance workers engaged in bargaining to enhance their power was to have the line broken. Such little paradoxes may be as important as forms of paradox staged with drama.

System-level paradoxes may have micro-level effects – and vice versa – and the tension between levels is aptly captured in the idea, full of Freudian resonance, of a lifelong tension between instincts and institutions (Petriglieri & Petriglieri, 2020). People's individual histories, with their inner motives and personal rivalries, influence the unfolding of institutions, including the largest (Cunha et al., 2018b; Petriglieri, 2020). In the case of the Troika intervention discussed above, macro-level interventions cascaded down, having very real consequences at the level of individuals, teams and organizations. For example, because of tighter budgetary controls, individuals felt more intense bureaucratic control, deepening the vicious circle of bureaucracy (Cunha & Tsoukas, 2015). In parallel, debates about the need for state reform coexisted with strengthening the existing model, closing a paradoxical loop uniting the macro and the micro. The resulting impasse contributes to explain the European failure to address increasing wealth inequalities, a feat that – despite its complexity – had been successfully achieved in the past (Piketty, 2020).

Growing inequality has increased social discontent that has been exploited by reactionary and xenophobic movements, further fuelling the vicious cycle.

Another example comes from Boeing: in the race against Airbus, Boeing rushed to run the 737 production line, in spite of concerns about safety, resulting in extremely concrete micro consequences. The content of an email sent by Ed Pierson, senior manager on the production line, to the head of the 737 programme months before the first fatal crash indicates the issues:

> Employees are fatigued from having to work at a very high pace for an extended period of time. This obviously causes stress on our employees and their families. Fatigued employees make mistakes. My second concern is scheduled pressure (combined with fatigue) is creating a culture where employees are either deliberately or unconsciously circumventing established processes. Right now all my internal warning bells are going off. And for the first time in my life, I'm sorry to say that I'm hesitant about putting my family on a Boeing airplane. (Stacey, 2019: 12)

Cultures result, in part, from leadership, although perhaps not quite so much as the leadership literature suggests. In this literature, the styles of leaders become cultural drivers and become, over time, hypostasized as the cultural signature of an organization (Petriglieri & Petriglieri, 2020). Macro-organizational behaviour (of leaders) creates a conception of cultures (of the organization) that cascade down (to the employees) in a given context. In the process, tensions are created, amplified, modified.

TENSIONS ACROSS LEVELS

As we have discussed, paradoxes occur at different levels, akin to Russian dolls, as expressed in the importance of the 'tone at the top', established by senior executives that strive to transmit it throughout the organization. Stein (2003) notes, for instance, that narcissistic leaders potentially create narcissistic organizational cultures, with each member competitively attentive to flattery of and from the leader. The integration among levels indicates that decisions made at one level produce tensions that will have an impact on different levels. As actors conduct their activities paradoxes interact with other paradoxes. Decisions made at the top travel through the organization, informed by their institutional context, in the process of which they meet responses produced by those at lower levels. Organizational action is always marked by an element of unpredictability in consequence; top-level ideas and institutional contexts rarely connect with street-level concerns, issues and grievances (Lipsky, 2010).

Sheep, Fairhurst and Khazanchi's (2017) work on knots in paradox indicates that paradoxes are interlinked, forming entanglements of interdependence. Paradoxes being entangled with other paradoxes means that paradoxes form interlinked tensions with other paradoxes. The way one paradox is tackled at a given level will have potential effects system wide. As Sheep and his colleagues indicated, knotted tensions may express amplifying or attenuating effects. In some cases, the failure to handle paradoxes productively will render their effects even more salient where deviation amplifying forces operate. In other cases, actions taken at one level may lead to amplification-reduction, directing the system towards more equilibrium.

The consideration of cross-level effects reveals that scholars need to consider not only isolated pairs of forces but also constellations of forces knotted, interwoven and entangled. Therefore, tensions form a mosaic in which multiple forces interact to produce emergent rather than mechanistically predictable outcomes. Paradoxes are always potentially surprising because the effects of a tension always extend beyond any pair of forces. Cross-level analysis based on tensional knots invites one to see synergies with caution. What appears as synergistic at one level may be disequilibriating at other levels. We next discuss amplification and attenuation effects.

Amplification Across Levels

Because tensions are not sealed within the confines of a level, it is necessary to consider how they may escalate across levels. If power-over defines "the ability to shape and define the experiences of others" (Petriglieri & Petriglieri, 2020: 14), leaders shape the tensions of others by defining those tensions that matter. Vicious circles arise when amplification of effects with decisions at one level cascade to other levels, involuntarily amplifying the effects of the paradox. The organization enters a dynamic of failure in which the measures taken to solve the problem end up aggravating it. Minor disturbances (desired or undesired) are amplified and may be registered as major consequences (Weick, 1979: 157). As Weick explained, "once a variable begins to move in a particular direction, either up or down, the variable will continue to move in that same direction until the system is destroyed or until some dramatic change occurs" (Weick, 1979: 72). The *vicious circle* is a deviation-amplifying loop that turns a bad situation to worse. An illustrative example is provided by George Orwell:

> A man may take to drink because he feels himself to be a failure, and then fail all the more completely because he drinks. It is rather the same thing that is happening to the English language. It becomes ugly and inaccurate because our thoughts are foolish, but the slovenliness of our language makes it easier for us to have foolish thoughts. (Orwell, 1968, in Tsoukas & Cunha, 2017)

The circularity of the process should be remarked: "an effect can become a cause, reinforcing the original cause and producing the same effect in an intensified form, and so on indefinitely" (Orwell, 1946: 3). This process resembles some organizational dynamics: the more an organization emphasizes control, the more distrust it begets, which drives defensiveness and turf wars, which result in the need for more controls, in a circle that feeds itself (Clegg & Dunkerley, 2013; Smith & Lewis, 2011; Tsoukas & Cunha, 2017).

A *virtuous circle* is the reverse of a vicious circle, being a deviation-amplifying loop that makes a good situation better. An interest-earning bank account is a deviation-amplifying loop: the amount of money in the account affects how much money comes into the account as interest; the more money you have, the more interest you earn; the more you practise ballet, the more you improve your ability to dance, which makes you enjoy it more and want to practice it even more. The more people experience positive emotions, the more they broaden their thought-action repertoires, which leads them to build enduring personal resources, which enable people to experience more positive emotions, and so on (Fredrickson, 2001).

Attenuation Across Levels

As Sheep, Fairhurst and Khazanchi (2017) have explained, there can also be attenuating effects across levels. In this case, the organization contains mechanisms that allow the system to correct itself. By "thinking outside the box" (Sheep, Fairhurst & Khazanchi, 2017) organizations engage in systems rich in corrective mechanisms. In organizations, such as the natural food co-op studied by Ashforth and Reingen (2014), inter-group conflict was instrumental to organizational-level harmony, a pattern also observed by Petriglieri, Petriglieri and Wood (2018). In macro-level systems, such as democracies, corrections may come from the separation of powers through checks and balances. In this case the system allows multiple logics to coexist and to inform one another without allowing any single logic to prevail. Another possibility for attenuating effects consists in developing loosely coupled systems, those in which systems have relative degrees of independence. This imbues the system with mechanisms that permit the system to counteract excesses.

More needs to be known about how different forms of governance (Sundaramurthy & Lewis, 2003) can be used to improve organizational competencies to manage paradox. It has been assumed by writers that we have discussed that some organizations handle paradox competently because of paradoxical mindsets and paradox savvy leaders. However, by seeing paradox as a cross-level phenomenon, a new possibility is revealed: the paradoxical mindset as a collective phenomenon, a relational form of collective heed to which different individuals bring different competencies rather than a process that happens in an individual's brain.

Paradoxes are sometimes produced as an organization formally adopts a practice that does not travel to the levels where it is supposed to be operationalized. For example, in the case of the Danish local branch of a global retail chain studied by Mikkelsen and Wahlin (2020), the authors found that policies intended to facilitate the recruitment of a diverse workforce were decoupled from actual practices. Organizational members supposedly benefitting from the policy were, in practice, submitted to dominant sensemaking processes that impeded them from voicing critical opinions about the policy that supposedly protected them. Certain forms of sensemaking, the authors pointed out, was forbidden, such that the dominant social order was ongoingly reproduced rather than made more diverse. An absurd situation was created in which a policy designed to protect some minorities worked in practice to dominate the workforce in order to obtain cheap loyalty. In this case the levels are decoupled; as predicted by Berti and Simpson (2019), being subject to a paradox can create an absurd and unmanageable situation. A company known for its exemplary diversity management techniques was in fact preventing its foreign-born employees from voicing their version of reality, one less romantic than the official version portrayed by the organization. The case has similarities with Padavic, Ely and Reid (2020), showing how cross-level effects may qualitatively change the nature of paradoxes.

The way the beliefs of managers and workers coexist defines the success or failure or organizational change initiatives (Repenning & Sterman, 2002). The organizational geographies of success and failure, however, are not uniform across organizations. The same initiative may produce diverse effects in different parts of an organizational system. The case of the adoption of the 'speak up' value (Cunha et al., 2019b) shows the case of differential effects across levels. A change decided at the top, assuring people that it was safe and wanted for them to speak up, was enacted differently at different levels. As the value cascaded down it was translated, with local circumstances, leadership relationships and relational patterns influencing the meaning of 'speak up'. At the end, the same value created different manifestations of tension, depending on how actors enacted the value. As the systems literature points out, seeing one issue at one level does not necessarily help to understand it in full as the same issue may be perceived differently at different levels. If inter-organizational collaborations are in future to tackle grand challenges, as has been suggested by responses to the United Nations (Daar et al., 2018), this will increase the need to understand cross-level effects that are often ambiguous, if not counter-intuitive. For instance, to understand and manage paradox beyond single-level dichotomies, organizations need to accept that tensions cross levels of analysis. An example of this necessity is provided by an organizational-level strategy devised to introduce work-family balance. The policy ended up derailing women's careers while projecting the image of the firm as generous and fair (Padavic, Ely & Reid, 2020).

STRATEGIES FOR MANAGING PARADOXICAL NESTED TENSIONS

In this section we discuss some possible strategies to manage paradoxes as nested, multilevel phenomena. Without the pretension of exhaustion, we focus on possible ways to navigate paradoxes: (1) within levels, (2) between levels, (3) between the organization and its environment, and (4) at the systemic level. The focus on boundaries is justified with the fact that, as open systems, organizations need to preserve an optimal level of permeability: porous enough to allow exchanges with the environment; closed enough to protect the system's integrity (Alderfer, 2011). Boundaries between management and workers, between departments and between the organization and its environment channel the socio-material bases of tensions, their intensity and responses to them. The strategies for managing paradoxes across levels aim to cultivate what Dodd and Favaro (2006) called "diagonal assets", mechanisms that connect and integrate parts and the whole.

In general, the nestedness of paradox reveals how paradoxes cannot, by definition, be 'managed', but only 'surfed'. The metaphor of surfing, with its emphasis on skill and flow, conveys the idea of exploiting complex and uncontrollable forces. Surfing a paradox is difficult because paradoxes are amalgams of processes that mix and mingle, partly lurking beneath the surface (Hatch, Schultz & Skov, 2015). What managers can do is to cherry-pick specific nested paradoxes, developing an understanding of organizations and their environments as fields of contradictions and paradoxical tensions. Managers frame those paradoxes most relevant to their organizations by constituting, selecting and manifesting them (Smets et al., 2019). Managers are makers rather than takers of paradoxes.

Within-level strategies: embrace paradoxical thinking. Organizations may stimulate their members to accept tension as inherent, learning to live with ambivalence as a necessary condition (Ashforth et al., 2014). Therefore, instead of seeing tension as dysfunctional, they can explore how tensions exist at the levels of individuals (e.g. work-family conflict), teams (e.g. individuality and belonging), organizations (e.g. exploration and exploitation) and systems (e.g. business prosperity vs. social and environmental sustainability). Instead of occluding or repressing tensions, they can be assumed. Practices such as co-leadership (Gibeau et al., 2019) and composing teams with people with diverse predispositions (Treffers, Klarner & Huy, 2020), as well as adopting balanced scorecard metrics (Kaplan & Norton, 1996a, 1996b), can be used to integrate competing logics. Even if they do not integrate them, at least the effort to do so makes the contradictions between logics manifest, thus countering the dangers of assuming unidimensional goals and logics. The adoption of paradoxical mindsets, co-leadership, ambidexterity and the acceptance of hybrid identities are forms of paradox management within levels. While they can be effective, they are difficult to sustain.

Between level strategies: practising pluralism. Between levels, organizations can manage nested paradoxes by breaking silos as silos create divisions. Silos are normally viewed as occurring between areas, but they also separate levels – as is well captured in the popular TV show *Undercover Boss* (in spite of/because of the show's "deeply fictional nature", discussed by Kirn, 2010) and expressed by Czarniawaska's epigraph to this chapter: because paradoxes come with different levels of intensity at different levels, levels need to communicate about their experiences of/with paradox.

By connecting teams with other teams, stimulating cross-functional thinking and cross-hierarchical dialogues, and finding shared understandings (Andriopoulos & Lewis, 2010), organizations nurture habituation with ambiguity and plurality, promoting acceptance of diverse views and avoiding the polarization that results from 'us vs. them' types of views. These mechanisms, sometimes called "linkages" (Goodman, 2000), are a powerful way of mixing views and ways of seeing. Organizations can counter by stimulating teams to see themselves as X-teams (Ancona, Bresman & Kaeufer, 2002). These X-teams are characterized by external activity, extensive ties, expandable structures, flexible membership and internal mechanisms for execution. Designing spaces can also stimulate a better appreciation of plurality and diversity (Gaim, Wåhlin & Jacobsson, 2019; Tett, 2015). If people with different roles, belonging to different areas, serendipitously bump into one another, conversations may be promoted and groups joined that tend to be separate.

Organization-environment strategies: cultivating openness to the world. Tensions often result from a growing focus on internal reliability and exploitation, which increasingly detaches the organization from its customers and competitors. Generative and regenerative tensions can be cultivated through interaction with the environment (listening, observation), including with partners (e.g. collectives; Soderstrom & Heinze, 2019), customers and benchmarking competitors. In fast-changing sectors, organizations can explore the periphery to challenge their dominant logics (Bettis & Prahalad, 1995). Instead of protecting themselves from customers (with rules, regulations and legalities), organizations may 'deep dive' into problems, assume the discomfort and engage with perturbations. Paradoxically, accepting discomfort may be critical to surviving.

System level strategies: seeing the bubble. Paradox management involves the need to see the forest and the trees (Wohlleben, 2016), the micro and the

Table 5.2   *Strategies for managing paradoxical nested tensions*

Level	Explanation	Symptoms	Strategies
Within-level strategies: cultivating paradoxical thinking	Some paradoxes are represented as taking place mainly at one single level (e.g. paradoxes of teams).	The unit shows unwanted destructive conflict. Tensions are perceived as unpleasant and degenerative. Internal competition is present. One goal excludes the others.	Accept that tensions are inevitable but that not all tensions are handled productively. Accept and manage tensions. Embrace a paradoxical vocabulary. Introduce irritations (e.g. devil's advocates) if the system is too stable. Introduce mediators if the system is too divided.
Between-level strategies: practising pluralism	Events at one level are unknown to the other levels. The organization drifts in the direction of 'thought worlds'	Cultures of blame. Turf wars and politicking. Isolation. Us vs. them.	Cultivate X-teams. Promote productive cross-level dialogues. Introduce cross-level. Define a uniting 'North Star'.
Organization-environment strategies: cultivating openness to the world	The organization grows increasingly isolated from the environment. Needs to expose itself to the environment.	Lack of innovation. Customer dissatisfaction. The organization protects itself from its customers.	Benchmark competitors. Deep dive problems to understand customer complaints.
System-level strategies: seeing the bubble	The system connects parts and wholes in complex ways.	Micro and macro concerns do not communicate. Stakeholder dissatisfaction.	Engage partners in reflecting on systemic issues. Train people to understand the bubble, i.e. to search for hidden connections.

macro, as well as the way they interact (Schad & Bansal, 2018). Because paradoxes confront people at different levels with different experiences, making sense of the different expressions of tension as well as the interactions among them may be critical for making sense of the nested nature of paradox as well as avoiding simple interpretations of the tensions at the material level. Zooming in and out may allow people to focus on concrete problems with the capacity to deal with minute details without missing the bigger picture (Nicolini, 2009). Organizations may also cultivate the critical ability of high reliability organizations of seeing the "bubble" (Roberts & Rousseau, 1989), managing an holistic understanding of a system which equips its members with the capacity to understand how events at multiple levels interact.

The strategies discussed in Table 5.2 have one fundamental goal: to foster a sense of connectedness between both the different parts of an organization and with its environment, countering the tendency to search for clarity and uniformity. While clarity and predictability are comfortable, they introduce rigidity via categories. The cultivation of the capacity to recognize paradox reminds people that the world is ambiguous and that navigating organizational ambiguity is challenging. The alternative often consists in the search for a Great Man (it is usually a male) who offers a sense of protection to a dependent organization (Petriglieri & Petriglieri, 2020), one seemingly capable of bulldozing ambiguity, offering a sense of wholeness and the capacity to contain inner contradictions. As tensions shift, organizations may use these and other diagonal assets to cultivate a collective paradoxical mindset, one that sees the organization as a whole – rather than individuals – as the unit where paradoxes can be uncodified and embraced.

CONCLUSION

Nestedness can portray paradox as an impossible situation: wherever you turn there is a paradox. As such, because paradox is everywhere, it becomes an impossible problem, an infinite paradox. Pragmatically, as discussed in Chapter 2, paradoxes understood as endless persistence become paralysing, circles that cannot be overcome (Masuch, 1985). Seeing paradox as strong process, the succession of paradoxes is not a problem if only because paradoxes enable flow and constitute organizational riddles in search of action. Enacted as expressions of systemic complexity, paradoxes are a source of dynamism and transformation as they function as triggers of change. Systems are too complex to be apprehended via linear relations. Paradox nestedness helps to explain complexity: processes articulate with other processes in a fluid dynamic that never stabilizes. Viewed as static tensions or impossible choices, paradoxes are paralysing; viewed as dynamic processes that never cease to move, paradoxes become energizing, even when they are irritating and difficult to understand.

6. Paradoxes of power, control and empowerment

Organizations have been described as "deep pools of conflicting motives and interests" (Alvarez et al., 2020: 713). These pools are stirred, agitated and occasionally overwhelmed by power dynamics. Power is frequently conceived as a negative corrupting force, or as a distanced position in a hierarchical structure wielding significant control over organizational resources. To contemporary scholars, however, power is a construct of multiple dimensions that is a fundamental enabling and restricting factor in any system or structure (Clegg, 1989). Power consists, essentially, of social relations among people, moulding the facilitation or inhibition of choice, capabilities and change as people struggle for meaning (Clegg, Courpasson & Phillips, 2006). Paradoxes of power explored in this chapter relate to the counter-intuitive effects of power's deployment. The fundamental paradox of concern has been described by Smith and Lewis (2011: 383) as the *paradox of organizing* involving tensions between control and autonomy where "[s]tructuring and leading foster collaboration and competition, empowerment and direction, and control and flexibility". Organizing paradoxes arise when inconsistencies are embedded by organizational systems within processes designed for achieving specific organizational outcomes.

Two related nested paradoxes are the paradox of control and the paradox of autonomy. The *paradox of control* arises when managers assert *power-over* subordinates to ensure conformity, yet the more overtly that power is imposed, the more likely it is to elicit resistance and the need for further use of coercive power. Such coercive power may restrict an individual's body but not their mind or will. The *paradox of autonomy* concerns another dimension of power, autonomous empowerment (*power-to*), a capacity that enables working collective endeavours (Arendt, 1972). This empowerment comes with a catch; apparent autonomy and freedom is provided to the body of employees, but the organization strives to colonize their mind and sentiments to constitute their subjectivity in approved ways. Subjectification through induction, training, culture programmes, adherence to strategies is a common counterpart to empowerment (Alvesson & Willmott, 2002; Willmott, 1993). This leads critical voices to argue that "empowerment means that you were somehow disempowered", and then "they usually hand you a stack of work to do" (Boje & Dennehy, 1993: 270).

Traditional management orthodoxy operating as bureaucracy drew upon the power of control over a panoply of offices and rules relating and binding them. More recently, power has been exerted in increasingly more subtle ways in organizations, through the affordances of empowerment granting the power-to what previously had not been ceded. In this chapter we explore the tensions and paradoxes that emerge from each of these approaches to power. We conclude that each of these positions is paradox denying (or at least paradox ignoring). Instead, we propose a third approach of accepting and meeting the organizing paradox through genuine democratic power sharing arrangements, where power is shared with others. *Power-with* others extends the insights of the other two approaches while also accepting, meeting and transcending the needs of the underlying tensions (Table 6.1).

PARADOXES OF CONTROL: POWER-OVER

Max Weber, a German scholar of the early 1900s, is the classic scholar who gave systematic attention to power relations within what in his day were characteristic modern organizations: bureaucracies (Lounsbury & Carberry, 2005). Weber (1978) had a number of concepts that he used to discuss power relations, including domination, legitimacy, authority and power, which he defined as "the probability that one actor within a social relationship will be in a position to carry out his or her own will despite resistance, regardless of the basis on which this probability rests" (Weber, 1978: 53). Domination, when acceded to by those subject to it, assumes legitimacy, enacted through an individual's voluntary consent to what is thus titled authority. Weber described three forms of authority premised on the power of charisma, tradition and rational-legality. Charismatic power is reliant upon exceptional individual qualities of heroism, character or humanity which attract followers. Traditional power draws upon belief in the authority of culture, conventions and customs that claim legitimacy from the sanctity ascribed to historical tradition, such as the feudal transmission of the right to rule over an estate or country, premised on intergenerational primogeniture by an authority that tradition deems sov-

Table 6.1   Three modes of organizational power relations with related paradox manifestations or responses

Power relation	Description	Paradox (control vs. autonomy)
Power-over	Coercive *power-over* is enacted by force whereas authoritative *power-over* relies on voluntary submission.	"an over reliance on the direct control of employee behaviour only emphasises the need for employee empowerment" (Lewis, Brown & Sutton, 2019: 488).
Power-to	Facilitative empowerment supports an individual's *power-to* act and enact their will without interference.	"there is a fundamental paradox in the idea of people empowering people because the very institutional structure that puts one group in a position to empower others also works to undermine the act of empowerment" (Gruber & Trickett, 1987: 370).
Power-with	Coactive *power-with* facilitates personal and organizational development and growth through collaborative and democratic governance practices.	"Circular behaviour is the basis of integration. If your business is so organized that you can influence a co-manager while he is influencing you, so organized that a workman has an opportunity of influencing you as you have of influencing him, if there is an interactive influence going on all the time between you, power-with may be built up" (Follett, 1995: 107).

ereign. Rational-legal power draws upon the legitimacy conveyed by rational rules, policies and systems, including the legitimacy afforded to those in positions of authority, giving them control over resources, all organized for achieving defined objectives.

Of these three forms of power Weber (1978) held rational-legal power to be that which afforded the greatest stability and efficiency. Being founded on systems of rational rules that transcend individual authority it could most easily handle succession of authority; it depended neither on the vagaries of fertility or genetic inheritance nor on the promotion of extraordinary qualities whose extinction might lead to problems with the routinization of charisma. Charismatic rule might be routinized on the basis of tradition, as has happened with the heirs of Kim Il-sung in North Korea, now in the third generation of the dynasty. However, it was the rational-legal mode of power that Weber saw as underpinning the bureaucratic mode of organizing. Bureaucracy arose in Germany through the domination of Prussia in the state formation of 48 principalities into the German nation through the bureaucratic apparatus of the military and the state (Clegg, Courpasson & Phillips, 2006; Clegg, 1990). With Germany's late participation in the Industrial Revolution and the advance of capitalism towards the end of the 19th century, bureaucracy was adopted as an industrial model. Bureaucracy had no single source of origin. The organization of the East India Company could lay claim to devising it; something similar to German bureaucracy was being promulgated elsewhere as well, for instance in the United States, under the influence of West Point, the famous military and engineering academy. Bureaucratic organizing requires rules to be written as a way of ensuring that their application is universal, accountable and rational. In a well-organized bureaucracy, all component parts operate in unison as a force aimed at achieving defined objectives. The individual's role is to submit to playing their part as an essential component in the greater system, as a cog in a large organizational machine. By designating bureaucratic organization as a type of power, Weber redefined how power was understood, from being viewed as a position or title with which an individual person or group of people could realize their will in social relations, towards viewing power as systemically embedded within dense structures informing what people were authorized to do or not do organizationally. Weber recognized that, despite its benefits, the limitations of bureaucratic power included the stifling of individual autonomy, freedom and creativity. Later writers added to its offences, rule tropism, where rules are followed for their own sake while forgetting their originally intended purpose (Merton, 1936). These tensions arise from bureaucracy as a system of power-over those subject to it. The paradox of bureaucracy and of power-over more generally is that the more effective any bureaucracy is as a system of control and productivity, the more it is likely to undermine its future prospects due to stifling individual autonomy, creativity, motivation and well-being.

In modern organizations power-over employees, originally embedded in the files and the bureau of an organization, where they were written down, initially in longhand, later mechanically by typewriters, is today embedded digitally and virtually. The bureau is increasingly enacted through technologies that seek to optimize workforce performance by monitoring, directing, evaluating and rewarding employee behaviours (Dewettinck & Buyens, 2006), increasingly digitally, through 'digitocracy' (Ballesteros, 2020). Control mechanisms in the past sought to ensure employees observed formal policies and procedures (Tyler & Blader, 2005) put in place by an organizational hierarchy that operated as a complex dynamic command and control system (Harris & White, 1987). Four levers of control pulled by managers, described by Simons (1995) across varied situations, include systems of belief, boundaries, diagnosis and interaction. Lewis, Brown and Sutton (2019: 488) identify the paradox of control being that "an over reliance on the direct control of employee behaviour only emphasises the need for employee empowerment". Recognizing the limits of managerial control, Streatfield (2001: 7) observes a "paradoxical position in which managers find themselves, namely, that of being simultaneously 'in control' and 'not in control'". A mechanism here is that "agents increasingly perceive controls as indications of distrust, further motivating them to reduce their effort" (Sundaramurthy & Lewis, 2003: 405), an observation supported by evidence. Taylor (2010) found that external control forced on individuals diminishes goal-oriented behaviour, followed by trust levels and subsequently performance. Falk and Kosfeld (2006) observed that most individuals demonstrate control adverse behaviour, suggesting that organizations ought to carefully consider control's hidden costs. Pay-offs from tighter control tend to be achieved more quickly, more easily and with greater certainty. Consequently, organizations have tended to favour control over autonomy. Across the globe, organizations have accordingly adopted tools for controlling employee performance such as Kaplan and Norton's (1996a, 1996b) balanced scorecard management tool (see also Kaplan & McMillan, 2020). Control tends to be used as a default management approach (Harris & White, 1987), despite its being experienced by employees as rigid, stifling, coercive and suffocating (Adler & Borys, 1996; Ritzer, 1993). These costs of hard power-over drive organizations to seek paradoxically to achieve the same performance objectives by leaning towards remedies of autonomy and empowerment, otherwise described by sociologists as power-to.

PARADOXES OF EMPOWERMENT: POWER-TO

Talcott Parsons, a Harvard University researcher, brought Weber to the attention of English-speaking audiences. In Parsons' (1963, 1964) view power is the positive force of empowerment facilitating an individual's power to act. His perspective on power is hierarchical in that it is bestowed by legitimate managerial authority with the power to allocate resources for attaining collective objectives. Critics of Parsons argue that although his power might appear as a positive force for those aligned with collective managerial goals, it is oppressive and illegitimate for those with values and objectives that differ from the prevailing majority (Clegg, Courpasson & Phillips, 2006; Clegg, 1990). Further, the consensual basis of legitimate authority is seldom built upon a basis of collective objectives. This gives rise to a paradox that undermines Parsons' notion of empowerment, as described by Gruber and Trickett (1987: 370): "there is a fundamental paradox in the idea of people empowering people because the very institutional structure that puts one group in a position to empower others also works to undermine the act of empowerment". Eylon (1998: 21) adds, "the very fact that one group is in the position to judge if others are dis-empowered and then to decide what to 'give' so that they will become 'empowered' indicates that true empowerment is not occurring". Howcroft and Wilson (2003: 10) similarly observe: "if one depends on someone else to be the giver of that power, then one does not have power". In this section we will look into paradoxes of empowerment from various perspectives, including Michael Foucault's analysis of power/knowledge as a technology of domination, organizational culture management initiatives and post-bureaucratic organizational design.

Michel Foucault, a French sociologist, viewed power-to as a soft form of domination (Clegg, 1994). Soft power achieves the same objectives as hard power but not by coercive force: it causes another to act in a manner they would not ordinarily do, by shaping their sense of self, their values, attitudes and beliefs. Foucault also described this as a form of 'power/knowledge' (Foucault, 1980) that he used to explicate how power shapes our sense of normalcy and truth, taming individuals and rendering the member of a society docile subjects. Power/knowledge is an efficient type of domination as it normalizes power to the extent that it is made imperceptible, inducing a false experience of freedom and engendering trust, loyalty and commitment from those who are dominated (Foucault, 1984). Both the dominators and the dominated are accomplices in these power relations which incorporate members of society through fixed relations of traditional families, schools and hierarchical organizational structures that strive to achieve subjectification of those humans that pass through them. Older traditions of sociology might have referred to this as 'socialization'. Dominators are not 'puppeteers': they are not immune to those power effects that shape and constrain their identities and choice; think of the British Royal Family. Yet, power/knowledge dynamics disproportionately favour those who have to gain from the preservation of the status quo.

Foucault's (1977) initial views of the disciplinary power/knowledge word drew on Scottish moral philosopher Jeremy Bentham's discussion of panoptical design, which he initially experienced in a Moscow manufactory directed by his brother Samuel. Cells are arranged in a circular shape around a central watchtower so that inmates would feel under the constant gaze of their guardians (Bentham, 2017a). The effect of an ability to exercise surveillance unseen would be to ensure the automatic functioning of power. Bentham (2017b: 225) envisaged his design:

> The Building *circular* – The Cells occupying the Circumference – The Keepers etc – the Centre – an *intermediate annular Well* all the way up … By *blinds*, and other contrivances, the *Keeper concealed* from the observation of the Prisoners, unless where he thinks fit to shew himself: hence the sentiment of a sort of invisible omnipresence.

The desired effect would be for prisoners to internalize the dominant social gaze, objectifying themselves from the standpoint of society's expectations and value judgements, ensuring their enactment of self-surveillance and self-regulation.

Foucault (1977) viewed the panopticon as a metaphor for modern disciplinary society, which has as its aims human docility and utility for the system.

To him the panoptical design, which informed the design of 54 prisons in Victorian Britain and many others around the world (Andrzejewski, 2008; Switek, 2016), as well as libraries, asylums and workhouses, was not just a building but a technology of power. Foucault (1977) similarly viewed modern society's structures as colonizing citizen's minds and souls with power/ knowledge through ongoing social observation by family, peers, educational institutions, workplaces and all other social arenas where people are subject to socialization processes and internalize social expectations, all while ostensibly providing freedom. The panoptic was especially salient in dictatorial regimes such as Khmer Rouge Kampuchea (Clegg, Cunha & Rego, 2012) but technological advances such as the internet, social media and artificial intelligence algorithms, which leave trails of meta data, would suggest that since Foucault formulated his ideas in the 1970s and 1980s, society's constantly observing eye has broadened its reach and deepened its colonizing effects, reaching from the university (Waycott et al., 2017) to the workplace (Upchurch & Grassman, 2016) to the home (van Zoonen, Verhoeven & Vliegenthart, 2016).

Culture management is an arena where scholars of management and organizations draw parallels between Foucault's observations concerning the domination of society through power/knowledge with organizational efforts (Carter, McKinlay & Rowlinson, 2002). Since the 1970s and 1980s organizations have sought to engender employee trust, commitment, loyalty and engagement through soft power management initiatives, such as culture management (Wray-Bliss, 2003). By promoting the individual potential and values of 'excellence', 'involvement' and 'passion', culture management initiatives seek to define, promote and reinforce managerially sanctioned attitudes defining organizational membership, decision-making and behaviours, with the objective of reinforcing the attaining of defined organizational goals (Peters & Waterman, 1982). Organizational culture is an idea management has borrowed from anthropology, with a critical difference (Clegg et al., 2019). Anthropologists study existing cultures, while managers assume that they can engineer distinct organizational cultures and that employees embodying organizational cultural values such as initiative, engagement, service and responsibility will require little control or monitoring of their task performance as they are already compliant acculturated subjects.

Post-bureaucracy, a culture management-related initiative, rejects bureaucratic hierarchy, rigid process and policy adherence, top-down decision-making, one-way communication and the assumption employees are motivated extrinsically by their pay checks (Josserand, Teo & Clegg, 2006). Instead, post-bureaucracy favours heterarchy (Stark, 1999), team-based networked information sharing for decentralized decision-making and the flexible interpretation of rules in a manner that empowers initiative within the context of a subjectification that is oriented towards achieving organizational objectives through soft power (Courpasson, 2000). The assumption of post-bureaucracy is that employees are additionally motivated in their jobs by the intrinsic rewards of opportunities for personal growth, development, a sense of contribution and fulfilment. Post-bureaucratic organizing is preferred for facilitating enhanced agility, innovation and creativity within organizations, which is critical in a rapidly changing environment. Empowering employees with responsibilities as decision makers, initiative takers and team players in post-bureaucratic management has been described as a type of soft domination, with purported privileges, freedoms and authority deepening employee commitments, obligations and conformity (McKenna, Garcia-Lorenzo & Bridgman, 2010). Peer pressure and the desire for acceptance by peers in post-bureaucratic team-based network structures is further perceived as a mode of panoptical surveillance far more effective than direct managerial oversight (Crowley, Payne & Kennedy, 2014). In autonomous teams, employees enact self-monitoring and regulation to conform with organizational values, attitudes and beliefs and fit in with the group. Research has found that employees granted higher levels of autonomy experience greater well-being and job satisfaction and are more likely to demonstrate sustainably high performance (Pink, 2009; Hamel, 2007). Empirical studies into the association between employee autonomy and performance have been inconclusive (Verhoest et al., 2004). Baard, Deci and Ryan's (2004), study with 320 small businesses, where half relied on traditional control management and the other half granted workers autonomy, found that enterprises offering autonomy had four times the growth rate of control-oriented businesses. Langfred (2007) holds, however, that although employees might prefer the autonomy of self-managed work, it may nonetheless have a negative impact on the achievement of organizational objectives. Managers should not assume that increased employee responsibility, empowerment and autonomy necessarily corresponds with greater accountability, as it may also lead to increased feelings of being overwhelmed. Contradictions of power-to's empowering affordances are observed by Lewis, Brown and Sutton (2019: 488) as contributing to a paradox where "empowering employees serves to accentuate the need for direct effort towards organizational objectives and to coordinate autonomous workers or teams". Howcroft and Wilson (2003) identify five categories of contradiction and tension that ensue from power-to initiatives enacted to evoke compliance and provide cover for a status quo performance and productivity agenda: (1) rhetoric of empowerment, (2) rhetoric of involvement, (3) rhetoric of voice, (4) illusion of compatibility, and (5) outcome of participation.

Rhetoric of empowerment concerns the use of empowerment as a tool to disguise the intent of empowerment initiatives that are in reality undertaken for control purposes. The disconnection between rhetoric and practice sees relationships of power and powerlessness continue with the introduction of digital technologies of control and surveillance in the name of increasing employee autonomy. Digitocracy, suggests Ballesteros (2020: 12), is "a new way to rule an unprecedented number of people smartly and efficiently. This rule takes advantage of everybody's free use of digital devices". In the digitocracy, subjects become their own self-managers but also subject to online exercises that they must do when 'invited' to do so by a machine-enabled invitation, the peculiar efficiency of the power of this digital technology resides in its exploitation of what are positioned as individual choices.

Digitocratic organizations have been able to hybridize economic interests with the blurring of distinctions between artefacts and humans. Devices that require black-boxed algorithms give rise to new forms of discrimination that depend on algorithms. Prompted by algorithms, organizations encourage sharing and posting as preferred ways of acting. Human resource management is increasingly machine enabled and consists of subjects passing online tests of their subjectification, often using simplistic game-like scenarios that the subjects have to interpret correctly in terms of pre-defined categories. Digital devices are the new media of communication and subjectification; subjects that perform in ways that run counter to their presumed subjectification can be seen as deficient and deviant, in need of further subject formation. Bureaucratic rules take on a strongly ethical quality that is not imposed but self-managed; that is, self-managed in accord with organizational precepts that have already been algorithmically determined.

A *rhetoric of involvement* accompanies the digitocratic organization. The rhetoric concerns tensions that arise when employees play a relatively passive role in decision-making despite the strong organizational emphasis on employee involvement. Tensions are particularly found in the levels and types of participation. Howcroft and Wilson (2003: 14) observe: "A paradox that arises from the wielding of the term 'empowerment' is that managers can employ a variety of tactics to enrol employees in the process of participation, with no intention of genuine influence sharing." As an example, despite the rhetoric of involvement, employees are generally not invited to participate in prescribing and controlling at which levels and areas employee may be involved, they are not consulted about the digitocratic gateways through which they must pass as obligatory passage points that assure their continuing conformance with being an organizational subject.

Exclusion of dissent concerns the non-inclusion of employee disagreement or protest as legitimate types of employee involvement; there is, for instance, no opportunity to be a Bartleby (Ten Bos & Rhodes, 2003) and say that one would prefer not to have to take these tests or play these games. That would be taken as illegitimate resistance and indications of a lack of employee understanding of their subject position. Organizational initiatives of employee involvement are often inauthentic as they only include compliant members;

they are designed to produce compliant members through their "voluntary" subjectification.

An *illusion of compatibility* concerns the conflict between the benefits of employee empowerment proffered to employees as increased self-autonomy and improved working conditions on the one hand, with the benefits anticipated by management in terms of increased employee compliance and productivity. Management justify employee empowerment in terms of increased productivity, aided by digitalizing much of their work and most of the communication to which they are subject, through Microsoft Teams, email, WhatsApp and messaging, revealing assumptions about not only the primacy of production over people but also the necessary subjection of employees to digital devices. The Nazis had the gall to inscribe *Arbeit Macht Frei* over the gates of Auschwitz; today's managerial autocrats might as well inscribe *Digitocracy Makes us Free* over their realms.

Outcome of participation concerns the tensions arising when the benefits of empowerment fail to deliver managerially anticipated productivity gains on account of system inefficiencies; digital systems that do not communicate with each other; digital systems that are rapidly superseded as IT consultants bring new algorithmic dazzlement to dazzle management while the hordes, the multitude, have to learn new systems – all in the name of efficiency and self-management. Regardless of the claims made for the benefits of employee empowerment and participation as a means of ensuring enhanced productivity, research findings indicate mixed outcomes (Verhoest et al., 2004).

These tensions and paradoxes of power-to as empowerment in the digitocracy arise when power is deployed in a manner different from power-over in its appearance but with even greater intrusions and more subtle objectives. When empowerment is underpinned by the assumption that one individual or group (the powerful) has the legitimate authority to give power-to or empower another individual or group (the powerless), it is always partial, just enough to maintain the status quo. Sewell and Wilkinson (1992: 102) described their findings of a study where managerial empowerment was provided within a narrowly defined and closely monitored sphere, as having the effect of "empowerment as rhetoric and the centralization of power and control as the reality" (Sewell & Wilkinson, 1992: 102). These tendencies are accelerated mightily when empowerment moves from teams, absent their supervisor, to individuals whose digital devices exercise veillance over those that are subjects (Zorina et al., 2021).

Incompatibility between the intentions and expectations of each party with respect to empowerment and autonomy means that there is a disconnect between what is espoused and what is intended and expected, giving rise to dissonance, anxiety and frustration (see Chapter 4 on pragmatic paradoxes). A fundamental problem of empowerment is glossing over these contradictions in the paradox of organizing, where control and autonomy are constantly competing for dominance (Smith & Lewis, 2011). Another approach to power is power-with, which manages these tensions initially by acknowledging them. Power-with, or coactive power, is the topic of the next section.

ORGANIZING PARADOX THROUGH POWER-WITH

Mary Parker Follett, an American political scientist sometimes described as the mother of organization studies (Clegg et al., 2019), was a person ahead of her time (Drucker, 1995; Schilling, 2000). Writing in the 1920s and 1930s, Follett (1924, 1995) saw enterprise as a social setting rather than merely an economic one. In some respects, it has been argued, there were some continuities between her arguments and those deployed much later by Foucault (Carlsen et al., 2020).

Follett sought to manage tensions in the perennial conflict between owners of capital (shareholders and managers employed to represent their interests) and labour (workers) by harmonizing power relations, writing: "What is the central problem of social relations? It is the question of power; this is the problem of industry, of politics, of international affairs" (Follett, 1924: xii). Follet described genuine power not as coercive power-over, but as coactive power-with, writing: "This kind of power, power-with, is what democracy should mean in politics or industry" (p. 187). Managers and workers in conflict seeking outcomes where a single side wins, is in fact a loss for both sides, as the whole has been depleted rather than enriched.

Follett's (1941 [2003]) circular theory of power describes managers and workers influencing each another in a complex social relational web. She espoused democratic authority that sees the replacement of bureaucratic institutions with networks of people analysing, producing and taking responsibility for outcomes at each stage of organizational processes. Circular power updates the facts accounted for in an evolving context, accommodating new interpretations, experiences and insights across time. Follett held that power cannot be delegated by managers within organizations as genuine power is not a 'thing' that the powerful can bestow upon the powerless.

Conditions allowing a single individual or group to empower others, as in power-to, can be just as likely to also undermine the notion implied by empowerment (Gruber & Trickett, 1987; Kizilos, 1990; Simon, 1990). Follett instead conceptualizes power as a democratic accomplishment that managers can facilitate workers in growing. At the organizational level, the objective of circular coactive power-with is not power sharing but to increase power: "our task is not to learn where to place power; it is how to develop power ... Genuine power can only be grown, it will slip from every arbitrary hand that grasps it" (pp. xii–xiii).

Follett's writings anticipate current discussions on empowerment (Eylon, 1998) and resolving the empowerment paradox (Smith & Lewis, 2011). Her philosophy of management was founded on resolving the organizing paradox: she believed that a definitive driver of human behaviour is the desire for self-governance in directing one's own affairs, yet this desire is incompatible with the collective participation necessary for realizing an individual's full potential. Central to this paradox is the assumption of a clear division between managers and employees, between those with power and those without. In the view of Follett, genuine empowerment will only occur when all parties perceive one another as equal partners. Under these conditions, individuals can contribute their unique knowledge, abilities and experiences to the collective. Resolving the empowerment paradox requires organizational management seeking to be, and remaining, adaptive to member contributions. Management has a responsibility to orchestrate a collaborative environment that is adaptive to "the law of the situation" (Follett, 1924: 152).

In Follett's (1924) view, the empowerment paradox can be overcome only when there is a willingness to undertake a long-term commitment, including through the implementation of significant changes at functional and structural levels. The intention to collaborate and integrate is insufficient for the transfer of formalized power, in Follett's view. Rather, the removal of all structural impediments to the full participation of the organization's members in all activities of responding to the law of the situation is the only means of achieving true democratic power. Follett wrote: "Many persons' idea of increased democracy within the cooperative movement is to democratize the organization: to have it less hierarchical than at present, to have more democratic elections, etc. This is not enough, to elect the officials and then to listen to their policy and consent. The farmers must also contribute" (p. 215). Empowerment according to Follett's conceptualization is not the action of authorizing but rather a concerted action to build, develop and increase power through the coordination of relationships (Murrell, 1985; Thomas & Velthouse, 1990).

In the process of developing and increasing coactive power Follett (1995) paid due attention to language. She argued that words such as 'higher' and 'lower' or 'over' and 'under' were unhelpful in the organizational context in that they undermine specific individual contributions by placing some in positions where their contributions may be overlooked (p. 142). In contrast, words such as 'persuade' rather than 'convince' (p. 104) seek to clarify differences between management based on power-over, opposed to what she espoused as the only beneficial mode of organizational power, power-with. For Follett, organizations provide the context for such coordination.

Follett's concept of growing coactive power-with also bears a close relationship with her ideas concerning conflict, where she sees the most sustainable solutions are those obtained by understanding and satisfying the needs of both parties. "A business should be so organized", Follett (1995: 76) writes, "... that full opportunity is given in any conflict, in any coming together of different desires, for the whole field of desire to be viewed". Eylon (1998: 23) sees Follett's "win-win" view of conflict as at the core of her approach to resolving the paradox of empowerment. Unless power is understood as coactive it will involve zero-sum perceptions of one party's winning as another party losing. Achieving power-with outcomes, however, requires all parties putting aside the expectation that 'their' perspective or issue must prevail. Instead relationships must be understood in terms of commonality, integration and circularity:

> Circular behaviour is the basis of integration. If your business is so organized that you can influence a co-manager while he is influencing you, so organized that a workman has an opportunity of influencing you as you have of influencing him, if there is an interactive influence going on all the time between you, power-with may be built up. (Follett, 1995: 107)

Reaching this level of coactive engagement requires a willingness for embracing solutions arrived at through dialectic synthesis, with all parties being comfortable not knowing in advance the likely form of any new solution.

Follett also further advocated the need for a free flow of information as vital to growing coactive power. Her notion of information flow goes beyond open communication by being associated with a notion of establishing respectful ongoing dialogue between all organizational members. To her credit, Follett acknowledges that her proposed dynamic approach to collective organization is not simple or easy. Rather, in correspondence with contemporary findings, she recognizes empowerment as a cyclical process (e.g. Thomas & Velthouse, 1990), where despite the challenges involved, it is the cycle itself that facilitates success within the process. Achieving coactive power requires recognizing empowerment as a dynamic and dialectic process. It is an iterative process of ongoing adaptation and adjustment between individual members and organizations defining the essential characteristics and functions of organizational practices and work.

To summarize, Follett resolves the organizing paradox of control and autonomy through an acceptance and engagement with these tensions via an awareness of structural challenges, language and conflict. This contrasts with the power-over response of denying the need for autonomy, or of power-to in offering a rhetoric of empowerment to disguise more subtle technologies of disempowerment and control. Paradox denial does not resolve the tensions but rather precipitates the occurrence of vicious circles, occurring when organizational inertia prevails over efforts for simultaneously engaging with both poles of a paradox by enacting changes at processual and structural levels (Lewis, Brown & Sutton, 2019). Other contributors to vicious circles include preferences for consistency and warding off the anxiety and defensiveness that tends to be fuelled by unmanaged conflict. Conditions such as these contribute towards organizational responses to salient paradoxical tensions that amplify contradictions and create self-reinforcing behavioural cycles in which individuals become more committed towards a single paradoxical pole rather than recognizing the inherent need for both poles (Smith & Lewis, 2011).

Follett (1995) describes genuine power not as the zero-sum game of power-over or even power-to but rather she proposes the self-developing capacity of power-with. This capacity is grown through cooperative democratic governance. Follett acknowledged that power-over will never be eliminated entirely. Accordingly, the empowerment paradox can never be perfectly resolved. Rather than trying to solve the tensions underpinning to organizing paradox, she advocates meeting them:

> What we need is some process for meeting problems. When we think we have solved a problem, well, by the very process of solving, new elements or forces come into the situation and you have a new problem on your hands to be solved. When this happens, men are often discouraged. I wonder why; it is our strength and our hope. We don't want any system that holds us enmeshed within itself. (Follett, 1995: 222)

Follett's insights concerning coactive power inform modern management approaches acknowledging stakeholder needs, the representation of workers on organizational boards, co-determination and participative management, where management consult with workers' councils on decisions relating to employee rights and status (Logue et al., 2015; Page, 2011) and profit-sharing initiatives. In a digitocracy premised on power-with, it is possible to reimagine the tools of the digitocracy as no longer centralized, as no longer affording big data opportunities for aggregation and exploitation of data (Clegg, van Rijmenam & Schweitzer, 2019) but as a distributed network enabling circular behaviour as the basis of integration – much as Tim Berners Lee intended the World Wide Web to be. His vision was that it would be decentralized, non-discriminatory, bottom-up in design, universal and premised on democratic consensus. A different digitocracy, one that is increasingly remote as a possibility.

Follett reminds us that truly understanding and implementing empowerment requires first understanding underlying individual and organizational assumptions concerning power (Eylon, 1998). She further provides helpful starting points from which to seek to meet rather than resolve the empowerment paradox.

CONCLUSION

We explored the organizing paradoxes underlying tensions of control and empowerment, where greater control calls for greater autonomy and greater autonomy calls for greater control. Our analysis is informed by a deep engagement with the power literature, distinguishing between power that is oppressive and imposed to power that is coactive and mutually beneficial. In our analysis, we have conceived of power as a multidimensional construct, that operates at individual, organizational and systemic societal levels. More specifically, we have analysed power using a three-part framework of power-over, power-to and power-with.

Our analysis of power-over focused on the ideas of the classical theorist of power, Max Weber, who described three types of authoritative power while emphasizing the efficient, predictable rational legal power of bureaucracy. We discussed bureaucracy as an almost mechanical system of organizational control that can be experienced as inhibiting individual freedom, creativity and autonomy. A paradox of power-over is that its successful enactment as a mode of control highlights the need for greater autonomy as power-to.

In considering power-to, we reviewed current culture management approaches that emphasize empowerment of employees. Drawing on Foucault, we also considered the rhetoric of empowerment as contradiction laden, a disguised mode of domination by those with power to bestow over those without, encouraged to become "empowered". Analysis revealed the objectives of power-over and power-to as one and the same, achieving greater organizational control. With power-to, control is paradoxically achieved through empowerment that relies on self-surveillance to achieve greater levels of conformity by promoting values of organizational commitment, trust, engagement and productivity. We considered how contemporary bureaucracy is transitioning into digitocracy in which employees' consent is self-managed as they subject themselves to various management controls designed as quizzes and games that one has to have passed to be considered a subject in conformance with organizational requirements. These are premised on a form of subjectification that creates the compliant employee.

Finally, we considered power-with, drawing upon the ideas of Mary Parker Follett. Genuine power, according to Follett, is not the zero-sum game of power-over, but rather a democratic cooperative process of governance. Follett did not seek to solve the organizing paradox but to meet it through a constant process of engaged dialogue, adaptation and collaboration. Critical to this endeavour is recognition that an empowerment programme must be developed and executed involving all of those affected in its deployment. Giving authority is not what is vital for empowerment but the cultivation of methods for facilitating components of empowerment such as circularity, responsibility, adaptive responsiveness, dialectic and synthesis. Digital opportunities exist to do this but run counter to the ways in which digitocracy has developed.

7.   The sociological futures of paradox: incorporating grand challenges

We are being afflicted with a new disease ... namely, technological unemployment.
This means unemployment due to our discovery of means of economising the use of
labour outrunning the pace at which we can find new uses for labour. But this is only
a temporary phase of maladjustment. All this means in the long run that mankind is
solving its economic problem.
(Keynes, 1930 [1963]: 364)

Capital itself is the moving contradiction, [in] that it presses to reduce labour time to
a minimum, while it posits labour time, on the other side, as sole measure and source
of wealth.
(Marx, 1973: 706)

Almost all contemporary definitions of paradox in philosophy agree that
a paradox is composed of meaningful statements (Priest, Berto & Weber,
2018). Extending the idea of paradox from philosophy one might say that
almost all contemporary definitions of paradox in practice are composed of
meaningful tensions. If we were to ask how paradoxes emerge, philosophers
who have thought much about these things tell us the following: "Paradoxes
emerge organically from the growth of new beliefs" (Sorensen & Sainsbury,
2020: 158). Translating paradox from the ideational to the material world, one
might conclude that it is the case that paradoxes emerge organically from the
growth of new practices. These new practices, such as exploration in search
of innovation, if successful, produce further new practices that may clash with
those practices already being exploited. Established practices are not free from
contradictions; however, ways to work through them may already have been
organically incorporated in practices, so that paradoxes remain latent, coped
with tacitly.

The growth of new practices is not just a matter of materiality, however.
Certainly, new ways of doing things, and of doing new things, require learning
and have an ideational component. Learning is hardly the only issue, though;
of more import is legitimacy. Doing new things or doing old things in new
ways always runs the risk of being seen as illegitimate, because these doings
are not embedded in past practices. Let us make the argument more substantive
by zooming out and looking at the macro context of paradox and organization,
namely the social, economic and material world where paradoxes germinate.

For the future, management and organization scholars may need to zoom out before zooming in, that is, to situate paradoxes in their sociological context and to explore their nestedness (as discussed in Chapter 5) in the broader societal issues, including grand challenges. In this chapter we focus especially on the capitalist system in which the vast majority of our organizations are nested and the contradictions that this system generates. We do so by studying the paradoxes inherent in the International Monetary Fund (IMF), a global financial organization headquartered in Washington DC, formed of 190 countries coordinating monetary operations. From there we draw ramifications to other themes, such as the COVID-19 pandemic and the digital transformation in process.

THE CENTRAL CONTRADICTION OF CAPITALISM

The central contradiction of capitalism, according to Piketty (2014), is what he calls $r > g$, where r stands for the return on capital invested and g is the economy's growth rate. The latter, Piketty suggests, is what determines wage growth rates. The central contradiction, he elaborates, is that since returns to capital exceeding returns to labour is at the core of a successful capitalist system, so too is rising inequality. A practical example of this contradiction is the annual growth of the US economy over a ten-year period from 1997 to 2007 while also seeing millions of job losses. Gapper (2011) of the *Financial Times* observes: "The problem with US manufacturing is not that it has been shrinking—despite the 'offshoring' of textile and electronics manufacturing to China, US manufacturing output rose by 3.9 per cent a year between 1997 and 2007. However, productivity grew 6.8 per cent annually in the same period, so millions of jobs were lost." In Marx's (1973) terms, more value was extracted from labour processes using less people and more technology domestically and through globalizing other elements of labour to offshore sites in which more 'efficient' labour could be supplied through outsourcing contracts. Efficiency in this context is defined in terms of the cost controls of an outsourced supply chain.

It should be noted that Piketty's (2014) argument has been contested (Wood & Hughes, 2015); nonetheless, it has clearly registered in high places. The Deputy Director of the IMF Research Department, Jonathan Ostry, in collaboration with others, has collated a range of IMF and other research to highlight the adverse effects of austerity on inequality and on growth (Ostry, Loungani & Furceri, 2016) in the wake of the Global Financial Crisis (GFC). Consequently, the macroeconomic implications of relative deprivation are on the IMFs' radar. Increasingly, the IMF urges the use of progressive income tax as a key macroeconomic policy for durable growth and stability. In some quarters, given the IMFs past record of policy prescriptions subsequent to its surveillance of national economies, prescriptions that have been orthodoxly neoliberal focused on minimizing public expenditures rather than minimizing inequality, critics have borrowed a leaf from Brunssons's (2002) book and accused the IMF of 'organized hypocrisy' (Kentikelenis, Stubbs & King, 2016). In this case, organized hypocrisy is signified by a gap between the Fund's words and the Fund's deeds. The gap becomes a paradox to be explained; should we believe the words or believe in the deeds?

PARADOXES AND LEGITIMATION GAPS: THE IMF

Paradoxes emerge from gaps between past and present words, between past and present practices, as well as between present words and present practices. Such gaps can open up tensions of legitimation: should one trust the words or the deeds (Schulz, Hatch & Larsen, 2000)? These gaps arise, in part, for reasons that have been well established in institutional theory. Meyer and Rowan (1977) argued that legitimacy can result from appearing to cohere with norms of 'rational effectiveness', 'legal mandates' and 'collectively valued purposes, means, goals, etc.'. Such coherence insulates organizations from external pressures. Applying this framework, we might infer that the IMF's past practices, while they may have conformed with rational effectiveness, increasingly were out of kilter with changing collective values, post-GFC. On the one hand, the assumption that neoliberal austerity policies were more rational; on the other hand, a strong ideological push justifying the rising levels of inequality (Piketty, 2020). The IMF, in its concern with the paradoxical central contradiction of capitalism, has engaged in buttressing its legitimacy in the face of changing times (Oxfam Canada, 2016). Legitimacy, as we have learned from Suchman (1995), is premised on perceptions that can be strategically managed to help achieve organizational goals. In the IMF's case, the paradox of its present words and past practices not being resolved by correspondence augured if not a potential legitimation crisis (Habermas, 1975), at least a gap. In essence, this is the argument of Clift and Robles (2020: 2) who maintain that "the IMF's quest for political legitimation in part explains efforts to reorient its prescriptive discourse towards more progressive, egalitarian territory".

We have now a further implication of organizations that deal in paradoxes. Holding to both-anding as a way of embracing paradox on the part of organizations can hoist these organizations on the petard of a legitimation gap. Clift and Robles put it well:

> The IMF's technocratic compulsions operate in ways that paradoxically exacerbate the IMF's problems. Its reorientation operates within restrictive economistic param-

eters that undermine policy efficacy, reflecting orthodox economic ideas deeply imbued in the Fund's mind-set. (Clift & Robles, 2020: 2–3)

Clift and Robles explain the back story to the emergence of this paradox in terms of the impact of Ostry, Loungani and Furceri's (2016) argument that excessive levels of inequality (e.g. an increased concentration of wealth in the wealthiest 1% of the population) hinder economies from growing more strongly and sustainably. The effective aggregate demand of the 1%, largely conspicuous consumption of positional goods (Hirsch, 1978; Veblen, 1899 [2007]), is insufficient in sustaining economic growth compared to the effective aggregate demand of the 99%, oriented towards a broad range of more ordinary goods and services. Such an assessment is confirmed by the historical data presented by Piketty (2020), which shows that aggressive redistributive policies do not stifle stronger economic growth; on the contrary, they appear to support it. These observations are relevant to the ongoing debate on the nature of the firm. The importance of purpose and the impact of firms on the quality of democracy seem inescapable themes for the future of paradox theory. The need to deepen workplace democracy (Davis, 2020) and to emphasize purpose (Mayer, 2020) should be part of this process. The change in the direction of organizations reducing the number of their employees, minimizing physical assets, asserting a global presence through extensive use of ethically questionable supply chains, as well as their enhanced panoptical potential in the era of AI and big data analytics (Zuboff, 2019), should be part of a paradox theory.

Diminishing inequalities through fiscal redistributions of elite wealth and income through the tax system aids growth, rather than hampering it, as rival 'trickle down' approaches maintain, in justification of tax cuts for capitalists that allegedly spur investment and employment. In the United States, where state governments have made significant cuts to taxes on capitalists, there is extensive data analysis concluding that these "tax cuts have little to no positive impact on gross state product, job creation, personal income, poverty rates, and business establishments" (Prillaman & Meier, 2014: 364).

Kentikelenis, Stubbs & King (2016) find that IMF programmes and institutional rhetoric were mis-matched. On the face of it, the paradox of words and deeds in the IMF position it as striving for legitimacy while continuing to articulate familiar policy prescriptions from the past. However, this is to assume a high degree of organic unity and coordinated strategy in what is a very large and complex organization. The IMF appears to be increasingly characterized by internal contestation and divergence of view, as it struggles to navigate legitimation challenges and institutional barriers (Clift & Robles, 2020).

To compound this picture of organizational fragmentation in a major global institution there is a further paradox. The IMF's legitimacy rests on its macroeconomic analyses' technical and objective accomplishment. These models are well versed in doing what the IMF traditionally does but as Clift and Robles (2020: 5) note, "the IMF is continually surprised by events outside the parameters of its models". Which brings us to COVID-19.

COVID-19: AN EXOGENOUS ENVIRONMENTAL CONTINGENCY ON A GRAND SCALE

The IMF website presents an impressive list of questions and answers about its response to the crisis caused by COVID-19. It is an event exogenous to both national and IMF policies; it is environmental both in terms of its origins in nature and as a factor external to those many organizations that have to deal with it, as well as being a contingency that cannot be ignored, using criteria developed by Clegg (1989). Directing organizations to be resilient and embrace paradox (Giustiniano et al., 2020), it is useful but also insufficient when dealing with a pandemic.

The IMF website is an impressive rhetorical document, and rhetoric has been shown to be an effective tool to work through paradox, at least temporarily (Abdallah, Denis & Langley, 2011; Bednarek, Paroutis & Sillince, 2017). The question, however, is whether rhetoric and action align, especially in light of the IMF's recent commitment to a more inclusive conception of macro-criticality as something that "affects, or has the potential to affect, domestic or external stability, or global stability" (IMF, 2015: 36), which COVID-19 undoubtedly does.

To answer this question, we turn to analysis by Oxfam (2020). The headline indicates that IMF embracing of paradox is purely rhetorical: 84% of the COVID-19 loans the IMF has made "require, poor countries hard hit by the economic fallout from the pandemic to adopt more tough austerity measures in the aftermath of the health crisis" (Oxfam, 2020: n.p.). The IMF has negotiated 91 loans with 81 countries since the pandemic was declared. In 76 of these loans, Oxfam's analysis reveals, there is a "push for belt-tightening that could result in deep cuts to public healthcare systems and pension schemes, wage freezes and cuts for public sector workers such as doctors, nurses and teachers, and unemployment benefits, like sick pay". The International Interim Executive Director of Oxfam, Chema Vera, states that the IMF is "steering countries to pay for pandemic spending by making austerity cuts that will fuel poverty and inequality". Moreover, as is pointed out, this is despite IMF research showing that austerity worsens poverty and inequality. COVID-19, as the International Labour Organization explains in its *Global Wage Report* (ILO, 2020), has caused average wages to fall in two-thirds of the countries it tracked in the first half of 2020, with lower-paid workers – disproportionately women – most affected by a loss of working hours.

These outcomes are occurring in many countries where prior policy prescriptions for austerity that followed those of the IMF had significantly weakened public services, especially healthcare, through a "policy agenda that seeks to balance national budgets through cuts to public services, increases in taxes paid by the poorest, and moves to undermine labor rights and protections". Such an outcome is not without precedent but rather in keeping with the IMF's track record, indicating that while rhetoric may have changed, historical practices continue. Rowden's (2013) work, titled *The Deadly Ideas of Neoliberalism: How the IMF has Undermined Public Health and the Fight Against AIDS*, makes the case that the IMF monetarist approach of prioritizing low inflation with low budget deficits had undermined developing nations' efforts to scale up investment in public health. Consequently, public health services have been chronically underfunded, creating demoralizing working conditions and fuelling a 'brain drain' of medical professionals, further undermining general public health and developing nations' efforts to defeat HIV/AIDS.

The paradox is evident: a commitment to social inequality as a key element in macro-criticality is not served by policy prescriptions that stress austerity measures and cuts to public services. At the same time, a solution that has worked in the past, the application of progressive taxation on wealth and income, is not even mentioned as a viable possibility (Piketty, 2020). How does one begin to explain this apparent contradiction? Is it a case of both-anding in which the IMF both articulates a commitment and fails to follow through on it? Is it a sign of a legitimation gap? Or does it signify some combination of these factors?

We think the latter is the case. To explain why this is so we must return to a fundamental point about the IMF as a complex organization.

COMPLEX ORGANIZATION AND CONTRADICTIONS

The IMFs legitimacy is built on the reputation of its economists' technical competence. Clift and Robles (2020) note this as a reputation that is seemingly apolitical, scientific and technocratic, premised on depoliticization of political economy by the economization of all questions; that is, translating any issue into the terms of economic modelling: "The desire to remain camped on familiar economistic ground so as to enhance its technical authority helps explain why the IMF's operationalization of inequality as macro-critical takes the form it does", as Clift and Robles (2020: 4) put it. Thus, one element of the paradoxical contradictions that are associated with the macro-criticality of social inequality for the IMF resides in the sensemaking apparatus that employment and socialization in the IMF privileges, creating an institutionally intellectual mobilization of bias (Schattschneider, 1960) towards technocratic and economistic analysis.

Despite frequent pleas in the positive literature on paradox theory in management and organization studies to 'embrace' paradoxes, a fundamental fact is that an organization's members cannot embrace what they fail to make sense of. All organization contains a mobilization of bias and the IMF's is institutionalized in certain forms of economic thought. However, and this is the important point, no system of thought is ever hegemonic – if it were, then social inequality would never have made it on to the IMF agenda. Yet, for a paradox to be taken 'seriously' (i.e. not as the expression of flawed reasoning, communication breakdown or ambiguous definitions), it is necessary that both the contrasting logics that underpin the opposite and interdependent poles are acknowledged as important, legitimate and salient. If one logic is only paid lip service to, the paradox will be 'rhetorically', rather than practically, salient.

The IMF is a very large, very complex, very privileged and very bureaucratic organization. It has deeply embedded operating procedures that are nested, professionally, in some of the best and brightest graduates of the economics discipline, most often from those North American and European schools that produce conservative macroeconomists (Momani, 2010). These professionals are not well equipped, on the whole, to deal with issues of social inequality and the analysis of *political* economy that they entail. Moreover, they are not notably diverse in terms of gender, regional and academic backgrounds. The policy frameworks and strategies that the IMF has developed to try and enable consistency across its operations are intendedly acontextual, while they must be applied in radically variable national contexts. Across these different contexts, common sensemaking is largely made through variants of mainstream macroeconomics, although, in the wake of the GFC, there was some recruitment of more Keynesian-oriented economists. It is for this reason, one thinks, that the macro-criticality of social inequality made it into the rhetoric, if not always the practice, of the IMF.

The results are laid out clearly by Clift and Robles (2020: 10):

> It follows, firstly, that PhDs from leading institutions (the gene pool from which the IMF routinely recruits) will not have focused on [inequality] issues; and, secondly, that the leading macroeconomics journals will not offer models or insights to help the Fund in tackling inequality through macroeconomic policy. This in turn limits the intellectual and 'scientific' authority behind its policy propositions. On what evidential basis within macroeconomics can Fund missions advance the case for any particular per cent additional spending on social protection, or specific taxation changes aimed at tackling inequality? … The inequality agenda thus raises to new levels tensions between the Fund's technocratic compulsions and its legitimacy pressures. In substance, the IMF remains centred on its rigid technocratic orientation which thereby bolsters its authority to act as an arbiter of sound policy and custodian of economic stability. This also allows it to maintain only a narrow and shallow

engagement in areas (such as inequality) beyond its established areas of expertise. However, the Fund has thus far failed to recognize fully the difficulties underlying the paradox of seeking political legitimation within these economistic parameters.

Its policy paradoxes over issues of macro-criticality are not limited to issues of inequality; there are also issues associated with a rapidly warming planet and its implications for policy prescriptions premised on economic growth through exploitation of resources.

THE IMF AND CLIMATE CHANGE

The IMF has also been active in striving to assert legitimacy in its relation to one other of the grand challenges of the day: climate change. Climate change is another major macro-critical factor that one would think is necessarily at the heart of contemporary economic calculation if only because a rapidly warming planet threatens not only the carbon basis of the global economy to which IMF prescriptions apply but also because it threatens the assumption of economic growth as the underlying engine of infinite progress and growth.

The paradox that presents itself when we look at IMF policies related to sustainability is that matters of life itself are refracted through an economistic lens. In a recent IMF blog, Guérin, Natalucci and Suntheim (2020) draw a link between COVID-19 and sustainability issues. It is how they do it that is paradoxical. First, they note that in the absence of a green investment push "tighter financial constraints and adverse economic conditions can be detrimental to firms' environmental performance, reducing green investments, and potentially slowing down the transition to a low-carbon economy" (Guérin, Natalucci & Suntheim, 2020: n.p.). Second, they propose that sustainable finance policies (led by international cooperation and the IMF) will be key, including standardized corporate sustainability reporting systems allowing investors to determine actual exposures of companies to climate-related financial risks, together with a standardized definition of what constitutes a sustainable investment fund (Guérin, Natalucci & Suntheim, 2020).

In this analysis the climate crisis is treated discursively through the lens of sustainable finance policies. Sustainability that was initially premised as being a matter for green investment and a low carbon economy is translated into a matter of standardized reporting and disclosure in order to instil confidence in investors that sustainability is not a financial risk. Quite how this will save the limits of life on Earth being breached is not at all clear. The climate crisis being experienced in an ascending curve of global warming this century signifies that these limits are being breached. These limits can be thought of in terms of the Planetary Boundaries (PBs) that make life liveable. The PBs framework encompasses nine Earth system thresholds, the standing conditions for life on Earth, the consequences of crossing which are potentially catastrophic. At least four system boundaries (rate of biodiversity loss, climate change, human interference with the nitrogen cycle, and land-system change) appear to have already been transgressed in ways that cannot be repaired or will be extremely challenging to reverse. The consistent corporate responses that Guérin, Natalucci and Suntheim (2020) call for entail that, ideally, at each level of the nine Earth systems identified, a systematic audit should be conducted in terms of the construction of a future perfect scenario in which minimization of harm is the purpose to be achieved, cascading through organizational levels to the framing of the individual. For responsible management in contemporary times the precautionary principle needs to be paramount in relation to all stakeholder agencies, in addition to human agents, in various ecological systems. New sets of rules and meanings in terms of audit accountabilities need to be routinized.

Despite the volume of growing published evidence, the majority of contemporary business organizations and institutions have demonstrated that they are not prepared to take the idea of material boundaries into consideration any more than the IMF appears to do so. That this should be the case is hardly surprising; as Methmann (2010: 357) researched, the IMF in concert with other global institutions seeks "to remedy the dislocatory effects of climate change while not altering their practices …[they] … seek to establish a relation of equivalence between, for example, growth, free trade and climate protection". Methmann (2010: 357) goes on to say that climate protection and sustainability are used as "empty signifiers" that are constructed through specific discursive strategies. The first of these is to constitute the issue as one outside the remit of sovereign states because it is a global problem that requires a global approach; second, there is the issue of action necessarily being subordinated to the emergence of a global consensus. A third strategy is to note the limited resources and capabilities of the nations that are set to suffer most immediately from the results of climate change, while a fourth strategy is to discuss climate change as an externality problem, one of the tensions that accompany global growth.

The concept of externalities was originally developed in the 1920s by Pigou (2013), who argued that a tax (later called a 'Pigouvian tax') on negative externalities can be used to reduce their incidence. That technical externalities require government regulation and taxation to prevent or lessen them has been intensely debated after Pigou's seminal work.

> Externalities pose fundamental economic policy problems when individuals, households, and firms do not internalize the indirect costs of or the benefits from their economic transactions. The resulting wedges between social and private costs or returns lead to inefficient market outcomes. In some circumstances, they may prevent markets from emerging. Although there is room for market-based corrective solutions, government intervention is often required to ensure that benefits and costs are fully internalized. (Helbling, 2020: n.p.)

What might be the nature of this government intervention? It will involve the task of connecting causalities on multiple scales. Institutional legislative and regulatory measures will need rethinking, with the state having a prime function in tackling climate change, especially in terms of negotiating international treaties and enforcing them.

Currently, both abundant information as well as management tools are available for reducing the use of natural resources and climate emissions; nonetheless, management thinking and action have yet to demonstrate the required will to overcome management's cultural constraints. Temporally, short-term thinking focused on achieving profitability tends to prevail. Effective action in response to the challenges of the PBs requires not only highly collaborative and insightful ways of enacting responsible agency (rather than merely publishing attractive reports on corporate sustainability) but also political will and direction, a strong public sector and an ensuring state (nationally and internationally).

Business leaders should be astutely aware of their power since 147 global companies control 40% of the economic value of global business via a complicated web of ownership relations. In close connection with state actors, the elite group of global business organizations has successfully strengthened their agency and power globally. While some individual members of this group are taking sustainability action with the support of, for example, multiregional input-output models, these perform inadequately as a network in relation to the challenges that face us. Establishing an effective management response requires a collective effort, through which business actors gain momentum by assembling alliances whose agency demands changes in the industry and supports democratic mechanisms to ignite change at large.

Democracy derives from the people but devolves to the state and its elected governments. The powers of the state include the monopoly of the right to taxation. As such, taxation changes are contingencies with which organizations are obliged to deal. At present, some jurisdictions, including the United States and Australia, extend the right to tax profits globally. Taxing the foreign profits of transnational companies (TNCs) on a global basis could be extended in a number of ways.

First, it could be recognized, as the French government has proposed, that companies lacking physical presence in a country in which they are accruing profits through large numbers of online users or customers should be taxed at the same rate as bricks and mortar businesses. If this proposal were adopted by various national governments then the beginnings of a global tax scheme would be in place. Such a scheme could be extended to include ecological taxation – ecotax – that could be levied as an excess and additional tax on those business actions whose activities anywhere in the world were breaching any of the nine PBs. The state is also the only actor that could establish caps on production either directly or through Pigouvian taxes, which are necessary to guarantee policy success for sustainable change.

Managers in TNCs can be motivated in terms of enlightened self-interest; for instance, global trajectories of action can be nudged in more ecologically responsible directions through devices such as ecotaxation. A model of the Global Resources Dividend (GRD) might be the answer. Businesses would pay a tax on any services or resources that they use or sell rated proportionately to the harm that they create in extraction or production. Those business organizations that could establish that they had enacted policies that minimized the harm to the lowest-rated harm decile of the tax register would pay a disproportionately lower tax than those businesses that could not so demonstrate that they qualified. Proportionality would vary with the demonstration of performance. Those organizational actors that could demonstrate commitment to circular economy principles would clearly be advantaged. The aim would be to move away from voluntarist and weak sustainability typical of compliance and business-centred corporate approaches towards regenerative and co-evolutionary sustainability, where the emphasis is on absolute reductions of production and consumption activities.

The onus should be on business organizations to demonstrate why they should not be taxed at the highest band. Tax will act as a nudge to the adoption of policies with transformative potential. Put differently, companies should demonstrate the precautionary principle in practice; those that fail to do so would be subject to highly discriminate taxes. If the majority of organizations were paying their GRD, the tax benefits of doing so would help deter deviance as self-interest drove responsible action. There would be added pressure on each country to enforce the gathering of GRD funds within its borders because of the tax advantages of so doing; the hosting of rogue businesses by non-compliant states could lead to these businesses being singled out for preferential and discriminatory tax treatment in the more developed states that implemented the ecotax principles.

Planetary boundaries are not simply here and now; they are also temporal in that where the boundary is drawn today has potentially profound effects on the boundaries of tomorrow – the essence of the case for action against global warming. Establishing boundaries is of crucial importance in highlighting the uniqueness of actors and acknowledging responsibilities. To the extent that the boundary blurring between human and non-human actors signifies a retreat from anthropocentrism, the chances of life remaining within planetary boundaries increases. In other words, if the needs of non-human stakeholders are taken into account and met, the rate of biodiversity loss may begin to diminish, and climate change slowed. Similar desired effects might be expected in terms of the other ecological boundaries.

The paradox is that there are global institutions such as the IMF that have the global reach and in principle capabilities to instruct states in Pigouvian taxes but that seem reluctant to do so, despite advice from senior analysts such as Helbling (2020). The small number of very large transnational organizations that are mainly responsible for the root emissions and erosions of the planetary boundaries could be effectively subject to ecotaxation. As Helbling (2020) states, it is a Gordian knot, a knotted paradox, that can only be cut by government of the state. The paradox is that since Pigou, it is clear what is to be done; it is equally clear that it has hardly been done. There can be no both-anding in these domains: we cannot continue both to exploit and pollute the planet and also save it. These are paradoxes to which paradox scholars need to turn their attention, perhaps in a less scholastic and more practically oriented manner than some of the discussions that have been conducted thus far. Indeed, the area of public policy, not only with respect to the IMF, is one to which paradox scholars might well turn their intellectual acumen if only because paradoxes aplenty abound therein, given a heightened impetus because of the COVID-19 pandemic and responses to it. We will briefly mention a few of these.

First, there is the tension between the norms and practices of different sciences and those of politics. Nowhere has this been more evident than in the politics of the United Kingdom in which, as Baines (2020: n.p.) notes, "during a time of immeasurable medical uncertainty" probability modelling of different scenarios, based on more or less strict quarantining of the population, is the standard policy setting. However, quarantining is not necessarily a popular option with politicians, particularly those of a libertarian bent, of whom there are a number amongst the government benches, because it is electorally unpopular with those voters that do not appreciate restrictions on their freedoms of movement and sociality. The paradox resides in doing what the pragmatic science suggests and the decision-making powers that reside in politicians susceptible to their perceptions of electoral pressure. The science is based on scenarios offering degrees of certainty in a probable range of contagion and death. The political implementation of the science through policymaking has to take place in the specific national context in which it is to be implemented. At this point we reconnect with the arguments from the IMF, to articulate why these decision-making powers were severely tested during the pandemic. At the root of these was a lack of resilience capabilities on the part of the British state as a result of policy prescriptions that accorded with the standard recipes of the IMF.

At the start of 2020, Britain had been through 10 years of austerity following the 2008 financial crash – another great international crisis that hit the country harder than almost anywhere else. The NHS was stretched and fragmented, its lines of authority and responsibility tangled by years of regulatory tinkering. Outside

London, the country's economy was unproductive and poor, and its elderly-care system an unreformed national disgrace. The civil service, which believed itself to be the best in the world, had become a shadow of its former self, almost entirely shorn of the ability to act operationally or think strategically, its center hollowed out, weak, and ineffective. The country itself seemed divided and angry, unable to agree on a unifying national story […] When the pandemic hit, then, Britain was not the strong, successful, resilient country it imagined, but a poorly governed and fragile one. The truth is, Britain was sick before it caught the coronavirus. (McTague, 2020: n.p.).

At the outset of the pandemic many of Britain's elderly were moved to care homes, which are not part of the public sector, as is the health service, in order to free up hospital capacity. As the renowned strategist Lawrence Freedman (2020) argued, the initial response that was made to the pandemic was rapidly overwhelmed, in part because the strategy was predicated on a model devised for a flu outbreak. In effect, potentially infected elderly and vulnerable patients were being moved into situations in which infection controls were far laxer than in the public hospitals they were evacuated from. These patients were not tested for COVID-19 beforehand. As entities that seek to minimize costs and maximize revenues, care homes are largely staffed by exploited, largely female low-paid workers, often in insecure employment, who make ends meet by working across multiple providers. When any of these people caught the virus, they transmitted it into several situations in which fragile, ill and elderly people resided in close contact with employees who would often have to physically handle the residents. With the pandemic, the two systems of public health and private care came into conflict, with the public health system being protected but at the cost of placing vulnerable people in extremely vulnerable situations (McTague, 2020) because of the way that the labour market was constructed as a result of a privatized care system in which those 'in care' were a source of value best maximized by cheapening its cost as much as possible. The results of this are well known; the UK had one of the worst records in Europe in terms of infection and death rates. In terms of inequality, one result of the response to the pandemic such as lockdowns and social isolating, while necessary to preserve life and health, has been to deepen already existing levels of inequality. Disproportionately, it is female labour in the secondary labour market of retail, hospitality and service employment that has suffered the impact of the coronavirus pandemic in terms of unemployment (Ro, 2020). Of course, many other factors were in play in addition to poor decision- and policymaking. The civil service appeared unprepared for the task; it was beset by organizational changes and politics that the Prime Minister's special political advisor, Dominic Cummings, exacerbated; Cummings' example in breaching curfew was also another factor in alienating the populace from a rhetoric that it appeared was not felt as an obligatory limit on behaviour by elites.

Contradiction aplenty: between public health and private care; between austerity oriented to protect wealth creation through cutting government imposts generating a lack of health protection; between advice based on epidemiological modelling and its probabilities and the perceived probabilities of electoral discontent if these policies were followed. These were not all. Where central global institutions influence policymaking and decision-making in national governments then they can set in train unanticipated consequences posing contradictions for the future, as in the case in the British response to COVID-19:

> Expert advisory committees proved too slow and ponderous, with not enough dissenting voices; crisis-response cells could not cope and had to be bypassed; the Cabinet Office buckled under the strain; the NHS had no adequate way of sharing data; authorities could not meet the sudden need for mass testing; the Foreign Office could not get people home fast enough; the Department of Health could not design a contact-tracing app that worked; the government overall could not sufficiently procure key pandemic equipment; and Downing Street generally gave the impression of lurching from one crisis to another. (McTague, 2020: n.p.)

CONCLUSION

The discussion of paradox in this chapter has been conducted in terms that thus far have not troubled paradox scholars, possibly because research has mainly focused on the organizational level of analysis. Fragmentation and heterogeneity of sensemaking apparatuses in organizations, however limited, can open up the agendas of organizations such that they make commitments to innovative ventures. However, when it comes to implementing the rhetoric of the new into the customary practices of the past, forms of default mechanism come into play, not necessarily through mendacity but through trained incapacities and institutional legacies, ensuring an institutionalized mobilization of bias. Trained incapacities and institutionalized mobilizations of bias thus produce a legitimation gap between rhetoric and practice, exposing a paradox between what an organization such as the IMF says and does. At one level, this 'organized hypocrisy' enables organizations to both-and. Nonetheless, the paradox of the fundamental contradiction between words and deeds remains. Commitments can be espoused while in practice they are framed in such a way as to ensure their contradiction remains.

Returning to Piketty (2014) again, what we have is contradiction on contradiction, a double helix of contradictions cycling out viciously. The irresolution of the paradox of the IMF means that the policy prescriptions that might orient nations towards resolving the paradoxes of successful capitalism are greatly lessened. Recall that this contradiction is premised on returns to capital exceeding returns to labour producing inequality, restricting wage growth of the 99%, which in the long term undermines the production of profit, as surplus value is ever more concentrated, relatively, in fewer and fewer hands and aggregate effective demand diminished by a lack of wage growth. This is, indeed, a paradox; in a system that requires effective demand, which is the preserve of the many, as well as maximizing profits, which is the preserve of the few, there is a long-term tendency to paradoxical outcomes with deleterious effects for health, wealth and climate.

In the midst of the Fourth Industrial Revolution, the current threat posed by a global pandemic and in the face of an even bigger climate crisis, we need a stronger and bolder paradox theory. A paradox perspective should not be leveraged only as a technocratic tool aimed at balancing tensions and maintaining the status quo. Rather, paradox should be increasingly treated as a heuristic tool, revealing the intrinsic contradictions of any 'grand theory' aimed at organizing society (be it neoliberal, socialist or any 'third way'). Its potential is not just to reveal problems in rhetorically perfect but practically flawed models but to stress that, instead of considering reified, packaged solutions, we should focus on the processes by which problems are set and solutions are sought. Acknowledging paradoxes drives us to appreciate the interdependence and interrelatedness of issues, the need to iteratively adjust and cope with the side effects caused by our remedies, as well as the necessity critically to scrutinize strategies and learn from experience. In this, it can also help in improving the quality of the political debate, moving away from simplistic, dumbed-down solutions to wicked problems (such as sustainable development, migration, sovereignty, etc.). The promise of paradox theory has only just begun to be realized.

References

Abdallah, C., Denis, J.-L., & Langley, A. (2011). Having your cake and eating it too: Discourses of transcendence and their role in organizational change dynamics. *Journal of Organizational Change Management, 24*(3): 333–348.

Abrams, D., & Hogg, M. A. (2004). Metatheory: Lessons from social identity research. *Personality and Social Psychology Review, 8*(2): 98–106.

Adler, P. S., & Borys, B. (1996). Two types of bureaucracy: Enabling and coercive. *Administrative Science Quarterly, 41*: 61–89.

Ahrne, G., & Brunsson, N. (2005). Organizations and meta-organizations. *Scandinavian Journal of Management, 21*(4): 429–449.

Alderfer, C. (2011). *The practice of organizational diagnosis: Theory and methods.* New York, NY: Oxford University Press.

Allen, V. L. (1975). *Social analysis: A Marxist critique and alternative.* New York, NY: Longman.

Alvarez, S. A., Zander, U., Barney, J. B., & Afuah, A. (2020). Developing a theory of the firm for the 21st century. *Academy of Management Review, 45*(4): 711–716.

Alvesson, M., & Sandberg, J. (2011). Generating research questions through problematization. *Academy of Management Review, 36*(2): 247–271.

Alvesson, M., & Spicer, A. (2012). A stupidity-based theory of organizations. *Journal of Management Studies, 49*(7): 1194–1220.

Alvesson, M., & Willmott, H. (2002). Identity regulation as organizational control: Producing the appropriate individual. *Journal of Management Studies, 39*: 619–644.

Alvesson, M., & Willmott, H. (2012). *Making sense of management: A critical introduction.* London, UK: Sage.

Ancona, D., Bresman, H., & Kaeufer, K. (2002). The comparative advantage of X-teams. *MIT Sloan Management Review, 43*(3): 33–39.

Andriopoulos, C., & Lewis, M. W. (2009). Exploitation-exploration tensions and organizational ambidexterity: Managing paradoxes of innovation. *Organization Science, 20*(4): 696–717.

Andriopoulos, C., & Lewis, M. W. (2010). Managing innovation paradoxes: Ambidexterity lessons from leading product design companies. *Long Range Planning, 43*(1): 104–122.

Andrzejewski, A. V. (2008). *Building power: Architecture and surveillance in Victorian America.* Knoxville: University of Tennessee Press.

Aoki, K. (2020). The roles of material artifacts in managing the learning-performance paradox: The Kaizen case. *Academy of Management Journal, 63*(4): 1266–1299.

Appelrouth, S. (2005). Body and soul: Jazz in the 1920s. *American Behavioral Scientist, 48*(11): 1496–1509.

Arendt, H. (1972). *Crisis of the republic.* New York, NY: Harcourt, Brace & Co.

Argan, G. C. (1968). *Storia dell'arte italiana.* Vol. 2 *Da Giotto a Leonardo.* Sansoni.

Argyris, C. (1994). Good communication that blocks learning. *Harvard Business Review, 72*(4): 77–85.

Aroles, J., & McLean, C. (2016). Rethinking stability and change in the study of organizational routines: Difference and repetition in a newspaper-printing factory. *Organization Science, 27*(3): 535–550.

Ashby, M. N., Riad, S., & Davenport, S. (2019). Engaging with paradox, striving for sustainability: Relating to public science and commercial research. *Organization & Environment, 32*(3): 255–280.

Ashforth, B. (1994). Petty tyranny in organizations. *Human Relations, 47*(7): 755–778.

Ashforth, B. E., & Reingen, P. H. (2014). Functions of dysfunction: Managing the dynamics of an organizational duality in a natural food cooperative. *Administrative Science Quarterly, 59*(3): 474–516.

Ashforth, B. E., Rogers, K. M., Pratt, M. G., & Pradies, C. (2014). Ambivalence in organizations: A multilevel approach. *Organization Science, 25*(5): 1453–1478.

Azoulay, P., Repenning, N. P., & Zuckerman, E. W. (2010). Nasty, brutish, and short: Embeddedness failure in the pharmaceutical industry. *Administrative Science Quarterly, 55*(3): 472–507.

Baard, P. P., Deci, E. L., & Ryan, R. M. (2004). Intrinsic need satisfaction: A motivational basis of performance and well-being in two work settings. *Journal of Applied Social Psychology, 34*(10): 2045–2068.

Bacharach, S. B. (1989). Organizational theories: Some criteria for evaluation. *Academy of Management Review, 14*: 496–515.

Bachmann, C., Habisch, A., & Dierksmeier, C. (2018). Practical wisdom: Management's no longer forgotten virtue. *Journal of Business Ethics, 153*(1): 147–165.

Bahcall, S. (2019). *Loonshots*. New York, NY: St. Martin's Press.

Baines, D. (2020). What 16,000 missing coronavirus cases tell us about how the UK is handling the pandemic. *The Conversation*, 7 October 2020, https://theconversation.com/what-16-000-missing-coronavirus-cases-tell-us-about-how-the-uk-is-handling-the-pandemic-147539 (accessed 3 December 2020).

Baker, D. (2013). Service quality and customer satisfaction in the airline industry: A comparison between legacy airlines and low-cost airlines. *American Journal of Tourism Research, 2*(1): 67–77.

Ballesteros, A. (2020). Digitocracy: Ruling and being ruled. *Philosophies, 5*(2): 1–9.

Bansal, P., & Song, H.-C. (2017). Similar but not the same: Differentiating corporate sustainability from corporate responsibility. *Academy of Management Annals, 11*(1): 105–149.

Bansal, P., Kim, A., & Wood, M. O. (2018). Hidden in plain sight: The importance of scale in organizations' attention to issues. *Academy of Management Review, 43*(2): 217–241.

Barad, K. (2003). Posthumanist performativity: Toward an understanding of how matter comes to matter. *Signs, 28*: 801–831.

Barney, J. B. (2018). Why resource-based theory's model of profit appropriation must incorporate a stakeholder perspective. *Strategic Management Journal, 39*(13): 3305–3325.

Barton, M. A., & Kahn, W. A. (2018). Group resilience: The place and meaning of relational pauses. *Organization Studies, 40*(9): 1409–1429.

Bateson, G. (1972). *Steps to an ecology of mind: Collected essays in anthropology, psychiatry, evolution, and epistemology*. Aylesbury, UK: Intertext.

Bateson, G., Jackson, D. D., Haley, J., & Weakland, J. H. (1956). Toward a theory of schizophrenia. *Behavioral Science, 1*(4): 251–264.

Battilana, J., Besharov, M., & Mitzinneck, B. (2017). On hybrids and hybrid organizing: A review and roadmap for future research. In R. Greenwood, C. Oliver, T. B.

Lawrence, & R. Meyer (eds), *The SAGE handbook of organizational institutionalism* (2nd edn, pp. 133–169). Los Angeles, CA: Sage.

Beckett, S. (1958 [2009]). *Three novels. Molloy. Malone dies. The unnamable.* New York, NY: Grove Press.

Bednarek, R., Chalkias, K., & Jarzabkowski, P. (2020). Managing risk as a duality of harm and benefit: A study of organizational risk objects in the global insurance industry. *British Journal of Management.* First published: 28 November 2019, https://doi.org/10.1111/1467-8551.12389

Bednarek, R., Paroutis, S., & Sillince, J. (2017). Transcendence through rhetorical practices: Responding to paradox in the science sector. *Organization Studies, 38*(1): 77–101.

Bednarek, R., Cunha, M. P., Schad, J., & Smith, W. K. (eds) (2021). Both-anding paradox theory. *Research in the sociology of organizations,* forthcoming.

Beech, N., Burns, H., de Caestecker, L., MacIntosh, R., & MacLean, D. (2004). Paradox as invitation to act in problematic change situations. *Human Relations, 57*(10): 1313–1332.

Benders, J., & Van Veen, K. (2001). What's in a fashion? Interpretative viability and management fashions. *Organization, 8*(1): 33–53.

Bennis, W. G. (2000). *Managing the dream: Reflections on leadership and change.* New York: Basic Books.

Benson, J. K. (1977). Organizations: A dialectical view. *Administrative Science Quarterly, 22*(1): 1–21.

Bentham, J. (2017a). *Correspondence of Jeremy Bentham, volume 1: 1752 to 1776.* Edited by Timothy L. S. Sprigge & J. H. Burns. London, UK: UCL Press.

Bentham, J. (2017b). *Correspondence of Jeremy Bentham, volume 4: October 1788 to December 1793.* Edited by A. T. Milne & J. R. Dinwiddy. London, UK: UCL Press.

Berg Johansen, C., & De Cock, C. (2018). Ideologies of time: How elite corporate actors engage the future. *Organization, 25*(2): 186–204.

Berti, M. (2017). *Elgar introduction to organizational discourse analysis.* Cheltenham, UK: Edward Elgar Publishing.

Berti, M. (2021). Logic(s) and paradox. *Research in the sociology of organizations,* forthcoming.

Berti, M., & Simpson, A. V. (2019). The dark side of organizational paradoxes: The dynamics of disempowerment. *Academy of Management Review.* Published online: 26 November 2019. DOI: 10.5465/amr.2017.0208.

Berti, M., & Simpson, A. V. (2020). On the practicality of resisting pragmatic paradoxes. *Academy of Management Review.* Published online: 24 July 2020. DOI: 10.5465/amr.2020.0258

Berti, M., Simpson, A. V., & Clegg, S. R. (2018). Making a place out of space: The social imaginaries and realities of a Business School as a designed space. *Management Learning, 49*(2): 168–186.

Besharov, M. L., & Smith, W. K. (2014). Multiple institutional logics in organizations: Explaining their varied nature and implications. *Academy of Management Review, 39*(3): 364–381.

Bettis, R. A., & Prahalad, C. K. (1995). The dominant logic: Retrospective and extension. *Strategic Management Journal, 16*(1): 5–14.

Bhaskar, R. (1975). *A realist theory of science.* Leeds, UK: Leeds Books.

Bion, W. R. (1946). The leaderless group project. *Bulletin of the Menninger Clinic, 10*(3): 77–81.

Blau, P. M. (1954). Co-operation and competition in a bureaucracy. *American Journal of Sociology, 59*(6): 530–535.

Boje, D. M., & Dennehy, R. F. (1993). *Managing in the postmodern world: America's revolution against exploitation.* Dubuque, IA: Kendall/Hunt.

Boulding, K. E. (1956). General systems theory—the skeleton of science. *Management Science, 2*(3): 197–208.

Braverman, H. (1975). *Labor and monopoly capital: The degradation of work in the twentieth century.* New York, NY: Monthly Review Press.

Brenkert, G. G. (2009). Google, human rights, and moral compromise. *Journal of Business Ethics, 85*(4): 453–478.

Brooks, D. (2019, 18 June). Harvard's false path to wisdom. *The New York Times.*

Brown, N. J. L., Sokal, A. D., & Friedman, H. L. (2014). The persistence of wishful thinking: Response to "updated thinking on positivity ratios". *American Psychologist, 69*: 629–632.

Brown, S. L., & Eisenhardt, K. M. (1997). The art of continuous change: Linking complexity theory and time-paced evolution in relentlessly shifting organizations. *Administrative Science Quarterly, 42*(1): 1–34.

Brown, S. L., & Eisenhardt, K. M. (1998). *Competing on the edge: Strategy as structured chaos.* Boston, MA: Harvard Business Press.

Brunsson, N. (1989). *The organization of hypocrisy: Talk, decisions and actions in organizations.* Chichester, UK: Wiley.

Brunsson, N. (2002). *The organization of hypocrisy.* Copenhagen: Copenhagen Business School Press.

Bufford, R. K. (2006). Paradox. https://digitalcommons.georgefox.edu/gscp_fac/305 (accessed 1 December 2020).

Bussing, A., Bissels, T., Fuchs, V., & Perrar, K.-M. (1999). A dynamic model of work satisfaction: Qualitative approaches. *Human Relations, 52*(8): 999–1028.

Byggeth, S., & Hochschorner, E. (2006). Handling trade-offs in ecodesign tools for sustainable product development and procurement. *Journal of Cleaner Production, 14*(15–16): 1420–1430.

Cameron, K. S. (1986). Effectiveness as paradox: Consensus and conflict in conceptions of organizational effectiveness. *Management Science, 32*(5): 539–553.

Cameron, K. S. (2008). Paradox in positive organizational change. *The Journal of Applied Behavioral Science, 44*(1): 7–24.

Cameron, K. S. (2011). Responsible leadership as virtuous leadership. *Journal of Business Ethics, 98*(1): 25–35.

Cameron, K. S. (2017a). Cross-cultural research and positive organizational scholarship. *Cross Cultural & Strategic Management, 24*(1): 13–32.

Cameron, K. S. (2017b). Paradox in positive organizational scholarship. In W. K. Smith, M. W. Lewis, P. Jarzabkowski, et al. (eds), *The Oxford handbook of organizational paradox* (pp. 216–238). Oxford, UK: Oxford University Press.

Cameron, K. S., & Lavine, M. (2006). *Making the impossible possible: Leading extraordinary performance: The Rocky Flats story.* San Francisco, CA: Berrett-Koehler.

Cameron, K. S., & Quinn, R. E. (1988). *Paradox and transformation: Toward a theory of change in organization and management.* Cambridge, MA: Ballinger Publishing Company.

Cameron, K. S., & Spreitzer, G. M. (2012). *The Oxford handbook of positive organizational scholarship.* Oxford, UK: Oxford University Press.

Cameron, K. S., Dutton, J., & Quinn, R. E. (2003a). *Positive organizational scholarship: Foundations of a new discipline.* San Francisco, CA: Berrett-Koehler.

Cameron, K. S., Dutton, J. E., & Quinn, R. E. (2003b). Foundations of positive organizational scholarship. In K. S. Cameron, J. E. Dutton, & R. E. Quinn (eds), *Positive organizational scholarship: Foundations of a new discipline* (pp. 3–13). San Francisco, CA: Berrett-Koehler.

Cameron, K. S., Quinn, R. E., DeGraff, J., & Thakor, A. V. (2014). *Competing values leadership*. Cheltenham, UK: Edward Elgar Publishing.

Campbell, P., Keohane, D., & Inagaki, K. (2019, 9 December). Staying together. *Financial Times*, 17.

Camus, A. (1955). *The myth of Sisyphus, and other essays*. New York, NY: Alfred A. Knopf.

Cappellaro, G., Compagni, A., & Vaara, E. (2021). Maintaining strategic ambiguity for protection: Struggles over opacity, equivocality, and absurdity around the Sicilian mafia. *Academy of Management Journal, 64*(1): 1–37.

Capra, F. (1975). *The Tao of physics: An exploration of the parallels between modern physics and eastern mysticism*. Boulder, CO: Shambhala.

Carlsen, A., & Sandelands, L. (2015). First passion: Wonder in organizational inquiry. *Management Learning, 46*(4): 373–390.

Carlsen, A., Clegg, S. R., Pitsis, T. S., & Mortensen, T. F. (2020). From ideas of power to the powering of ideas in organizations: Reflections from Follett and Foucault. *European Management Journal*, https://doi.org/10.1016/j.emj.2020.03.006

Carter, C., McKinlay, A., & Rowlinson, M. (2002). Introduction: Foucault, management and history. *Organization, 9*(4): 515–526.

Cassidy, J. (2020, 17 September). How Boeing and the F.A.A. created the 737 MAX catastrophe. *The New Yorker*, https: //www.newyorker.com/news/our-columnists/how-boeing-and-the-faa-created-the-737-max-catastrophe (accessed 30 November 2020).

Chen, M. J. (2002). Transcending paradox: The Chinese "middle way" perspective. *Asia Pacific Journal of Management, 19*(2–3): 179–199.

Child, C. (2019). Whence paradox? Framing away the potential challenges of doing well by doing good in social enterprise organizations. *Organization Studies, 41*(8): 1147–1167.

Cho, C. H., Laine, M., Roberts, R. W., & Rodrigue, M. (2015). Organized hypocrisy, organizational façades, and sustainability reporting. *Accounting, Organizations and Society, 40*, 78–94.

Chytry, J. (2003). Between polis and poiēsis: On the 'Cytherean' ambiguities in the poetry of James G. March. *Industrial and Corporate Change, 12*(4): 943–960.

Clair, J. A., & Dufresne, R. L. (2007). Changing poison into medicine: How companies can experience positive transformation from a crisis. *Organizational Dynamics, 36*(1): 63–77.

Clark, C. M., Tan, M. L., Murfett, U. M., Rogers, P. S., & Ang, S. (2019). The call center agent's performance paradox: A mixed-methods study of discourse strategies and paradox resolution. *Academy of Management Discoveries, 5*(2): 152–170.

Clarke, C. A., & Knights, D. (2014). It's a bittersweet symphony, this life: Fragile academic selves and insecure identities at work. *Organization Studies, 35*(3): 335–357.

Clarke, C., Knights, D., & Jarvis, C. (2012). A labour of love? Academics in business schools. *Scandinavian Journal of Management, 28*: 5–15.

Clegg, S. R. (1989). *Frameworks of power*. London, UK: Sage.

Clegg, S. R. (1990). *Modern organizations: Organization studies in the postmodern world*. London, UK: Sage.

Clegg, S. R. (1994). Weber and Foucault: Social theory for the study of organizations. *Organization, 1*(1): 149–178.

Clegg, S. R. (ed.) (2002). *Management and organization paradoxes.* Amsterdam: John Benjamins.

Clegg, S. R., & Cunha, M. P. (2017). Organizational dialectics. In W. K. Smith, M. W. Lewis, P. Jarzabkowski, & A. Langley (eds), *The Oxford handbook of organizational paradox* (pp. 105–124). Oxford, UK: Oxford University Press.

Clegg, S. R., & Dunkerley, D. (2013). *Organization, class and control.* London, UK: Routledge.

Clegg, S. R., Courpasson, D., & Phillips, N. (2006). *Power and organizations.* London, UK: Sage.

Clegg, S. R., Cunha, M. P., & Berti, M. (2020). Research movements and theorizing dynamics in management and organization studies. *Academy of Management Review.* Published online: 29 October 2020, https://doi.org/10.5465/amr.2018.0466t

Clegg, S. R., Cunha, J. V., & Cunha, M. P. (2002). Management paradoxes: A relational view. *Human Relations, 55*(5): 483–503.

Clegg, S. R., Cunha, M. P., & Rego, A. (2012). The theory and practice of utopia in a total institution: The pineapple panopticon. *Organization Studies, 33*(12): 1735–1757.

Clegg, S. R., van Rijmenam, M. H., & Schweitzer, J. (2019). The politics of openness. In D. Seidl, G. von Krogh, & R. Whittington (eds), *Cambridge handbook of open strategy,* vol. 1 (pp. 307–325). Cambridge, UK: Cambridge University Press.

Clegg, S. R., Cunha, M. P., Rego, A., & Dias, J. (2013). Mundane objects and the banality of evil: The sociomateriality of a death camp. *Journal of Management Inquiry, 22*(3): 325–340.

Clegg, S. R., Kornberger, M., Pitsis, T., & Mount, M. (2019). *Managing and organizations: An introduction to theory and practice* (5th edn). London, UK: Sage.

Clegg, S. R., Simpson, A., Berti, M., & Cunha, M. P. (2020). Artificial intelligence and the future of practical wisdom in business management. In B. Schwartz, C. Bernacchio, C. González-Cantón, et al. (eds), *Handbook of practical wisdom in business and management.* Cham, Switzerland: Springer.

Clegg, S. R., Cunha, M. P., Munro, I., Rego, A., & Sousa, M. O. (2016). Kafkaesque power and bureaucracy. *Journal of Political Power, 9*(2): 157–181.

Clift, B., & Robles, T. A. (2020). The IMF, tackling inequality, and post-neoliberal 'reglobalization': The paradoxes of political legitimation within economistic parameters. *Globalizations, 18*(1): 39–54.

Clifton, D. O., & Harter, J. K. (2003). Investing in strengths. In K. Cameron, J. Dutton, & R. Quinn (eds), *Positive organizational scholarship: Foundations of a new discipline* (pp. 111–121). Oakland, CA: Berrett-Koehler.

Cohen, S., & Taylor, L. (2003). *Escape attempts: The theory and practice of resistance in everyday life.* London, UK: Routledge.

Collins, J. C. & Porras, J. I. (2005). *Built to last: Successful habits of visionary companies.* New York, NY: Random House.

Coman, S., & Casey, A. (2021). The enduring presence of the founder. In M. Maclean, S. R. Clegg, R. Suddaby, & C. Harvey (eds), *Historical organization studies: Theory and applications* (pp. 131–148). London, UK: Routledge.

Cooper, R. (1986). Organization/disorganization. *Social Science Information, 25*(2): 299–335.

Cooren, F., & Seidl, D. (2020). Niklas Luhmann's radical communication approach and its implications for research on organizational communication. *Academy of Management Review*, *45*(2): 479–497.

Corritore, M., Goldberg, A., & Srivastava, S. B. (2020). The new analytics of culture. *Harvard Business Review*, *98*(1): 76–83.

Courpasson, D. (2000). Managerial strategies of domination. Power in soft bureaucracies. *Organization Studies*, *21*(1): 141–161.

Crossan, M., Mazutis, D., & Seijts, G. (2013). In search of virtue: The role of virtues, values and character strengths in ethical decision making. *Journal of Business Ethics*, *113*(4): 567–581.

Crowley, M., Payne, J. C., & Kennedy, E. (2014). Working better together? Empowerment, panopticon and conflict approaches to teamwork. *Economic and Industrial Democracy*, *35*(3): 483–506.

Crozier, M. (1964). *The bureaucratic phenomenon*. London, UK: Tavistock.

Cuganesan, S. (2017). Identity paradoxes: How senior managers and employees negotiate similarity and distinctiveness tensions over time. *Organization Studies*, *38*(3–4): 489–511.

Cunha, M. P., & Clegg, S. R. (2019). Improvisation in the learning organization: A defense of the infra-ordinary. *The Learning Organization*, *26*(3): 238–251.

Cunha, M. P., & Putnam, L. L. (2019). Paradox theory and the paradox of success. *Strategic Organization*, *17*(1): 95–106.

Cunha, M. P., & Tsoukas, H. (2015). Reforming the state: Understanding the vicious circles of reform. *European Management Journal*, *33*(4): 225–229.

Cunha, M. P., Clegg, S. R., Rego, A., & Berti, M. (2021). *Paradoxes of power and leadership*. Cheltenham, UK: Routledge.

Cunha, M. P., Clegg, S. R., Rego, A., & Lancione, M. (2012). The Organization (Ângkar) as a state of exception: The case of the S-21 extermination camp, Phnom Penh. *Journal of Political Power*, *5*(2): 279–299.

Cunha, M. P., Giustiniano, L., Rego, A., & Clegg, S.R. (2019a). Heaven or Las Vegas: Competing institutional logics and individual experience. *European Management Review*, *16*(3): 781–798.

Cunha, M. P., Guimarães-Costa, N., Rego, A., & Clegg, S. R. (2010). Leading and following (un)ethically in limen. *Journal of Business Ethics*, *97*(2): 189–206.

Cunha, M. P., Rego, A., Simpson, A. V., & Clegg, S. R. (2020). *Positive organizational behaviour: A reflective approach*. London, UK: Routledge.

Cunha, M. P., Simpson, A. V., Clegg, S., & Rego, A. (2019b). Speak! Paradoxical effects of a managerial culture of "speaking up". *British Journal of Management*, *30*(4): 829–846.

Cunha, M. P., Neves, P., Clegg, S. R., Costa, S., & Rego, A. (2018a). Paradoxes of organizational change in a merger context. *Qualitative Research in Organizations and Management: An International Journal*, *14*(3): 217–240.

Cunha, M. P. Cardona, M. J., Clegg, S.R., Gomes, J. F., Matallana, M., Rego, A., & Sánchez, I. D. (2018b). Through the looking glass: Leader personhood and the intersubjective construction of institutions. *Journal of Political Power*, *11*(3): 378–402.

Currie, G., Lockett, A., & Suhomlinova, O. (2009). The institutionalization of distributed leadership: A 'catch-22'in English public services. *Human Relations*, *62*(11): 1735–1761.

Czakon, W., Srivastava, M. K., Le Roy, F., & Gnyawali, D. (2020). Coopetition strategies: Critical issues and research directions. *Long Range Planning*, *53*(1): 101874.

Czarniawska, B. (1997). *Narrating the organization: Dramas of institutional identity.* Chicago, IL: University of Chicago Press.

Daar, A. S., Chang, T., Salomon, A., & Singer, A. (2018). Grand challenges in humanitarian aid. *Nature*, July: 169–173.

D'Adderio, L., Glaser, V., & Pollock, N. (2019). Performing theories, transforming organizations: A reply to Marti and Gond [letter to the editor]. *Academy of Management Review, 44*(3): 676–679.

Davies, A. (2019). Water wars: Will politics destroy the Murray-Darling Basin plan – and the river system itself? *The Guardian*, 14 December, https://www.theguardian .com/australia-news/2019/dec/14/water-wars-will-politics-destroy-the-murray -darling-basin-plan-and-the-river-system-itself (accessed 29 November 2020).

Davis, G. F. (2020). Corporate purpose needs democracy. *Journal of Management Studies*. Online first. DOI: 10.1111/JOMS.12659

Davis, M. S. (1971). That's interesting! Towards a phenomenology of sociology and a sociology of phenomenology. *Philosophy of the Social Sciences, 1*(2): 309–344.

De Rond, M. (2012). *There is an I in team: What elite athletes and coaches really know about high performance.* Boston, MA: Harvard Business Press.

Dekker, S. (2012). *Just culture: Balancing safety and accountability.* Farnham, UK: Ashgate Publishing Ltd.

Denis, J.-L., Langley, A., & Rouleau, L. (2007, 01/01). Strategizing in pluralistic contexts: Rethinking theoretical frames. *Human Relations, 60*, DOI: 10.1177/0018726707075288

Dewettinck, K., & Buyens, D. (2006). Linking behavioral control to employee outcomes: Testing two explanations using motivation theories. In *Academy of Management Proceedings*. Best conference paper.

Diamond, J. (2005). *Collapse: How societies choose to fail or succeed.* London, UK: Penguin.

Diamond, M. A. (1986). Resistance to change: A psychoanalytic critique of Argyris and Schon's contributions to organization theory and intervention. *Journal of Management Studies, 23*(5): 543–562.

Dodd, D., & Favaro, K. (2006). Managing the right tension. *Harvard Business Review, 84*(12): 62–74.

Dopson, S., & Neumann, J. E. (1998). Uncertainty, contrariness and the double-bind: Middle managers' reactions to changing contracts. *British Journal of Management, 9*(3): S53–S70.

Dougherty, D. (1992). Interpretive barriers to successful product innovation in large firms. *Organization Science, 3*(2): 179–202.

Douglas, M. (1986). *How institutions think.* Syracuse, NY: Syracuse University Press.

Drucker, P. F. (1995). Introduction: Mary Parker Follett: Prophet of management. In P. Graham (ed.), *Mary Parker Follett prophet of management: A celebration of writings from the 1920s* (pp. 1–10). Washington, DC: Beard Books.

Duran, J. (1993). Escher and Parmigianino: A study in paradox. *The British Journal of Aesthetics, 33*(3): 239–246.

Dutton, J. E., & Glynn, M. A. (2008). Positive organizational scholarship. In C. Cooper & J. Barling (eds), *Handbook of organizational behavior* (pp. 693–712). Thousand Oaks, CA: Sage.

Dylan, B. (1966). Stuck inside of Mobile (with the Memphis blues again). *Blonde on blonde.* New York, NY: Columbia CD.

Dylan, B. (2020). I contain multitudes. *Rough and rowdy ways.* New York, NY: Columbia CD.

Eden, C., Jones, S., Sims, D., & Smithin, T. (1981). The intersubjectivity of issues and issues of intersubjectivity. *Journal of Management Studies, 18*(1): 37–47.

Edmondson, A. C. (2018). *The fearless organization: Creating psychological safety in the workplace for learning, innovation, and growth.* New York, NY: John Wiley & Sons.

Edmondson, A. C., & Lei, Z. (2014). Psychological safety: The history, renaissance, and future of an interpersonal construct. *Annual Review of Organizational Psychology and Organizational Behavior, 1*(1): 23–43.

Ehrig, T., & Schmidt, J. (2019). Making biased but better predictions: The tradeoffs strategists face when they learn and use heuristics. *Strategic Organization.* Published online first. DOI: 10.1177/1476127019869646

Eisenberg, E. M. (1990). Jamming: Transcendence through organizing. *Communication Research, 17*(2): 139–164.

Eisenhardt, K. M. (2000). Paradox, spirals, ambivalence: The new language of change and pluralism. *Academy of Management Review, 25*(4): 703–705.

Ekman, S. (2012). *Authority and autonomy: Paradoxes in modern knowledge work.* Basingstoke, UK: Palgrave Macmillan.

Engeström, Y., & Sannino, A. (2011). Discursive manifestations of contradictions in organizational change efforts: A methodological framework. *Journal of Organizational Change Management, 24*(3): 368–387.

Escher, M. C. (2000). *MC Escher: The graphic work.* Köln: Taschen.

Es-Sajjade, A., Pandza, K., & Volberda, H. (2020). Growing pains: Paradoxical tensions and vicious cycles in new venture growth. *Strategic Organization.* First published 21 June 2020. DOI: 10.1177/1476127020929003

Ewing, J. (2017). *Faster, higher, farther: The inside story of the Volkswagen scandal.* New York, NY: Random House.

Eylon, D. (1998). Understanding empowerment and resolving its paradox. *Journal of Management History, 4*(1): 16–28.

Fairhurst, G. T. (2019). Reflections: Return paradox to the wild? Paradox interventions and their implications. *Journal of Change Management, 19*(1): 6–22.

Fairhurst, G. T., & Grant, D. (2010). The social construction of leadership: A sailing guide. *Management Communication Quarterly, 24*(2): 171–210.

Falk, A., & Kosfeld, M. (2006). The hidden costs of control. *The American Economic Review, 96*(5): 1611–1630.

Farjoun, M. (2010). Beyond dualism: Stability and change as a duality. *Academy of Management Review, 35*(2): 202–225.

Farjoun, M. (2019). Strategy and dialectics: Rejuvenating a long-standing relationship. *Strategic Organization, 17*(1): 133–144.

Farjoun, M., Smith, W., Langley, A., & Tsoukas, H. (eds) (2018). *Dualities, dialectics, and paradoxes in organizational life.* Oxford, UK: Oxford University Press.

Farson, R. (1996). *Management of the absurd.* New York, NY: Simon and Schuster.

Feather, N. T. (1989). Attitudes towards the high achiever: The fall of the tall poppy. *Australian Journal of Psychology, 41*(3): 239–267.

Feldman, M. S., & Orlikowski, W. J. (2011). Theorizing practice and practicing theory. *Organization Science, 22*: 1240–1253.

Fineman, S. (2006). On being positive: Concerns and counterpoints. *Academy of Management Review, 31*(2): 270–291.

Fiol, C. M. (2002). Capitalizing on paradox: The role of language in transforming organizational identities. *Organization Science, 13*(6): 653–666.

Fisher, C. D. (2010). Happiness at work. *International Journal of Management Reviews*, *12*(4): 384–412.

Fleming, P. (2013). 'Down with Big Brother!' The end of 'corporate culturalism'? *Journal of Management Studies*, *50*(3): 474–495.

Fleming, P., & Spicer, A. (2014). Power in management and organization science. *The Academy of Management Annals*, *8*(1): 237–298.

Follett, M. P. (1924). *Creative experience*. London: Longmans, Green and Company.

Follett, M. P. (1941 [2003]). *Dynamic administration: The collected papers of Mary Parker Follett: Early sociology of management and organizations*. Abingdon, UK: Routledge.

Follett, M. P. (1995). *Mary Parker Follett prophet of management: A celebration of writings from the 1920s*. Edited by P. Graham. Washington, DC: Beard Books.

Foucault, M. (1977). *Discipline and punish: The birth of the prison*. Trans. A. Sheridan. New York, NY: Pantheon.

Foucault, M. (1980). *Power/knowledge: Selected interviews and other writings, 1972–1977*. New York, NY: Harvester Wheatsheaf.

Foucault, M. (1984). Truth and power. In P. Rabinow (ed.), *The Foucault reader* (pp. 51–75). New York, NY: Pantheon Books.

Francis, H., & Keegan, A. (2018). The ethics of engagement in an age of austerity: A paradox perspective. *Journal of Business Ethics*, *162*: 593–607. DOI: 10.1007/s10551-018-3976-1

Fredrickson, B. (2009). *Positivity*. New York, NY: Crown.

Fredrickson, B. (2013). Updated thinking on positivity ratios. *American Psychologist*, *68*(8): 814–822.

Fredrickson, B. L. (2001). The role of positive emotions in positive psychology: The broaden-and-build theory of positive emotions. *American Psychologist*, *56*(3): 218.

Freedman, L. (2020). Strategy for a pandemic: The UK and COVID-19. *The Survival Editors' blog*, https://www.iiss.org/blogs/survival-blog/2020/05/the-uk-and-covid-19 (accessed 3 December 2020).

Friedman, M. (1970 [2007]). The social responsibility of business is to increase its profits. In W. C. Zimmerli, M. Holzinger, & K. Richter (eds), *Corporate ethics and corporate governance* (pp. 173–178). Berlin: Springer.

Fu, N., Flood, P. C., Rousseau, D. M., et al. (2020). Line managers as paradox navigators in HRM implementation: Balancing consistency and individual responsiveness. *Journal of Management*, *46*(2): 203–233.

Gaim, M., Clegg, S., & Cunha, M. P. (2019). Managing impressions rather than emissions: Volkswagen and the false mastery of paradox. *Organization Studies*. DOI: 10.1177/0170840619891199 9

Gaim, M., Wåhlin, N., & Jacobsson, M. (2019). The role of space for a paradoxical way of thinking and doing: A study of idea work in architectural firms. *Creativity and Innovation Management*, *28*(2): 265–281.

Gaim, M., Clegg, S. R., Cunha, M. P., & Berti, M. (2020). Responding to paradox: The role of intensity. Unpublished manuscript.

Gannon, M. J., & Pillai, R. (2015). *Understanding global cultures: Metaphorical journeys through 34 nations, clusters of nations, continents, and diversity*. Los Angeles, CA: Sage.

Gapper, J. (2011). "America's turbulent jobs flight". *Financial Times*, 27 July, https://www.ft.com/content/1d467a7c-b883-11e0-8206-00144feabdc0 (accessed 10 December 2020).

Garfinkel, H. (1967). *Studies in ethnomethodology*. Englewood Cliffs, NJ: Prentice Hall.

Garland, T., Jr. (2014). Trade-offs. *Current Biology, 24*(2): R60–R61.

Garud, R., Gehman, J., & Tharchen, T. (2018). Performativity as ongoing journeys: Implications for strategy, entrepreneurship, and innovation. *Long Range Planning, 51*(3): 500–509.

Gherardi, S. (1994). The gender we think, the gender we do in our everyday organizational lives. *Human Relations, 47*(6): 591–610.

Gherardi, S. (2012). *How to conduct a practice-based study: Problems and methods*. Northampton, MA: Edward Elgar Publishing.

Ghoshal, S. (2005). Bad management theories are destroying good management practices. *Academy of Management Learning & Education, 4*: 75.

Gibeau, É., Langley, A., Denis, J. L., & van Schendel, N. (2019). Bridging competing demands through co-leadership? Potential and limitations. *Human Relations, 73*(4). DOI: 0018726719888145

Gibson, C. B., & Birkinshaw, J. (2004). The antecedents, consequences, and mediating role of organizational ambidexterity. *Academy of Management Journal, 47*(2): 209–226.

Gimpl, M. L., & Dakin, S. R. (1984). Management and magic. *California Management Review, 27*(1): 125–136.

Giustiniano, L., Clegg, S. R., Cunha, M. P., & Rego, A. (2018). *Elgar introduction to theories of organizational resilience*. Cheltenham, UK: Edward Elgar Publishing.

Giustiniano, L., Cunha, M. P., Simpson, A. V., Rego, A., & Clegg, S. (2020). Resilient leadership as paradox work: Notes from COVID-19. *Management and Organization Review*. Online first: DOI: 10.1017/mor.2020.57

Goffman, E. (1959). *The presentation of self in everyday life*. New York, NY: Anchor Books for Doubleday.

Goldstein, J., Hazy, J. K., & Lichtenstein, B. B. (2010). The innovative power of positive deviance. In *Complexity and the nexus of leadership* (pp. 125–146). New York, NY: Palgrave Macmillan.

Goldstein, L. (1996). Reflexivity, contradiction, paradox and M. C. Escher. *Leonardo, 29*(4): 299–308.

Gondo, M. B., & Amis, J. M. (2013). Variations in practice adoption: The roles of conscious reflection and discourse. *Academy of Management Review, 38*(2): 229–247.

Goode, E. (1991). Positive deviance: A viable concept? *Deviant Behavior, 12*(3): 289–309.

Goodman, P. S. (2000). *Missing organizational linkages: Tools for cross-level research*. Thousand Oaks, CA: Sage.

Graen, G. B., & Uhl-Bien, M. (1995). Relationship-based approach to leadership: Development of leader-member exchange (LMX). Theory of leadership over 25 years: Applying a multi-level multi-domain perspective. *The Leadership Quarterly, 6*(2): 219–247.

Grebner, S., Semmer, N. K., & Elfering, A. (2005). Working conditions and three types of well-being: A longitudinal study with self-report and rating data. *Journal of Occupational Health Psychology, 10*(1): 31.

Greiner, L. E. (1998). Evolution and revolution as organizations grow. *Harvard Business Review, 76*(3): 55–64.

Gruber, J., & Trickett, E. J. (1987). Can we empower others? The paradox of empowerment in the governing of an alternative public school. *American Journal of Community Psychology, 15*(3): 353–371.

Guérard, S., Langley, A., & Seidl, D. (2013). Rethinking the concept of performance in strategy research: Towards a performativity perspective. *M@n@gement*, *16*(5): 566–578.

Guérin, P., Natalucci, F., & Suntheim, F. (2020). Firms' environmental performance in times of crisis. IMF Blog, 26 October 2020, https://blogs.imf.org/2020/10/26/firms-environmental-performance-in-times-of-crisis

Gümüsay, A. A., Smets, M., & Morris, T. (2020). "God at work": Engaging central and incompatible institutional logics through elastic hybridity. *Academy of Management Journal*, *63*(1): 124.

Gylfe, P., Franck, H., & Vaara, E. (2019). Living with paradox through irony. *Organizational Behavior and Human Decision Processes*, *155*: 68–82.

Habermas, J. (1975). *Legitimation crisis*. Boston, MA: Beacon Press.

Hahn, T., & Knight, E. (2019). The ontology of organizational paradox: A quantum approach. *Academy of Management Review*. Published online: 30 September 2019. DOI: 10.5465/amr.2018.0408

Hahn, T., Figge, F., Pinkse, J., & Preuss, L. (2010). Trade-offs in corporate sustainability: You can't have your cake and eat it. *Business Strategy and the Environment*, *19*(4): 217–229.

Hahn, T., Figge, F., Pinkse, J., & Preuss, L. (2018). A paradox perspective on corporate sustainability: Descriptive, instrumental, and normative aspects. *Journal of Business Ethics*, *148*(2): 235–248.

Halse, C., Honey, A., & Boughtwood, D. (2007). The paradox of virtue: (Re) thinking deviance, anorexia and schooling. *Gender and Education*, *19*(2): 219–235.

Hamel, G. (2007). *The future of management*. Boston, MA: Harvard Business Press.

Hannan, M. T., & Freeman, J. (1984). Structural inertia and organizational change. *American Sociological Review*, *49*(2): 149–164.

Hargrave, T. (2021). The paradox perspective and the dialectics of contradiction research. In M. S. Poole & A. Van de Ven (eds), *The Oxford handbook of organizational change and innovation* (2nd edn). New York, NY: Oxford University Press.

Hargrave, T. J., & Van de Ven, A. H. (2017). Integrating dialectical and paradox perspectives on managing contradictions in organizations. *Organization Studies*, *38*(3–4): 319–339.

Harris, C. J., & White, I. (1987). *Advances in command, control and communication systems*. London, UK: Peregrinus.

Harrison, J. S., Phillips, R. A., & Freeman, R. E. (2020). On the 2019 Business Roundtable "Statement on the Purpose of a Corporation". *Journal of Management*, *46*(7): 1223–1237.

Harrison, S., Carlsen, A., & Skerlavaj, M. (2019). Marvel's blockbuster machine: How the studio balances continuity and renewal. *Harvard Business Review*, *97*(4): 136–145.

Hatch, M. J. (1997). Irony and the social construction of contradiction in the humor of a management team. *Organization Science*, *8*(3): 275–288.

Hatch, M. J., & Erhlich, S. B. (1993). Spontaneous humour as an indicator of paradox and ambiguity in organizations. *Organization Studies*, *14*(4): 505–526.

Hatch, M. J., Schultz, M., & Skov, A. M. (2015). Organizational identity and culture in the context of managed change: Transformation in the Carlsberg Group, 2009–2013. *Academy of Management Discoveries*, *1*(1): 58–90.

Hegel, G. W. F. (1812 [2010]). *The science of logic*. Cambridge, UK: Cambridge University Press.

Heil, J. F. (1996). Why is Aristotle's brave man so frightened? The paradox of courage in the "eudemian ethics". *Apeiron, 29*(1): 47.

Helbling, T. (2020). Externalities: Prices do not capture all costs. *Finance & Development*, https://www.imf.org/external/pubs/ft/fandd/basics/external.htm (accessed 3 December 2020).

Heller, J. (1961 [2010]). *Catch-22: A novel*. London, UK: Vintage Books.

Hengst, I.-A., Jarzabkowski, P., Hoegl, M., & Muethel, M. (2020). Toward a process theory of making sustainability strategies legitimate in action. *Academy of Management Journal, 63*(1): 246–271.

Hennestad, B. W. (1990). The symbolic impact of double bind leadership: Double bind and the dynamics of organizational culture. *Journal of Management Studies, 27*(3): 265–280.

Heracleous, L., & Wirtz, J. (2014). Singapore Airlines: Achieving sustainable advantage through mastering paradox. *The Journal of Applied Behavioral Science, 50*(2): 150–170.

Heracleous, L., Papachroni, A., Andriopoulos, C., & Gotsi, M. (2017). Structural ambidexterity and competency traps: Insights from Xerox PARC. *Technological Forecasting and Social Change, 117*: 327–338.

Hernes, T., & Bakken, T. (2003). Implications of self-reference: Niklas Luhmann's autopoiesis and organization theory. *Organization Studies, 24*(9): 1511–1535.

Hill, A. (2019, 2 December). Messy jargon can swamp lucid business thinking. *Financial Times*, 14.

Hirsch, F. (1978). *Social limits to growth*. London, UK: Routledge and Kegan Paul.

Hodson, R., Martin, A. W., Lopez, S. H., & Roscigno, V. J. (2013a). Rules don't apply: Kafka's insights on bureaucracy. *Organization, 20*(2): 256–278.

Hodson, R., Roscigno, V. J., Martin, A., & Lopez, S. H. (2013b). The ascension of Kafkaesque bureaucracy in private sector organizations. *Human Relations, 66*(9): 1249–1273.

Howcroft, D., & Wilson, M. (2003). Paradoxes of participatory practices: The Janus role of the systems developer. *Information and Organization, 13*(1): 1–24.

Huppert, F. A. (2009). Psychological well-being: Evidence regarding its causes and consequences. *Applied Psychology: Health and Well-Being, 1*(2): 137–164.

Huq, J.-L., Reay, T., & Chreim, S. (2017). Protecting the paradox of interprofessional collaboration. *Organization Studies, 38*(3–4): 513–538.

Huy, Q. N. (2001). In praise of middle managers. *Harvard Business Review, 79*(8): 72–79.

ILO (2020). Global Wage Report 2020–21: Wages and minimum wages in the time of COVID-19, https://www.ilo.org/global/publications/books/WCMS_762534/lang --en/index.htm (accessed 3 December 2020).

IMF (International Monetary Fund) (2015). Guidance note for surveillance under Article IV consultation (*IMF Policy Papers*), https://www.imf.org/~/media/Websites/IMF/ imported-full-text-pdf/external/np/pp/eng/2015/_031915.ashx (accessed 3 December 2020).

Irvine, A. D., & Deutsch, H. (2016). Russell's paradox. In E. N. Zalta (ed.), *The Stanford Encyclopedia of Philosophy*. Winter 2016 edn.

Jackall, R. (1988). *Moral Maze*. Oxford, UK: Oxford University.

Jamet, E. (2019, 16 May). Jacinda Ardern or inclusive leadership exemplified. *Forbes*.

Jansen, K. J. (2004). From persistence to pursuit: A longitudinal examination of momentum during the early stages of strategic change. *Organization Science, 15*(3): 276–294.

Janssens, M., & Steyaert, C. (1999). The world in two and a third way out? The concept of duality in organization theory and practice. *Scandinavian Journal of Management*, *15*(2): 121–139.

Jarzabkowski, P. A., & Lê, J. K. (2017). We have to do this and that? You must be joking: Constructing and responding to paradox through humor. *Organization Studies*, *38*(3–4): 433–462.

Jarzabkowski, P., Bednarek, R., & Lê, J. (2018). Studying paradox as process and practice: Identifying and following moments of salience and latency. In M. Farjoun, W. Smith, A. Langley, & H. Tsoukas (eds), *Perspectives on process organization studies: Dualities, dialectics and paradoxes in organizational life* (pp. 175–194). Oxford: Oxford University Press.

Jarzabkowski, P., Lê, J. K., & Van de Ven, A. H. (2013). Responding to competing strategic demands: How organizing, belonging, and performing paradoxes coevolve. *Strategic Organization*, *11*(3): 245–280.

Jay, J. (2013). Navigating paradox as a mechanism of change and innovation in hybrid organizations. *Academy of Management Journal*, *56*(1): 137–159.

Jeffries, F. L., & Reed, R. (2000). Trust and adaptation in relational contracting. *Academy of Management Review*, *25*: 873–882.

Jennings, P. D., & Hoffman, A. J. (2019). Three paradoxes of climate truth for the Anthropocene social scientist. *Organization & Environment*. DOI: 1086026619858857

Johnson, B. (2014). Reflections: A perspective on paradox and its application to modern management. *The Journal of Applied Behavioral Science*, *50*(2): 206–212.

Joosten, A., Van Dijke, M., Van Hiel, A., et al. (2014). Being "in control" may make you lose control: The role of self-regulation in unethical leadership behavior. *Journal of Business Ethics*, *121*(1): 1–14.

Josserand, E., Teo, S., & Clegg, S. R. (2006). From bureaucratic to post-bureaucratic: The difficulties of transition. *Journal of Organizational Change Management*, *19*(1): 54–64.

Kafka, F. (1925 [2007]). *The Trial*. Trans. D. Wyllie. Teddington, UK: Echo.

Kafka, F. (1926 [2009]). *The Castle*. Trans. A. Bell. Oxford, UK: Oxford University Press.

Kaminska, I. (2019, 27 November). Gig employers are undermining the social contract. *Financial Times*, 9.

Kaplan, S. (2019). *The 360° corporation: From stakeholder trade-offs to transformation*. Stanford, CA: Stanford University Press.

Kaplan, R. S., & McMillan, D. (2020). Updating the business scorecard for triple bottom line strategies. Harvard Business School Working Paper 21-028.

Kaplan, R. S., & Norton, D. P. (1996a). Linking the balanced scorecard to strategy. *California Management Review*, *39*(1): 53–79.

Kaplan, R. S., & Norton, D. P. (1996b). Using the balanced score card as a strategic management system. *Harvard Business Review*, *74*(1): 75–85.

Katz, D., & Kahn, R. (1978). *The social psychology of organizations* (2nd edn). New York, NY: Wiley.

Kaufman, A., & Englander, E. (2005). A team production model of corporate governance. *Academy of Management Executive*, *19*(3): 9–22.

Keller, J., & Chen, E. W. (2017). A road map of the paradoxical mind. In W. K. Smith, M. W. Lewis, P. Jarzabkowski, & A. Langley (eds), *The Oxford handbook of organizational paradox* (pp. 66–86). Oxford, UK: Oxford University Press.

Keller, J., Loewenstein, J., & Yan, J. (2017). Culture, conditions and paradoxical frames. *Organization Studies*, *38*(3–4): 539–560.

Keller, J., Wong, S.-S., & Liou, S. (2020). How social networks facilitate collective responses to organizational paradoxes. *Human Relations*, *73*(3): 401–428.

Kenny, K. (2019). *Whistleblowing: Toward a new theory.* Cambridge, MA: Harvard University Press.

Kentikelenis, A. E., Stubbs, T. H., & King, L. P. (2016). IMF conditionality and development policy space, 1985–2014. *Review of International Political Economy*, *23*(4): 543–582.

Kets de Vries, M. F. R. (1995). *Organizational paradoxes: Clinical approaches to management.* London, UK: Routledge.

Kets de Vries, M. F. R. (2011). *The hedgehog effect: The secrets of building high performance teams.* New York, NY: John Wiley & Sons.

Keynes, J. M. (1930 [1963]). Economic possibilities for our grandchildren. In *Essays in Persuasion* (pp. 358–373). New York, NY: W. W. Norton & Co.

Khorasani, S. T., & Almasifar, M. (2017). Evolution of management theory within 20 century: A systemic overview of paradigm shifts in management. *International Review of Management and Marketing, 7*(3).

Kilduff, M., Mehra, A., & Dunn, M. B. (2011). From blue sky research to problem solving: A philosophy of science theory of new knowledge production. *Academy of Management Review*, *36*(2): 297–317.

Kirn, W. (2010, 15 February). The fakery of CEOs undercover. *Bloomberg BusinessWeek*, 78–79.

Kizilos, P. (1990). Crazy about empowerment? *Training*, December: 47–56.

Knight, E., & Paroutis, S. (2017). Becoming salient: The TMT leader's role in shaping the interpretive context of paradoxical tensions. *Organization Studies*, *38*(3–4): 403–432.

Korczynski, M. (2011). The dialectical sense of humour: Routine joking in a Taylorized factory. *Organization Studies*, *32*(10): 1421–1439.

Kraatz, M. S., & Block, E. S. (2008). Organizational implications of institutional pluralism. In R. Greenwood, C. Oliver, R. Suddaby, & K. Sahlin-Andersson (eds), *The Sage handbook of organizational institutionalism* (pp. 243–275). London, UK: Sage.

Lado, A. A., Boyd, N. G., Wright, P., & Kroll, M. (2006). Paradox and theorizing within the resource-based view. *Academy of Management Review*, *31*(1): 115–131.

Langfred, C. W. (2007). The downside of self-management: A longitudinal study of the effects of conflict on trust, autonomy, and task interdependence in self-managing teams. *Academy of Management Journal*, *50*(4): 885–900.

Langley, A., Smallman, C., Tsoukas, H., & Van de Ven, A. H. (2013). Process studies of change in organization and management: Unveiling temporality, activity, and flow. *Academy of Management Journal*, *56*(1): 1–13.

Law, J. (2008). On sociology and STS. *The Sociological Review, 56*(4): 623–649.

Lawrence, P. R., & Lorsch, J. W. (1967). *Organization and environment.* Boston, MA: Harvard University Press.

Leonard-Barton, D. (1992). Core capabilities and core rigidities: A paradox in managing new product development. *Strategic Management Journal, 13*(S1): 111–125.

Leonardi, P. (2020). You're going digital – now what? *MIT Sloan Management Review*, *61*(2) (Winter): 28–30, 32–35.

Levinson, H. M. (1960). Pattern bargaining: A case study of the automobile workers. *The Quarterly Journal of Economics*, *74*(2): 296–317.

Lévi-Strauss C. (1967). *Structural anthropology.* New York, NY: Doubleday Anchor Books.

Lewis, M. W. (2000). Exploring paradox: Toward a more comprehensive guide. *Academy of Management Review, 25*(4): 760–776.

Lewis, M. W., & Dehler, G. E. (2000). Learning through paradox: A pedagogical strategy for exploring contradictions and complexity. *Journal of Management Education, 24*(6): 708–725.

Lewis, M. W., & Smith, W. K. (2014). Paradox as a metatheoretical perspective: Sharpening the focus and widening the scope. *Journal of Applied Behavioral Science, 50(*2): 127–149.

Lewis, M. W., Andriopoulos, C., & Smith, W. K. (2014). Paradoxical leadership to enable strategic agility. *California Management Review, 56*(3): 58–77.

Lewis, M., Smith, W. K., Jarzabkowski, P., & Langley, A. (eds) (2017). *The Oxford handbook of organizational paradox: Approaches to plurality, tensions, and contradictions* (pp. 105–124). New York, NY: Oxford University Press.

Lewis, R. L., Brown, D. A., & Sutton, N. C. (2019). Control and empowerment as an organising paradox: Implications for management control systems. *Accounting, Auditing & Accountability Journal, 32*(2): 483–507.

Li, J., & Hambrick, D. C. (2005). Factional groups: A new vantage on demographic fault lines, conflict, and disintegration in work teams. *Academy of Management Journal, 48*(5): 794–813.

Li, P. P. (1998). Towards a geocentric framework of organizational form: A holistic, dynamic and paradoxical approach. *Organization Studies, 19*(5): 829–861.

Li, P. P. (2014). The unique value of Yin-Yang balancing: A critical response. *Management and Organization Review, 10*(2): 321–332.

Li, P. P. (2016). Global implications of the indigenous epistemological system from the East: how to apply Yin-Yang balancing to paradox management. *Cross Cultural & Strategic Management, 23*(1): 42–77.

Li, X. (2020). Solving paradox by reducing expectation. *Academy of Management Review.* Published online:7 May 2020. DOI: 10.5465/amr.2020.0005

Lindberg, O., Rantatalo, O., & Hällgren, M. (2017). Making sense through false syntheses: Working with paradoxes in the reorganization of the Swedish police. *Scandinavian Journal of Management, 33*(3): 175–184.

Lindgreen, A., & Maon, F. (2019). Organization and management paradoxes. *International Journal of Management Reviews, 21*(2): 139–142.

Lipsky, M. (2010). *Street-level bureaucracy: Dilemmas of the individual in public service.* New York, NY: Russell Sage Foundation.

Liu, Y., Xu, S., & Zhang, B. (2020). Thriving at work: How a paradox mindset influences innovative work behaviour. *Journal of Applied Behavioral Science, 56*(3): 347–366.

Locke, E. A. (1969). What is job satisfaction? *Organizational Behavior and Human Performance, 4*(4): 309–336.

Lockwood, C., Giorgi, S., & Glynn, M. A. (2019). "How to do things with words": Mechanisms bridging language and action in management research. *Journal of Management, 45*(1): 7–34.

Logue, D. M., Jarvis, W. P., Clegg, S. R., & Hermens, A. (2015). Translating models of organization: Can the Mittelstand move from Bavaria to Geelong? *Journal of Management & Organization, 21*(01): 17–36.

Lopes, P. (2005). Signifying deviance and transgression: Jazz in the popular imagination. *American Behavioral Scientist, 48*(11): 1468–1481.

Lounsbury, M., & Carberry, E. J. (2005). From king to court jester? Weber's fall from grace in organizational theory. *Organization Studies*, *26*(4): 0170–8406.

Luhmann, N. (1986). The autopoiesis of social systems. In F. Geyer & J. van der Zouwen (eds), *Sociocybernetic paradoxes*, vol. 6 (pp. 172–192). London, UK: SAGE.

Luhmann, N. (1995a). *Social systems*. Stanford, CA: Stanford University Press.

Luhmann, N. (1995b). The paradoxy of observing systems. *Cultural Critique*, *31*: 37–55.

Luhmann, N. (2018). *Organization and decision*. Cambridge, UK: Cambridge University Press.

Lüscher, L. S., & Lewis, M. W. (2008). Organizational change and managerial sensemaking: Working through paradox. *Academy of Management Journal*, *51*(2): 221–240.

Luscombe, B. (2020). A year after Christchurch, Jacinda Ardern has the world's attention. How will she use it? *Time*, 20 February.

Maak, T., & Pless, N. M. (2006). Responsible leadership in a stakeholder society – a relational perspective. *Journal of Business Ethics*, *66*(1): 99–115.

Mahoney, J. (1998). Editorial adieu: Cultivating moral courage in business. *Business Ethics: A European Review*, *7*(4): 187–192.

Manson, M. (2016). *The subtle art of not giving a f*ck: A counterintuitive approach to living a good life*. New York, NY: HarperCollins.

March, J. G. (ed.) (1965 [2013]). *Handbook of organizations*. Chicago, IL: Rand McNally.

March, J. G. (1991). Exploration and exploitation in organizational learning. *Organization Science*, *2*(1): 71–87.

March, J. G. (2006a). Poetry and the rhetoric of management: Easter 1916. *Journal of Management Inquiry*, *15*(1): 70–72.

March, J. G. (2006b). Rationality, foolishness, and adaptive intelligence. *Strategic Management Journal*, *27*(3): 201–214.

March, J. G., & Simon, H. A. (1958). *Organizations*. New York, NY: Wiley.

March, J. G., & Weil, T. (2009). *On leadership*. New York, NY: John Wiley & Sons.

March, J. G., Schulz, M., & Zhou, X. (2000). *The dynamics of rules: Change in written organizational codes*. Stanford, CA: Stanford University Press.

Marti, E., & Gond, J.-P. (2018). When do theories become self-fulfilling? Exploring the boundary conditions of performativity. *Academy of Management Review*, *43*(3): 487–508.

Martin, R. (2009). *The design of business: Why design thinking is the next competitive advantage*. Boston, MA: Harvard Business School Press.

Marx, K. (1973). *Grundrisse*. New York, NY: Vintage.

Marx, K. (1976). *Capital* (Vol. 1). London: NLR/Penguin.

Masters, B. (2019). Boeing will pay for cosy relations with regulators. *Financial Times*, 4 December, 13.

Masuch, .M (1985). Vicious circles in organizations. *Administrative Science Quarterly*, *30*(1): 14–33.

Mayer, C. (2020). The future of the corporation and the economics of purpose. *Journal of Management Studies*. DOI: 101111/JOMS.12660

McCabe, D. (2016). 'Curiouser and curiouser!': Organizations as Wonderland – a metaphorical alternative to the rational model. *Human Relations*, *69*(4): 945–973.

McKenna, B., Rooney, D., & Boal, K. B. (2009). Wisdom principles as a meta-theoretical basis for evaluating leadership. *The Leadership Quarterly*, *20*(2): 177–190.

McKenna, S., Garcia-Lorenzo, L., & Bridgman, T. (2010). Managing, managerial control and managerial identity in the post-bureaucratic world. *Journal of Management Development, 29*(2): 128–136.

McNulty, J. K., & Russell, V. M. (2010). When "negative" behaviors are positive: A contextual analysis of the long-term effects of problem-solving behaviors on changes in relationship satisfaction. *Journal of Personality and Social Psychology, 98*(4): 587–604.

McTague, T. (2020). How the pandemic revealed Britain's national illness. *The Atlantic*, 12 August 2020, https://www.theatlantic.com/international/archive/2020/08/why-britain-failed-coronavirus-pandemic/615166/ (accessed 3 December 2020).

Mease, J. J. (2019). Applied tensional analysis: Engaging practitioners and the constitutive shift. *Management Learning, 50*(4): 409–426.

Merton, R. K. (1936). The unanticipated consequences of purposive social action. *American Sociological Review, 1*(6): 894–904.

Metcalf, W. (1940). The reality of the unobservable. *Philosophy of Science, 7*(3): 337–341.

Methmann, C. P. (2010). 'Climate protection' as empty signifier: A discourse theoretical perspective on climate mainstreaming in world politics. *Millennium, 39*(2): 345–372.

Meyer, J. W., & Rowan, B. (1977). Institutionalized organizations: Formal structure as myth and ceremony. *American Journal of Sociology, 83*(2): 340–363.

Meyerson, D. E., & Scully, M. A. (1995). Crossroads tempered radicalism and the politics of ambivalence and change. *Organization Science, 6*(5): 585–600.

Miao, Q., Newman, A., Yu, J., et al. (2013). The relationship between ethical leadership and unethical pro-organizational behavior: Linear or curvilinear effects? *Journal of Business Ethics, 116*(3): 641–653.

Michel, A. (2014). The mutual constitution of persons and organizations: An ontological perspective on organizational change. *Organization Science, 25*(4): 1082–1110.

Mikkelsen, E. N., & Wahlin, R. (2020). Dominant, hidden and forbidden sensemaking: The politics of ideology and emotions in diversity management. *Organization, 27*(4): 557–577.

Miller, D. (1993). The architecture of simplicity. *Academy of Management Review, 18*(1): 116.

Miller, D., & Friesen, P. H. (1980). Momentum and revolution in organizational adaptation. *Academy of Management Journal, 23*(4): 591–614.

Miller, D., & Le Breton-Miller, I. (2005). *Managing for the long run: Lessons in competitive advantage from great family businesses.* Boston, MA: Harvard Business Press.

Miron-Spektor, E., Gino, F., & Argote, L. (2011). Paradoxical frames and creative sparks: Enhancing individual creativity through conflict and integration. *Organizational Behavior and Human Decision Processes, 116*(2): 229–240.

Miron-Spektor, E., Ingram, A., Keller, J., Smith, W. K., & Lewis, M. W. (2018). Microfoundations of organizational paradox: The problem is how we think about the problem. *Academy of Management Journal, 61*(1): 26–45.

Miska, C., & Mendenhall, M. E. (2018). Responsible leadership: A mapping of extant research and future directions. *Journal of Business Ethics, 148*(1): 117–134.

Momani, B. (2010). Internal or external norm champions: The IMF and multilateral debt relief. In S. Park & A. Vetterlein (eds), *Owning development: Creating policy norms in the IMF and the World Bank* (pp. 29–47). New York, NY: Cambridge University Press.

Morgan, G. (2011). Reflections on images of organization and its implications for organization and environment. *Organization & Environment, 24*(4): 459–478.

Murnighan, J. K., & Conlon, D. E. (1991). The dynamics of intense work groups: A study of British string quartets. *Administrative Science Quarterly, 36*(2): 165–186.

Murrell, K. L. (1985). The development of a theory of empowerment: Rethinking power for organization development. *Organization Development Journal*, Summer: 34–38.

Nagel, T. (1986). *The view from nowhere.* New York, NY: Oxford University Press.

Neumann, J. E., James, K. T., & Vince, R. (2019). Key tensions in purposive action by middle managers leading change. In A. B. Shani & D. A. Noumair (eds), *Research in Organizational Change and Development, 27*: 111–140.

Newark, D. (2018). Leadership and the logic of absurdity. *Academy of Management Review, 43*(2): 198–216.

Nguyen-Vo, T.-H. (2012). *The ironies of freedom: Sex, culture, and neoliberal governance in Vietnam.* Seattle, WA: University of Washington Press.

Nicolini, D. (2009). Zooming in and out: Studying practices by switching theoretical lenses and trailing connections. *Organization Studies, 30*(12): 1391–1418.

Nussbaum, M. C. (2003). *Upheavals of thought: The intelligence of emotions.* Cambridge, UK: Cambridge University Press.

Oakley, J. G. (2000). Gender-based barriers to senior management positions: Understanding the scarcity of female CEOs. *Journal of Business Ethics, 27*(4): 321–334.

Offe, C., & Wiesenthal, H. (1980). Two logics of collective action: Theoretical notes on social class and organizational form. *Political Power and Social Theory, 1*(1): 67–115.

O'Neill, O. A., Stanley, L. J., & O'Reilly, C. A. (2011). Disaffected Pollyannas: The influence of positive affect on salary expectations, turnover, and long-term satisfaction. *Journal of Occupational and Organizational Psychology, 84*(3): 599–617.

O'Reilly III, C. A., & Tushman, M. L. (2013). Organizational ambidexterity: Past, present, and future. *Academy of Management Perspectives, 27*(4): 324–338.

Orlikowski, W. J., & Scott, S. V. (2008). Sociomateriality: Challenging the separation of technology, work and organization. *Academy of Management Annals, 2*(1): 433–474.

Ortiz, J. T. (2020). Political leadership for peace processes: Juan Manuel Santos – between hawk and dove. *Leadership.* DOI: 10.1177/1742715020951229

Orwell, G. (1946) Politics and the English language. *Horizon* (April 1946 issue), http://www.public-library.uk/ebooks/72/30.pdf

Orwell, G. (1949). *Nineteen Eighty-Four.* London, UK: Martin Secker & Warburg.

Ostry, J. D., Loungani, P., & Furceri, D. (2016). Neoliberalism: Oversold. *Finance & Development, 53*(2): 38–41.

Owens, B. P., Johnson, M. D., & Mitchell, T. R. (2013). Expressed humility in organizations: Implications for performance, teams, and leadership. *Organization Science, 24*(5): 1517–1538.

Owens, B. P., Wallace, A. S., & Waldman, D. A. (2015). Leader narcissism and follower outcomes: The counterbalancing effect of leader humility. *Journal of Applied Psychology, 100*(4): 1203–1213.

Oxfam (2020). IMF paves way for new era of austerity post-COVID-19, https://www.oxfam.org/en/press-releases/imf-paves-way-new-era-austerity-post-covid-19 (accessed 30 November 2020).

Oxfam Canada (2016). *An economy for the 1%.* www.oxfam.ca/our-work/publications/ an-economy-for-the-1 (accessed 30 January 2020).

Pache, A.-C., & Santos, F. (2012). Inside the hybrid organization: Selective coupling as a response to competing institutional logics. *Academy of Management Journal, 56*(4): 972–1001.

Pacheco de Almeida, G., Henderson, J. E., & Cool, K. O. (2008). Resolving the commitment versus flexibility trade-off: The role of resource accumulation lags. *Academy of Management Journal, 51*(3): 517–536.

Padavic, I., Ely, R. J., & Reid, E. M. (2020). Explaining the persistence of gender inequality: The work–family narrative as a social defense against the 24/7 work culture. *Administrative Science Quarterly, 65*(1): 61–111.

Page, R. (2011). Co-determination in Germany – a beginners' guide. Arbeitspapiere, 33. Düsseldorf: Hans-Böckler-Stiftung.

Palmer, D. (2012). *Normal organizational wrongdoing: A critical analysis of theories of misconduct in and by organizations.* Oxford, UK: Oxford University Press.

Papachroni, A., & Heracleous, L. (2020). Ambidexterity as practice: Individual ambidexterity through paradoxical practices. *The Journal of Applied Behavioral Science, 56*(2): 143–165.

Parsons, T. (1963). On the concept of political power. *Proceedings of the American Philosophical Society, 107*(3): 232–258.

Parsons, T. (1964). Evolutionary universals in society. *American Sociological Review, 29*(3): 339–357.

Pascale, R. T., & Sternin, J. (2005). Your company's secret change agents. *Harvard Business Review, 83*(5): 72–81.

Pérezts, M., Bouilloud, J.-P., & de Gaulejac, V. (2011). Serving two masters: The contradictory organization as an ethical challenge for managerial responsibility. *Journal of Business Ethics, 101*(1): 33–44.

Perrow, C. (1977). The bureaucratic paradox: The efficient organization centralizes in order to decentralize. *Organizational Dynamics, 5*(4): 3–14.

Peters, T., & Waterman, R. H. (1982). *In search of excellence: Lessons from America's best-run companies.* New York, NY: Harper & Row.

Peterson, C., & Park, N. (2011). Character strengths and virtues: Their role in well-being. In S. I. Donaldson, M. Csikszentmihalyi, & J. Nakamura (eds), *Applied positive psychology: Improving everyday life, health, schools, work, and society* (pp. 49–62). New York, NY: Psychology Press.

Peterson, C., & Seligman, M. E. P. (2004). *Character strengths and virtues: A handbook and classification.* New York, NY: Oxford University Press.

Petriglieri, G. (2020). F**k science!? An invitation to humanize organization theory. *Organization Theory.* First published 23 January 2020. DOI: 10.1177/2631787719897663

Petriglieri, G., & Petriglieri, J. (2020). The return of the oppressed: A systems psychodynamic approach to organization studies. *Academy of Management Annals, 14*(1): 411–449.

Petriglieri, G., Petriglieri, J. L., & Wood, J. D. (2018). Fast tracks and inner journeys: Crafting portable selves for contemporary careers. *Administrative Science Quarterly, 63*(3): 479–525.

Pfeffer, J., & Sutton, R. I. (2006). *Hard facts, dangerous half-truths, and total nonsense: Profiting from evidence-based management.* Harvard, MA: Harvard Business School Press.

Pierce, J. R., & Aguinis, H. (2013). The too-much-of-a-good-thing effect in management. *Journal of Management, 39*(2): 313–338.

Pigou, A. C. (2013). *The economics of welfare.* London: Palgrave Macmillan.

Piketty, T. (2014). *Capital in the twenty first century.* Cambridge, MA: Harvard University Press.

Piketty, T. (2020). *Capital and ideology.* Cambridge, MA: Harvard University Press.

Pink, D. (2009). *Drive.* New York, NY: Penguin Books.

Pinkse, J., Hahn, T., & Figge, F. (2019). Supersized tensions and slim responses? The discursive construction of strategic tensions around social issues. *Academy of Management Discoveries, 5*(3): 314–340.

Pirson, M. (2019). A humanistic perspective for management theory: Protecting dignity and promoting well-being. *Journal of Business Ethics, 159*(1): 39–57.

Poole, M. S., & Van de Ven, A. H. (1989). Using paradox to build management and organization theories. *Academy of Management Review, 14*(4): 562–578.

Porter, E. (2002). *What is this thing called jazz? African American musicians as artists, critics, and activists.* Berkeley, CA: University of California Press.

Porter, M. E., & Kramer, M. R. (2011). Creating shared value. *Harvard Business Review, 89*(1/2): 62–77.

Pradies, C., Tunarosa, A., Lewis, M. W., & Courtois, J. (2020). From vicious to virtuous paradox dynamics: The social-symbolic work of supporting actors. *Organization Studies.* First published 18 March 2020. DOI: 10.1177/0170840620907200

Pratt, M. G., & Foreman, P. O. (2000). Classifying managerial responses to multiple organizational identities. *Academy of Management Review, 25*(1): 18–42.

Priest, G. (1979). The logic of paradox. *Journal of Philosophical Logic, 8*: 219–241.

Priest, G., Berto, F., & Weber, Z. (2018). Dialetheism. *The Stanford encyclopedia of philosophy* (Fall 2018 edn), https://plato.stanford.edu/entries/dialetheism/ (accessed 10 December 2020).

Prillaman, S. A., & Meier, K. J. (2014). Taxes, incentives, and economic growth: Assessing the impact of pro-business taxes on US state economies. *The Journal of Politics, 76*(2): 364–379.

Putnam, L. L. (1986). Contradictions and paradoxes in organizations. In L. Thayer (ed.), *Organization communications: Emerging perspectives* (pp. 151–167). Norwood, NJ: Ablex Publishing.

Putnam, L. L., & Ashcraft, K. L. (2017). Gender and organizational paradox. In W. K. Smith, M. W. Lewis, P. Jarzabkowski, & A. Langley (eds), *The Oxford handbook of organizational paradox* (pp. 331–352). Oxford, UK: Oxford University Press.

Putnam, L. L., Fairhurst, G. T., & Banghart, S. (2016). Contradictions, dialectics, and paradoxes in organizations: A constitutive approach. *Academy of Management Annals, 10*(1): 65–171.

Putnam, L. L., Myers, K. K., & Gailliard, B. M. (2014). Examining the tensions in workplace flexibility and exploring options for new directions. *Human Relations, 67*(4): 413–440.

Quinn, R. E. (1988). *Beyond rational management: Mastering the paradoxes and competing demands of high performance.* San Francisco, CA: Jossey-Bass.

Quinn, R. E. (2015). *The positive organization: Breaking free from conventional cultures, constraints, and beliefs.* San Francisco, CA: Berrett-Koehler Publishers.

Quinn, R. E., & Cameron, K. S. (1988). *Paradox and transformation: Toward a theory of change in organization and management.* New York, NY: Ballinger.

Quinn, R. E., & McGrath, M. R. (1985). The transformation of organizational cultures: A competing values perspective. In P. J. Frost, L. Moore, M. R. Louis, et al. (eds), *Organizational culture*. Thousand Oaks, CA: Sage.

Raisch, S., Hargrave, T. J., & Van De Ven, A. H. (2018). The learning spiral: A process perspective on paradox. *Journal of Management Studies, 55*(8): 1507–1526.

Raisch, S., Birkinshaw, J., Probst, G., & Tushman, M. L. (2009). Organizational ambidexterity: Balancing exploitation and exploration for sustained performance. *Organization Science, 20*(4): 685–695.

Ramarajan, L. (2014). Past, present and future research on multiple identities: Toward an intrapersonal network approach. *Academy of Management Annals, 8*(1): 589–659.

Ramoglou, S., & Tsang, E. W. (2016). A realist perspective of entrepreneurship: Opportunities as propensities. *Academy of Management Review, 41*(3): 410–434.

Raza-Ullah, T., Bengtsson, M., & Kock, S. (2014). The coopetition paradox and tension in coopetition at multiple levels. *Industrial Marketing Management, 43*(2): 189–198.

Reardon, K. (2007). Courage as a skill. *Harvard Business Review*, January: 58–64.

Reay, T., & Hinings, C. R. (2009). Managing the rivalry of competing institutional logics. *Organization Studies, 30*(6): 629–652.

Rego, A., Cunha, M. P., & Clegg, S. R. (2012). *The virtues of leadership: Contemporary challenges for global managers.* Oxford, UK: Oxford University Press.

Rego, A., Owens, B., Yam, K. C., et al. (2019). Leader humility and team performance: Exploring the mediating mechanisms of team PsyCap and task allocation effectiveness. *Journal of Management, 45*(3): 1009–1033.

Repenning, N. P., & Sterman, J. D. (2002). Capability traps and self-confirming attribution errors in the dynamics of process improvement. *Administrative Science Quarterly, 47*(2): 265–295.

Rescher, N. (1960). Choice without preference. A study of the history and of the logic of the problem of "Buridan's Ass". *Kant-Studien, 51*(1–4): 142–175.

Rescher, N. (2001). *Paradoxes: Their roots, range, and resolution.* Chicago, IL: Open Court.

Ritzer, G. (1975). *Sociology: A multiple paradigm science.* Boston, MA: Allyn & Bacon.

Ritzer, G. (1990). Metatheorizing in sociology: The basic parameters and the potential contributions of postmodernism. *Sociological Forum, 5*(1): 3–15.

Ritzer, G. (1993). *The McDonaldization of society.* London, UK: Pine Forge Press.

Riviezzo, A., Garofano, A., Napolitano, M. R., & Marino, V. (2015). Moving forward or running to standstill? Exploring the nature and the role of family firms' strategic orientation. *Journal of Family Business Strategy, 6*(3): 190–205.

Rizio, S. M., & Skali, A. (2019). How often do dictators have positive economic effects? Global evidence, 1858–2010. *The Leadership Quarterly*. Published 1 June 2019.

Ro, C. (2020). The Covid-19 recession is unique among modern economic shocks in its harm to women's finances and prospects. Can this be reversed? https://www.bbc.com/worklife/article/20201021-why-this-recession-disproportionately-affects-women (accessed 5 December 2020).

Roberts, K. H., & Rousseau, D. M. (1989). Research in nearly failure-free, high-reliability organizations: Having the bubble. *IEEE Transactions on Engineering Management, 36*(2): 132–139.

Roberts, L. M. (2006). Shifting the lens on organizational life: The added value of positive scholarship. *Academy of Management Review, 31*(2): 292–305.

Romanelli, E., & Tushman, M. L. (1994). Organizational transformation as punctuated equilibrium: An empirical test. *Academy of Management Journal, 37*(5): 1141–1166.

Rowden, R. (2013). *The deadly ideas of neoliberalism: How the IMF has undermined public health and the fight against AIDS*. London, UK: Zed Books.

Sandelands, L. E., & Carlsen, A. (2013). The romance of wonder in organization studies. *Journal of Management, Spirituality & Religion, 10*(4): 358–379.

Sasaki, I., Ravasi, D., & Micelotta, E. (2019). Family firms as institutions: Cultural reproduction and status maintenance among multi-centenary shinise in Kyoto. *Organization Studies, 40*(6): 793–831.

Schabram, K., & Maitlis, S. (2017). Negotiating the challenges of a calling: Emotion and enacted sensemaking in animal shelter work. *Academy of Management Journal, 60*(2): 584–609.

Schad, J. (2017). Ad Fontes. Philosophical foundations of paradox research. In W. K. Smith, M. W. Lewis, P. Jarzabkowski, & A. Langley (eds), *The Oxford handbook of organizational paradox* (pp. 27–47). Oxford, UK: Oxford University Press.

Schad, J., & Bansal, P. (2018). Seeing the forest and the trees: How a systems perspective informs paradox research. *Journal of Management Studies, 55*(8): 1490–1506.

Schad, J., & Smith, W. K. (2019). Addressing grand challenges' paradoxes: Leadership skills to manage inconsistencies. *Journal of Leadership Studies, 12*(4): 55–59.

Schad, J., Lewis, M. W., & Smith, W. K. (2019). Quo vadis, paradox? Centripetal and centrifugal forces in theory development. *Strategic Organization, 17*(1): 107–119.

Schad, J., Lewis, M. W., Raisch, S., & Smith, W. K. (2016). Paradox research in management science: Looking back to move forward. *The Academy of Management Annals, 10*(1): 5–64.

Schattschneider, E. E. (1960). *The semi-sovereign people*. New York, NY: Holt, Reinhart, and Winston.

Schilling, M. A. (2000). Decades ahead of her time: Advancing stakeholder theory through the ideas of Mary Parker Follett. *Journal of Management History, 6*(5): 224–242.

Schulz, M., Hatch, M. J., & Larsen, M. H. (eds) (2000). *The expressive organization: Linking identity, reputation and the corporate brand*. Oxford, UK: Oxford University Press.

Schütz, A. (1974). *The structures of the life-world*. London, UK: Heinemann.

Schwartz, B. (2011). Practical wisdom and organizations. *Research in Organizational Behavior, 31*: 3–23.

Seidl, D. (2004). Luhmann's theory of autopoietic social systems. Working paper. Ludwig-Maximilians-Universität München-Munich School of Management, https://www.zfog.bwl.uni-muenchen.de/files/mitarbeiter/paper2004_2.pdf. (accessed 9 December 2020).

Seidl, D., & Mormann, H. (2014). Niklas Luhmann as organization theorist. In P. Adler, P. du Gay, G. Morgan, & M. Reed (eds), *Oxford handbook of sociology, social theory and organization studies: Contemporary currents* (pp. 125–157). Oxford, UK: Oxford University Press.

Seltzer, L. F. (1986). *Paradoxical strategies in psychotherapy: A comprehensive overview and guidebook*. New York, NY: John Wiley & Sons.

Seo, M., Putnam, L. L., & Bartunek, J. M. (2004). Dualities and tensions of planned organizational change. In M. S. Poole & A. H. Van de Ven (eds), *Handbook of organizational change and innovation* (pp. 73–107). New York, NY: Oxford University Press.

Sewell, G., & Wilkinson, B. (1992). Empowerment or emasculation? Shopfloor surveillance in a Total Quality Organization. In P. Blyton & P. Turnbull (eds), *Reassessing human resource management* (pp. 97–115). London, UK: Sage.

Shapira, Z. (2011). "I've got a theory paper – do you?": Conceptual, empirical, and theoretical contributions to knowledge in the organizational sciences. *Organization Science*, *22*(5): 1312–1321.

Sharma, G., & Bansal, P. (2017). Partners for good: How business and NGOs engage the commercial–social paradox. *Organization Studies*, *38*(3–4): 341–364.

Sheep, M. L., Fairhurst, G. T., & Khazanchi, S. (2017). Knots in the discourse of innovation: Investigating multiple tensions in a reacquired spin-off. *Organization Studies*, *38*(3–4): 463–488.

Shenhav, Y. (1995). From chaos to systems: The engineering foundations of organization theory, 1879–1932. *Administrative Science Quarterly*, *40*: 557–585.

Silva, T., Cunha, M. P., Clegg, S. R., Neves, P., Rego, A., & Rodrigues, R. A. (2014). Smells like team spirit: Opening a paradoxical black box. *Human Relations*, *67*(3): 287–310.

Simon, B. L. (1990). Rethinking empowerment. *Journal of Progressive Human Services*, *1*(1): 27–39.

Simon, H. (1996). *The sciences of the artificial*. Cambridge, MA: The MIT Press.

Simons, R. (1995). *Levels of control*. Boston, MA: Harvard Business School Press.

Simpson, A. V., & Berti, M. (2020). Transcending organizational compassion paradoxes by enacting wise compassion courageously. *Journal of Management Inquiry*, *29*(4): 433–449.

Simpson, A. V., Clegg, S., & Freeder, D. (2013). Power, compassion and organization. *Journal of Political Power*, *6*(3): 385–404.

Simpson, A. V., Clegg, S., Lopes, M. P., et al. (2014a). Doing compassion or doing discipline? Power relations and the Magdalene Laundries. *Journal of Political Power*, *7*(2): 253–274.

Simpson, A. V., Clegg, S., & Pitsis, T. (2014b). Normal compassion: A framework for compassionate decision making. *Journal of Business Ethics*, *119*(4): 473–491.

Skousen, M., & Taylor, K. C. (1997). *Puzzles and paradoxes in economics*. Cheltenham, UK: Edward Elgar Publishing.

Smets, M., Jarzabkowski, P., Burke, G. T., & Spee, P. (2015). Reinsurance trading in Lloyd's of London: Balancing conflicting-yet-complementary logics in practice. *Academy of Management Journal*, *58*(3): 932.

Smets, M., Moss Cowan, A., Athanasopoulou, A., Moos, C., & Morris, T. J. (2019). Taking to making paradox: A multi-level perspective on how CEOs balance nested paradoxes. *Academy of Management Proceedings*, 2019(1): 18917.

Smith, I.H., & Kouchaki, M. (2018). Moral humility: In life and at work. *Research in Organizational Behavior*, *38*: 77–94.

Smith, K. K., & Berg, D. N. (1987). *Paradoxes of group life: Understanding conflict, paralysis, and movement in group dynamics.* San Francisco, CA: Jossey-Bass.

Smith, W. K. (2014). Dynamic decision making: A model of senior leaders managing strategic paradoxes. *Academy of Management Journal*, *57*(6): 1592–1623.

Smith, W. K., & Besharov, M. L. (2019). Bowing before dual gods: How structured flexibility sustains organizational hybridity. *Administrative Science Quarterly*, *64*(1): 1–44.

Smith, W. K., & Lewis, M. W. (2011). Toward a theory of paradox: A dynamic equilibrium model of organizing. *Academy of Management Review*, *36*(2): 381–403.

Smith, W. K., & Lewis, M. W. (2012). Leadership skills for managing paradoxes. *Industrial and Organizational Psychology, 5*(2): 227–231.

Smith, W. K., & Tushman, M. L. (2005). Managing strategic contradictions: A top management model for managing innovation streams. *Organization Science, 16*(5): 522–536.

Smith, W. K., Lewis, M. W., & Tushman, M. L. (2016). Both/and leadership. *Harvard Business Review, 94*(5): 62–70.

Smith, W. K., Erez, M., Jarvenpaa, S., Lewis, M. W., & Tracey, P. (2017). Adding complexity to theories of paradox, tensions, and dualities of innovation and change: Introduction to Organization Studies special issue on paradox, tensions, and dualities of innovation and change. *Organization Studies, 38*(3–4): 303–317.

Smythe, J. (2019). Jacinda Ardern's 'solace and steel' seen uniting New Zealand. *Financial Times*, 22 March.

Soderstrom, S. B., & Heinze, K. L. (2019). From paradoxical thinking to practicing sustainable business: The role of a business collective organization in supporting entrepreneurs. *Organization & Environment.* First published 6 November 2019, DOI: 10.1177/1086026619885108

Sorensen, R., & Sainsbury, M. (2020). The number of unknown paradoxes. *Philosophy, 95*(2): 155–159.

Spreitzer, G. M., & Sonenshein, S. (2003). Positive deviance and extraordinary organizing. In K. S. Cameron, J. E. Dutton, & R. E. Quinn (eds), *Positive organizational scholarship* (pp. 207–224). San Francisco, CA: Berrett Koehler.

Spreitzer, G. M., & Sonenshein, S. (2004). Toward the construct definition of positive deviance. *American Behavioral Scientist, 47*(6): 828.

Stacey, K. (2019). Boeing staffer warned of 737 Max risk. *Financial Times*, 12 December, 12.

Stacey, R. D. (1996). *Complexity and creativity in organizations.* Oakland, CA: Berrett-Koehler Publishers.

Stacey, R. D., Griffin, D., & Shaw, P. (2002). *Complexity and management.* London, UK: Routledge.

Stadtler, L., & Van Wassenhove, L. N. (2016). Coopetition as a paradox: Integrative approaches in a multi-company, cross-sector partnership. *Organization Studies, 37*(5): 655–685.

Stark, D. (1999). Heterarchy: Distributing authority and organizing diversity. In J. H. Clippinger III (ed.), *The biology of business: Decoding the natural laws of enterprise* (pp. 153–179). San Francisco, CA: Jossey-Bass.

Stearns, S. C. (1989). Trade-offs in life-history evolution. *Functional Ecology, 3*(3): 259–268.

Stein, M. (2003). Unbounded irrationality: Risk and organizational narcissism at long term capital management. *Human Relations, 56*(5): 523–540.

Sterman, J. D., Repenning, N. P., & Kofman, F. (1997). Unanticipated side effects of successful quality programs: Exploring a paradox of organizational improvement. *Management Science, 43*(4): 503–521.

Stinchcombe, A. L. (1965). Social structure and organizations. In J. A. C. Baum & F. Dobbin (eds), *Economics meets sociology in strategic management. Advances in strategic management, volume 17* (pp. 229–259). Bingley, UK: Emerald.

Stohl, C., & Stohl, M. (2017). Clandestine/hidden organizations. In *The international encyclopedia of organizational communication* (pp. 1–9). Chichester, UK and New York, NY: London: John Wiley & Sons.

Stouten, J., Van Dijke, M., Mayer, D. M., et al. (2013). Can a leader be seen as too ethical? The curvilinear effects of ethical leadership. *The Leadership Quarterly, 24*(5): 680–695.

Streatfield, P. J. (2001). *The paradox of control in organizations.* London, UK: Routledge.

Strese, S., Meuer, M. W., Flatten, T. C., & Brettel, M. (2016). Examining cross-functional coopetition as a driver of organizational ambidexterity. *Industrial Marketing Management, 57*: 40–52.

Suchman, M. C. (1995). Managing legitimacy: Strategic and institutional approaches. *Academy of Management Review, 20*(3): 571–610.

Sull, D. N., & Eisenhardt, K. M. (2015). *Simple rules: How to thrive in a complex world.* Houghton Mifflin Harcourt.

Sundaramurthy, C., & Lewis, M. (2003). Control and collaboration: Paradoxes of governance. *Academy of Management Review, 28*(3): 397–415.

Switek, G. (2016). A simple idea in architecture: On the principles of projecting prisons. In J. Simon, T. Nicholas, & R. Tobe (eds), *Architecture and justice: Judicial meanings in the public realm.* Farnham, UK: Ashgate.

Takeuchi, H. T., Osono, E., & Shimizu, N. (2008). The contradictions that drive Toyota's success. *Harvard Business Review, 86*(6): 96–104.

Tantalo, C., & Priem, R. L. (2016). Value creation through stakeholder synergy. *Strategic Management Journal, 37*(2): 314–329.

Taylor, F. W. (1911). *Principles of scientific management.* New York, NY: W. W. Norton.

Taylor, M. (2010). Does locus of control predict young adult conflict strategies with superiors? An examination of control orientation and the organisational communication conflict instrument. *North American Journal of Psychology, 12*(3): 445–458.

Ten Bos, R., & Rhodes, C. (2003). The game of exemplarity: Subjectivity, work and the impossible politics of purity. *Scandinavian Journal of Management, 19*(4): 403–423.

Tetenbaum, T. J. (1998). Shifting paradigms: From Newton to chaos. *Organizational Dynamics, 26*(4): 21–33.

Tett, G. (2015). *The silo effect: The peril of expertise and the promise of breaking down barriers.* New York, NY: Simon and Schuster.

Thomas, K.W., & Velthouse, B.A. (1990). Cognitive elements of empowerment: An "interpretive" model of intrinsic task motivation. *Academy of Management Review, 15*(4): 666–681.

Thornborrow, T., & Brown, A. D. (2009). Being regimented: Aspiration, discipline and identity work in the British parachute regiment. *Organization Studies, 30*(4): 355–376.

Tracy, S. J. (2004). Dialectic, contradiction, or double bind? Analyzing and theorizing employee reactions to organizational tension. *Journal of Applied Communication Research, 32*(2): 119–146.

Treffers, T., Klarner, P., & Huy, Q. N. (2020). Emotions, time, and strategy: The effects of happiness and sadness on strategic decision-making under time constraints. *Long Range Planning, 53*(5): 101954.

Trevino, L. K., & Youngblood, S. A. (1990). Bad apples in bad barrels: A causal analysis of ethical decision-making behavior. *Journal of Applied Psychology, 75*(4): 378–385.

Trope, Y., & Liberman, N. (2003). Temporal construal. *Psychological Review, 110*(3): 403.

Tsoukas, H. (2017). Don't simplify, complexify: From disjunctive to conjunctive theorizing in organization and management studies. *Journal of Management Studies*, *54*(2): 132–153.

Tsoukas, H., & Chia, R. (2002). On organizational becoming: Rethinking organizational change. *Organization Science*, *13*(5): 567–582.

Tsoukas, H., & Cunha, M. P. (2017). On organizational circularity: Vicious and virtuous circles in organizing. In M. W. Lewis, W. K. Smith, P. Jarzabkowski, & A. Langley (eds), *The Oxford handbook of organizational paradox: Approaches to plurality, tensions, and contradictions* (pp. 393–412). New York, NY: Oxford University Press.

Tsoukas, H., Patriotta, G., Sutcliffe, K. M., & Maitlis, S. (2020). On the way to Ithaka: Commemorating the 50th anniversary of the publication of Karl E. Weick's *The social psychology of organizing. Journal of Management Studies, 57*(7): 1315–1330.

Tuckermann, H. (2018). Visibilizing and invisibilizing paradox: A process study of interactions in a hospital executive board. *Organization Studies*. DOI: 10.1177/0170840618800100

Tushman, M. L., & O'Reilly III, C. A. (1996). Ambidextrous organizations: Managing evolutionary and revolutionary change. *California Management Review*, *38*(4): 8–29.

Tye-Williams, S., & Krone, K. J. (2017). Identifying and re-imagining the paradox of workplace bullying advice. *Journal of Applied Communication Research*, *45*(2): 218–235.

Tyler, E. R., & Blader, S. L. (2005). Can business effectively regulate employee conduct? The antecedents of rule following in work settings. *Academy of Management Journal*, *48*(6): 1143–1158.

Upchurch, M., & Grassman, R. (2016). Striking with social media: The contested (online) terrain of workplace conflict. *Organization*, *23*(5): 639–656.

Vaill, P. B. (1998). *Spirited leading and learning: Process wisdom for a new age.* San Francisco, CA: Jossey-Bass Publishers.

Van Buren, M., & Safferstone, T. (2009). The quick wins paradox. *Harvard Business Review*, *87*(1): 54–61.

Van Dierendonck, D., & Patterson, K. (2015). Compassionate love as a cornerstone of servant leadership: An integration of previous theorizing and research. *Journal of Business Ethics*, *128*(1): 119–131.

van Zoonen, W., Verhoeven, J. W., & Vliegenthart, R. (2016). Social media's dark side: Inducing boundary conflicts. *Journal of Managerial Psychology*, *31*(8): 1297–1311.

Veblen, T. B. (1899 [2007]). *The theory of the leisure class.* New York, NY: Oxford University Press.

Verhoest, K., Peters, G., Boukart, G., & Vershuere, B. (2004). The study of organisational autonomy: A conceptual review. *Public Administration and Development*, *24*(2): 101–118.

Vignehsa, K. (2014). Stuckedness: On the organizational art of forbearance. University of Technology Sydney doctoral dissertation.

Vince, R., & Broussine, M. (1996). Paradox, defense and attachment: Accessing and working with emotions and relations underlying organizational change. *Organization Studies*, *17*(1): 1–21.

Vohnsen, N. H. (2015). Street-level planning: The shifty nature of "local knowledge and practice". *Journal of Organizational Ethnography*, *4*(2): 147–161.

Vohnsen, N. H. (2017). *The absurdity of bureaucracy: How implementation works.* Manchester, UK: Manchester University Press.

Voronov, M., & Weber, K. (2020). People, actors, and the humanizing of institutional theory. *Journal of Management Studies, 57*(4): 873–884.

Wagner, J. A. I. (1978). The organizational double bind: Toward an understanding of rationality and its complement. *Academy of Management Review, 3*(4): 786–795.

Waldman, D. A., & Bowen, D. E. (2016). Learning to be a paradox-savvy leader. *Academy of Management Perspectives, 30*(3): 316–327.

Waldman, D. A., Putnam, L. L., Miron-Spektor, E., & Siegel, D. (2019). The role of paradox theory in decision making and management research. *Organizational Behavior and Human Decision Processes, 155*(81): 1–6.

Walker, M., Fleming, P., & Berti M. (2020). "You can't pick up a phone and talk to someone": How algorithms function as biopower in the gig economy. *Organization*. Online first.

Wang, A. C. (2019). Developmental or exploitative? How Chinese leaders integrate authoritarianism and benevolence to cultivate subordinates. *Academy of Management Discoveries, 5*(3): 291–313.

Watzlawick, P. (1965). Paradoxical predictions. *Psychiatry, 28*(4): 368.

Watzlawick, P., Jackson, D. D., & Bavelas, J. B. (1967). *Pragmatics of human communication: A study of interactional patterns, pathologies, and paradoxes.* New York, NY: Norton.

Waycott, J., Thompson, C., Sheard, J., & Clerehan, R. (2017). A virtual panopticon in the community of practice: Students' experiences of being visible on social media. *The Internet and Higher Education, 35*: 12–20.

Weber, M. (1948). *From Max Weber: Essays in sociology.* Translated, edited and with introduction by H. H. Gerth and C. W. Mills. London, UK: Routledge & Kegan Paul.

Weber, M. (1978). *Economy and society: An outline of interpretive sociology.* Berkeley, CA: University of California Press.

Weick, K. E. (1979). *The social psychology of organizing* (2nd edn). Reading, MA: Addison-Wesley.

Weick, K. E. (1992). Agenda setting in organizational behavior: A theory-focused approach. *Journal of Management Inquiry, 1*(3): 171–182.

Weijers, I. (1999). The double paradox of juvenile justice. *European Journal on Criminal Policy and Research, 7*(3): 329–351.

Wendt, R. F. (1995). Women in positions of service: The politicized body. *Communication Studies, 46*(3–4): 276–296.

Wendt, R. F. (1998). The sound of one hand clapping: counterintuitive lessons extracted from paradoxes and double binds in participative organizations. *Management Communication Quarterly, 11*(3): 323–371.

Westenholz, A. (1993). Paradoxical thinking and change in the frames of reference. *Organization Studies, 14*(1): 37–58.

Whyte, W. H. (1956). *The organization man.* New York, NY: Simon and Schuster.

Wicks, A. C., Berman, S. L., & Jones, T. M. (1999). The structure of optimal trust: Moral and strategic implications. *Academy of Management Review, 24*(1): 99–116.

Wickstead, E. (2019). Why Jacinda Ardern is a leader for our times. *Vogue*, 21 March.

Wiedemann, N., Cunha, M. P., & Clegg, S. (2019). Rethinking resistance as an act of improvisation: Lessons from the 1914 Christmas truce. *Organization studies*. First published 12 December 2019. DOI: 10.1177/0170840619882957

Willmott, H. (1993). Strength is ignorance; slavery is freedom: Managing culture in modern organizations. *Journal of Management Studies, 30*(4): 515.

Willmott, H. (2013). The substitution of one piece of nonsense for another: Reflections on resistance, gaming, and subjugation. *Journal of Management Studies*, *50*(3): 443–473.

Wittgenstein, L. (1964). *Philosophical remarks*. Oxford, UK: Blackwell.

Wohlleben, P. (2016). *The hidden life of trees: What they feel, how they communicate—discoveries from a secret world*. Vancouver: Greystone Books.

Wolf, M. (2019). How to reform today's rigged capitalism. *Financial Times*, 4 December, 13.

Woo, D., & McDermott, K. W. (2019). Portrayals of unethical and unvirtuous workplace behaviors on TV: Implications for vocational anticipatory socialization. *International Journal of Communication*, *13*(19): 2859–2877.

Wood, G., & Hughes, S. (2015) (eds). *The central contradiction of capitalism? A collection of essays on capital in the twenty-first century*. London, UK: Policy Exchange.

World Economic Forum (2019). The universal purpose of a company in the Fourth Industrial Revolution. *Financial Times*, 2 December, 5.

Worline, M. C. (2012). Courage in organizations: An integrative review of the "difficult virtue". In K. M. Cameron & G. M. Spreitzer (eds), *The Oxford handbook of positive organizational scholarship* (pp. 304–315). New York, NY: Oxford University Press.

Wray-Bliss, E. (2003). Quick fixes, management culture and drug culture: Excellence and ecstasy, BPR and brown. *Culture and Organization*, *9*(3): 161–176.

Wray-Bliss, E. (2012). Leadership and the deified/demonic: A cultural examination of CEO sanctification. *Business Ethics: A European Review*, *21*(4): 434–449.

Yan, H. K. (2009). A paradox of virtue: The Daodejing on virtue and moral philosophy. *Philosophy East and West*, *59*(2): 173–187.

Yi, S., Knudsen, T., & Becker, M. (2016). Inertia in routines: A hidden source of organizational variation. *Organization Science*, *27*(3): 782–800.

Yong, E. (2016). *I contain multitudes: The microbes within us and a grander view of life*. London, UK: Bodley Head.

Zhang, Y., Waldman, D. A., Han, Y.-L., et al. (2015). Paradoxical leader behaviors in people management: Antecedents and consequences. *Academy of Management Journal*, *58*(2): 538–566.

Zheng, W., Kark, R., & Meister, A. L. (2018). Paradox versus dilemma mindset: A theory of how women leaders navigate the tensions between agency and communion. *The Leadership Quarterly*, *29*(5): 584–596.

Zorina, A., Belanger, F., Kumar, N., & Clegg, S. R. (2021). The Web of veillance: Enacting visibility in the digital age. *Organization Science*.

Zuboff, S. (2019). *The age of surveillance capitalism: The fight for a human future at the new frontier of power*. New York, NY: Public Affairs.

Index

Castle, The 64
catch-22 situations 63
categorization 16, 51
centralization/decentralization 81, 111
Cerf, V. 92
chaos 16, 55
charisma 103, 104
Chia, R. 16
China 26, 51, 119
circularity 96, 114, 117
Clark, C. M. 11
class
    conflicts 14, 23
    responses, of 37, 40
Clegg, S. R. 16, 22, 35, 71, 85, 122
Clift, B. 120–24
climate change
    business 127
    contradiction aplenty 131
    COVID-19 125, 129–31
    democracy 127
    externalities 126
    GRD 128
    PBs 125–6
    planetary boundaries 128
    sustainability 125–6
    TNCs 127–8
    United Kingdom 129–30
cognition 23, 25, 27, 43, 58
collaboration 20, 88, 97, 102, 116, 119
Collapse 12
commitment 21, 34, 40, 55, 70, 78, 84,
        107, 109, 113, 116, 122, 123, 128,
        131
communication 17
Communist Manifesto 78
competence 79, 123
complexity
    paradox as signal of 16–18
    systems 24, 79
compromise 39, 40, 52, 63, 90
conceptual coherence 22
conceptual core 4
conflict
    class 14, 23
    illusion of compatibility 111
    inter-group 96
    owners and labour, between 112
    win-win view 114
Conlon, D. E. 16, 88

constellation 79
contemporary organizations 78–9
contingency theory 122–3
contradictions 23–4, 123–5, 131–2
control
    Charismatic power 103
    domination 103
    power-over 103–6
    power-over employees 105–6
    rational-legal power 104–5
    traditional power 103–4
Cooper, R. 17
coopetition/cooperate/compete 91
coopetitive competency 91
coronavirus/COVID-19 122–3
    see also climate change
courage 55–6
crisis 45, 91, 92, 120, 122, 125, 129, 131
    see also coronavirus/COVID-19
cross-level analysis
    actors 83–4
    hybridity 82–3
    tensions reverberate 83
Crozier, M. 93
Cuganesan, S. 21
culture 94
    management 108
    narcissistic organizational 94
Cummings, D. 130
Cunha, M. P. 16, 22, 35, 71, 83
curvilinearity approach 53
customer 65, 78, 91, 99, 127

Dakin, S. R. 10
dark side (of paradox) 62–77
*Deadly Ideas of Neoliberalism: How
        the IMF has Undermined Public
        Health and the Fight Against
        AIDS, The* 123
Deci, E. L. 109
decision-making 67, 108, 110, 129, 131
defence mechanism 35
defensive responses 74
delegation 14
democracy 127
denial 74, 114
deparadoxify 17
De Rond, M. 88
Descartes 81
deviance